A WORLD OF
HER OWN MAKING

A World of
Her Own Making

KATHARINE SMITH REYNOLDS AND

THE LANDSCAPE OF REYNOLDA

CATHERINE HOWETT

University of Massachusetts Press   Amherst

in association with

Library of American Landscape History   Amherst

LC 2006028541
ISBN 10: 1-55849-520-7
ISBN 13: 978-1-55849-520-3

Designed by Jonathan D. Lippincott
Set in Goudy and Centaur
Printed and bound by C&C Offset Printing Co., Ltd.

Library of Congress Cataloging-in-Publication Data
Howett, Catherine M.
    A world of her own making : Katharine Smith Reynolds and the landscape
of Reynolda / Catherine Howett.
        p. cm.
    "In association with Library of American Landscape History, Amherst."
    Includes bibliographical references and index.
    ISBN-13: 978-1-55849-520-3 (cloth : alk. paper)
    ISBN-10: 1-55849-520-7 (cloth : alk. paper)
1. Reynolda House. 2. Landscape architecture—North Carolina—Winston-
Salem. 3. Reynolds, Katharine Smith. I. Library of American Landscape
History. II. Title.
    SB470.54.N65H69 2007
    712.09756'67—dc22

                                                              2006028541

British Library Cataloging in Publication data are available.

Opening photograph: *Aerial view of Reynolda, c. 1927, showing the village to the
left of Reynolda Road, the formal gardens, dairy, Lake Katharine, the bungalow, and
the golf course on the right.*

Facing title page: *Katharine Smith Reynolds, c. 1921.*

*Publication of this book was supported by generous underwriting
from Barbara B. Millhouse and a gift from Mr. and Mrs. Michael Jefcoat
in honor of Dr. Frederick Vogler.*

For John

and for Meghan, Maeve, Catherine, and Ciannat

Contents

Preface

✣

The subject of this book is Reynolda, the experimental farm, estate, and village in Winston-Salem, North Carolina, created by Katharine Smith Reynolds, wife of tobacco magnate R. J. Reynolds. Told with tender grace and enlivened by radiant insight, this multifaceted story illuminates subjects that range from scientific agriculture to the philosophy of the Arts and Crafts movement. As Catherine Howett observes in her introduction, however, "the real meaning of the landscape of Reynolda had less to do with its beauty or modernity than with the values and moral force with which a gifted and ambitious New Woman of the New South energetically invested it during her lifetime." *A World of Her Own Making* explores the intersection of these and many more themes through the lens of one of the most important women's projects of its era.

Kate Smith was educated at North Carolina's State Normal and Industrial College (today's University of North Carolina at Greensboro), where president Charles Duncan McIver framed the mission and goals of the "New Woman" in such a way that Kate could embrace this exciting ideal almost as a religious calling. Instead of being forced to choose between the life of a married southern lady and the tantalizing prospect of independence, Mrs.

Reynolds would achieve both. "Katharine would not be caught between these two worlds," as Howett writes; "she would live in a better world of her own making."

The story of the making of this world is told against the backdrop of the era's progressive ideals and the expanding personal horizons of its visionary, who was also the mother of four young children. Howett describes Katharine's purposes in planning, building, and administering her world, primary among which was to provide her family with "the good life lived close to nature." She also presents deftly limned portraits of the Philadelphia-based practitioners Charles Barton Keen, who designed the family bungalow and farm and village buildings, and Thomas S. Sears, the landscape architect who collaborated with Katherine Reynolds on the 1,000-acre estate.

Reynolda, like other estates of the day, was laid out according to British and American principles, set into open farmland and woods, with Italianate formal gardens where the public was welcomed and a large lake on whose shores village children once playacted the legend of Hiawatha. In addition to these more expected components of an American country place were a large farm operated profitably according to pioneering methods, model worker homes, a progressive school, and village church. Even in the context of the time—a period known among landscape historians as the country place era—Katharine Reynolds's initiative was bold, comparable, as Howett points out, to the architect Julia Morgan's work at San Simeon.

The Reynolda bungalow, home grounds and gardens, and farm buildings still exist today, adapted for contemporary use as the Reynolda House Museum of American Art and a cluster of shops and restaurants. In her emotionally stirring narrative Catherine Howett presents a strong case for the continued preservation of this rare and significant North American place. With *A World of Her Own Making*, the goal of LALH—to illuminate our landscape architectural past through exhaustive research and engaging analysis—has been memorably fulfilled.

*   *   *

Barbara Babcock Millhouse, the granddaughter of Katharine Reynolds and founder of Reynolda House Museum of American Art, first approached LALH with the idea of a monograph almost fifteen years ago. I am deeply grateful for her enthusiasm for such a book and for her support and patience while it was completed. I am also grateful to my esteemed colleague Catherine Howett for taking on this substantial project and her dedication to completing it over many years. In its complexity and beauty, Catherine's narrative far surpasses any expectations I had for this work. It has opened new worlds in my imagination, too.

I am indebted to Carol Betsch for photographing Reynolda so beautifully and for assembling other illustrations in the program; Jonathan Lippincott for bringing the words and pictures together with such finesse; Amanda Heller for her skillful editing; and the excellent staff of the Reynolda House Museum and Sherold Hollingsworth of Wake Forest University. Finally, I would like to thank our colleagues at the University of Massachusetts Press; the staff of the Library of American Landscape History; the LALH board of trustees, who followed the course of this project with such interest and optimism; and the many supporters of LALH, whose contributions make our good work possible.

Robin Karson, Executive Director
Library of American Landscape History
Amherst, Massachusetts

LALH

Library of American Landscape History, Inc., a nonprofit organization, produces books and exhibitions about North American landscape history. Our mission is to educate and thereby promote thoughtful stewardship of the land.

Acknowledgments

❧

So much gracious help has been provided me during the course of writing this book that I consider myself a beneficiary of the same spirit of cooperation in a shared endeavor that enlivened the original Reynolda community. That continuity is real and not imagined. Reynolda was a childhood home of Barbara Babcock Millhouse, founding director of the Reynolda House Museum of American Art, and it was she who, recognizing the importance of her grandmother's legacy, pursued the idea of a scholarly study of the landscape vision that had guided the estate's development. Robin Karson, executive director of the Library of American Landscape History, invited me to undertake a project that eventually engaged my mind and heart in ways I could never have anticipated. Throughout the long process of research and writing, Robin has been a steadfast source of encouragement, accommodation, and brilliantly insightful advice.

Historians and biographers learn to value whatever is saved from the past—the minutiae of daily life as much as more obviously significant sorts of documentation. Because Katharine Smith Reynolds was an instinctive saver and record-keeper whose family figured in public life over generations, a tradition of conservation rescued the estate from the ruin that Mary Reynolds Babcock had feared and created the archives that made this book possible. Archivist Richard Murdoch and his assistant, Todd Crumley, have stayed closely involved with the project, patiently helping me pursue new leads and interpret existing documentation. I have also used collections in the libraries of Wake Forest University, the University of North Carolina at Greensboro, and Davidson College that contain materials relevant to Katharine's story, and the Botany and Horticulture Library of the Smithsonian Institution, which houses photographic files from the estate of Thomas Sears. The ongoing research on the history of the estate by landscape architect Sherold Hollingsworth, personal assistant to Barbara Millhouse, and by Camilla Wilcox, curator of education for Reynolda Gardens, contributed significantly to the resources at my disposal, as did a seminal 1988 *North Carolina Historical Review* essay on Reynolda by Professor Margaret Supplee Smith of Wake Forest University.

Since a bracingly sharp editor brings a gift as rare as it is precious to any author, I was twice blessed in having Amanda Heller and Carol Betsch to work with. Equally important to readers will be Carol's expanded role as production editor in assembling the illustration program, searching out images that give the story its essential visual dimension. Crowning this remarkable effort, however, are a number of photographs of Reynolda today representing Carol's work as a distinguished landscape photographer. Graphic designer Jonathan Lippincott contributed his own exceptional gifts of eye and hand to this process.

Writing *A World of Her Own Making* proved to be a personal learning experience quite apart from its biographical and historical dimensions. I was surprised to discover, for example, that I came to a better understanding of Katharine's life and the nature of her achievement each time I tried to summarize the story for interested friends or perfect strangers. I am grateful for each of these conversations, too many to recall here, but I owe special thanks to Zachary Taylor Smith II, son of Katharine's brother

Eugene and now retired from a career in which he served as treasurer and director of the R. J. Reynolds Tobacco Company, president and director of the Mary Babcock Reynolds Foundation, and life trustee of the Zachary Smith Reynolds Foundation. Mr. Smith and Barbara Millhouse have served as my authorities on several aspects of family history. Geneologists Susan McIver Abernathy and Jack G. McIver assisted my search for materials related to the life and career of Charles Duncan McIver, and Preston Stockton responded to queries related to the planting plans of Thomas Sears.

Among all these generous listeners and contributors to my endless retellings of the Reynolda story, the most tirelessly enthusiastic and perceptive has been John Howett. This work is dedicated to him, and to four amazing New Women, our daughters.

Catherine Howett

A WORLD OF
HER OWN MAKING

Introduction

THE STORY OF ANY SINGLE HUMAN LIFE MIGHT BE TOLD from a myriad of perspectives, at least some of which will inevitably reveal connections between the person who is the subject of the story and significant historical events or cultural developments in the larger world. Even so, the case to be made here—that the achievement of Katharine Smith Reynolds in realizing the creation of Reynolda, her estate in Winston-Salem, North Carolina, deserves proper recognition within the history of American landscape architecture—may seem to stretch unreasonably the accepted boundaries of that history. She was not, after all, a professional landscape designer, nor even an amateur one. She was a woman of the American South born in 1880, who became the wife of one of the original southern tobacco tycoons. She subsequently devoted herself—as did most women of her class and place—to home, family, church, and community. Although, as her husband's fortunes expanded, she came to enjoy exceptional wealth and privilege, her social sphere remained fairly provincial; her life, moreover, was relatively brief. By the standards of any age she was a "doer," energetic and ambitious, but she never possessed the independence and the authority to act that made men like her husband influential figures in the world of business and public affairs, and ultimately earned them a place in history.

Few women, of course, even long after the achievement of suffrage early in the twentieth century, enjoyed educational or career opportunities equivalent to those of their brothers and husbands. In response to this reality, many contemporary historians have found it fruitful to examine the lives of women who devised strategies for attaining at least some measure of self-fulfillment by defying or subverting conventional expectations about their proper roles. Since the civil rights movement of the 1960s first helped heighten popular consciousness of historic inequalities, we have come to recognize the extent to which familiar and heretofore sacrosanct versions of the historical record are inevitably marred by omissions, distortions, subjective interpretation of "facts," and cultural bias. The consequence has been a wholesome revisionist temper within the academy and elsewhere, prompting research aimed at recovering missing or neglected narratives that can, by illuminating the work of those whom earlier histories ignored, provide a fuller and more nuanced understanding of the times in which they lived.[1]

The history of landscape architecture in the United States has offered a striking example of these fresh energies at work over the last thirty years or so. Up until then, contributions made by an admittedly small number of women to the profession, or more generally to the literature and practice of landscape design in America, were seldom formally acknowledged. Norman Newton's 1971 *Design on the Land*, for many years the standard text used in introductory survey courses in departments of landscape architecture, included mention of just three women practitioners.[2] Just as increasing numbers of young women had begun entering these programs, many of them drawn by environmental interests that were also an outgrowth of a 1960s sensibility, events and publications marking the 150th anniversary of the birth of Frederick Law Olmsted, revered as the "father of American landscape architecture," reintroduced this heroic nineteenth-century figure to new generations of Americans.[3] It would be fair to say, in fact, that these years marked the beginning of a gradual awakening, on the part of a whole class of educated Americans, to the realization that there were important connections between the quality of community and urban design and so-called quality of life. It was not long before women students, faculty, and professionals began to ask themselves, Where are the women? Who were they? What did they achieve, and how? Conferences, symposia, and a proliferation of publications, amounting by now to a substantial historical literature, have begun to explore the answers to those questions.

Not surprisingly, there were common threads of advantage that made it possible, from the late nineteenth century onward, for a small number of women to pursue careers related to some aspect of landscape design. Of the three women mentioned in Newton's classic text, Marian Cruger Coffin (1876–1957) remained unmarried throughout her career, while Annette Hoyt Flanders (1887–1946) and Beatrix Jones Farrand (1872–1959) were married but childless. Ellen Biddle Shipman (1869–1950), whom Newton ought certainly to have included, was married and a mother of three but divorced in 1927, when divorce was still rare enough to be thought scandalous. More important, all of these women, and most of the others of their generation who practiced or wrote about landscape design, belonged to a social class in which women were not expected to earn their own living, and in which opportunities to obtain a good education and to travel were much greater than was the norm for the vast majority of American women.

Katharine Smith Reynolds belonged to the same generation, even to the same class, but her achievement in conceiving and creating Reynolda—not just the physical place but, as we shall see, something of a utopian experiment—was a personal and singular project, her life's work. The only connection between this remarkable undertaking and the professional practice of landscape design was that Mrs. Reynolds was an enlightened client of architects, landscape architects, and others on whom she depended for the professional expertise that would help her realize her vision. What engages our attention is the mystery of how a young woman of her circumstances could possibly have tapped in, intellectually and imaginatively, to the most progressive ideas of her era, and then put these radical notions to work in a complex agricultural and social enterprise on the edge of a small southern city.

Ladies, Language, and Landscape

To understand the significance of Katharine Smith Reynolds's achievement, it may help to know something of the circumstances of her contemporaries who found access to more typical career paths as professional designers or influential writers on landscape subjects. There was just one woman among the ten professional landscape designers listed as charter fellows when the American Society of Landscape Architects was organized in January 1899.[4] Only a few years earlier, Charles Eliot, a brilliant younger partner in the preeminent firm of Frederick Law Olmsted, had discouraged a colleague from trying to form just such a "league of professional men" by arguing that there were scarcely four or five sufficiently accomplished practitioners in the entire country, while the profession itself was still "generally unrecognized by the public."[5] Ironically, it was Eliot's untimely death in 1897 that inspired his father, who was president of Harvard University, to establish there in 1900 the first academic program in landscape architecture. Until that time, the only avenue for a young man wishing to prepare for a career in the field was to find employment as an apprentice with an established firm.

At the turn of the twentieth century, opportunities for women to pursue either option—academic training or apprenticeship—were very few. Beatrix Cadwallader Jones, the lone woman among the founding members of the professional society (she became

Beatrix Farrand after her marriage in 1913), was so exceptionally fortunate in the circumstances of her birth, education, and social connections that her long and illustrious career merely dramatizes how difficult it was for women with fewer advantages even to imagine becoming, as Farrand preferred, modestly, to call herself, a "landscape gardener."[6] Her choice of this title for her design practice is significant, since the profession in this country had been renamed in 1863 by Olmsted and his partner Calvert Vaux, who began referring to themselves as "landscape architects" during the period when they were overseeing construction of Central Park in New York City.

Thirty years later, about the time that Beatrix Jones was living at Holm Lea, the Brookline, Massachusetts, estate of her mentor, Professor Charles Sprague Sargent of the Arnold Arboretum, another Brookline resident, Mrs. Schuyler Van Rennselaer, published *Art Out-of-Doors: Hints on Good Taste in Gardening*, a book so popular among American readers that it was reprinted in 1914 and revised in a second edition in 1925. The author set out to demonstrate that landscape design ought to be considered a "fourth art," equivalent in stature to architecture, painting, and sculpture, from which it followed that any genuinely cultured person should at least be familiar with its general principles and the most outstanding examples of its practice, both historic and contemporary. From this perspective, she maintained, Olmsted was clearly "the most remarkable artist yet born in America." Moreover, although her book was mostly concerned with recommendation for improving the artistic quality of "home grounds," Mrs. Van Rennselaer was at pains to make her readers aware of the wider, civic scope of Olmsted's profession, using as illustration his leadership role in planning the Chicago World's Fair, which opened the same year *Art Out-of-Doors* was published. She did quarrel, however, with the new usage "landscape architect." "Perhaps the best we can do," she proffered, "is to keep to 'landscape gardener,' trying to remember that it ought always to mean an artist, and an artist only."[7]

Beatrix Jones may have taken advantage of her mother's acquaintance with Mariana Griswold Van Rennselaer to seek the older woman's counsel during the time she resided in Brookline with the Sargent family.[8] She must certainly have read her book eagerly, responding to its author's passionate appreciation of the art of landscape design, even though nothing in the text explicitly suggested that women should be attracted to the profession, although for "many young men" the "chances for employment . . . are growing better year by year, and surely there is no profession whatsoever . . . that suggests to the imagination so delightful an existence."[9] Perhaps it was also Van Rennselaer's reservations about the designation "landscape architect" that prompted the younger woman's eventual decision to define herself instead as a landscape gardener. There is still another suggestion of the author's possible influence in a comment Jones later made in an interview published in the *New York Herald*, about a year after the founding of the American Society of Landscape Architects. After asserting that the business of landscape design is at once "hard work and perpetual pleasure," she observed that "with this grand art of mine I do not envy the greatest painter, or sculptor, or poet that ever lived. It seems to me that all arts are combined in this."[10]

Beatrix Jones would also have relished another sort of book with a landscape subject written by a woman and published in 1893, poet Celia Thaxter's *An Island Garden*, a volume delightfully illustrated with paintings of the author's house and garden and Thaxter herself by her friend, the American Impressionist Childe Hassam. Jones would have been familiar, from summer holidays at her family's vacation home in Bar Harbor, with the rocky island scoured by wind and waves—Appledore, within the Isles of Shoals in the southern Gulf of Maine—where Thaxter had created her garden. Although Celia Thaxter enjoyed a modest literary reputation in her own right, her celebrity was strongly identified with the place that had formed her artistic sensibility and remained the focus not just of her writing but of her life. Thaxter had inherited and continued to operate after her marriage a fashionable resort hotel, Appledore House, to which many distinguished writers and artists brought their families on summer holidays. She lived, gardened, and presided over what appears to have been a New England version of the European salon in a charming cottage adjacent to the inn. The spectacular profusion of the garden's flowers welcomed guests invited for an evening of conversation or music in her parlor. Here was a woman who had managed to define herself as an artist through a life devoted to letters and to what Victorian America recognized as the arts of the home, nurturing and domestic. In fact, Thaxter's life on Appledore curiously epitomizes a cultural understanding of the proper model for the lives of privileged women that had prevailed for most of the nineteenth century. The woman romantically rendered in Hassam's paintings is remote from the world of commerce and the stresses of urban life, focused instead on the creation and management of a beautiful home and garden—mistress of an island of refined culture sheltered from a harsh natural environment and the coarsening distractions of the world across the water.

From the perspective of that particular myth of femininity, it is significant that Celia Thaxter died the same year that *An Island Garden* was published, just as a new generation of women of her class were beginning, like Beatrix Jones, to seek educational and career opportunities beyond the traditional roles of wife and mother, teacher, or nurse. Thaxter's acknowledged accomplishments in horticulture and garden design were appreciated as those of a superbly gifted amateur. In fact, they so enhanced the perception of her femininity that what must have been the complicating realities of her working life as writer and innkeeper never shadowed the glowing image of the lady in the sunlit garden. The same social assumptions not only influenced Mariana Griswold Van Rennselaer's decision to publish her book under the name Mrs. Schuyler Van Rennselaer, but also made it impossible for her to acknowledge in print her belief that young women as well as young men ought to pursue careers as landscape architects. Yet in insisting on her preferences for calling that profession "landscape gardening," she was doing more than affirming its status as a form of art; consciously or not, she was emphasizing the historic traditions of horticulture, floriculture, and ornamental gardening as the foundation of landscape design. Precisely because these traditions had come to be increasingly associated with women's interests over the course of the nineteenth century, Olmsted and Vaux had opted for a more masculine-sounding identification of their profession with that of architecture.

Andrew Jackson Downing, the nineteenth century's most authoritative tastemaker in matters relating to home and garden, had addressed his popular *Treatise on the Theory and Practice of Landscape Gardening*, first published in 1841, to an audience of readers presumed to be exclusively male.[11] All of the estates Downing used to illustrate the principles of appropriate residential design belonged to "gentlemen of taste," many of whom he credited with having taken personal responsibility for design decisions relating to the architecture of the house and the layout of its grounds and gardens. American women, however, gradually took over a large part of such decision making as a natural extension of their responsibilities for household management and their proper interest in subjects related to the domestic sphere, which increasingly included residential design and the garden arts.

The marketing potential of this growing enthusiasm did not escape the attention of magazine publishers. In some instances, building and trade journals simply abandoned a predominantly male pool of subscribers in order to address the new audience of women eager for informative articles on architectural styles, interior and landscape design, and gardening. *Scientific American Building Monthly* became *American Homes and Gardens; Keith's Magazine on Home Building* became *Beautiful Homes Magazine.* The *Ladies' Home Journal*, which had begun publication in 1883 with a focus on fashions in clothing, manners, and cuisine, published illustrations of Frank Lloyd Wright's first Prairie Houses in 1901. *House Beautiful* was founded in 1896, followed just five years later by both *House and Garden*—subtitled *An Illustrated Monthly Devoted to Practical Suggestions on Architecture, Garden Designing and Planting Decoration, Home Furnishing and Kindred Subjects*—and *Country Life in America*. The latter venture, begun under the editorship of America's foremost horticulturist, Liberty Hyde Bailey, was modeled on the highly successful English magazine *Country Life*, which in 1901 first introduced its readers to the innovative design of the English plantswoman and garden writer Gertrude Jekyll, soon to become the doyenne of residential garden design on both sides of the Atlantic.

Jekyll was less well known, particularly in the United States, when Beatrix Jones chose her as one of the three gardeners she planned to visit on a study tour of great European gardens which she designed with the help of friends within the profession, then set out on in 1895 accompanied by her mother. The two spent a memorable morning with Miss Jekyll in the garden of her home, Munstead Wood. However brief this personal encounter, the example of Jekyll—a single woman, then in her fifties, who had come to garden design relatively late in life, having earlier devoted herself to painting—must have immeasurably reinforced the young American visitor's determination to establish herself as a professional landscape designer. There is no question that Jekyll's style of garden design, and particularly her superb skills as a plantswoman, had a lasting influence on the work of Beatrix Jones Farrand over the course of more than half a century of distinguished practice.

The "New Woman" and the Landscape Arts

In singling out such women as Mariana Griswold Van Rennselaer, Celia Thaxter, and Beatrix Jones Farrand, we are looking at women who, whatever difficulties they may have faced in moving beyond conventional expectations, were careful never to put their respectability at risk. On the contrary, they preserved their status as "ladies" within the familiar mores of a society in which men exercised superior authority not just in public affairs, but within the home as well. Many of the women who contributed to the burgeoning literature of gardening in this period actually took pains to portray themselves as nothing more than inoffensive amateurs, although they might subtly suggest that the male "experts" who wrote for the same audience could learn something from women with more hands-on experience of gardening.[12]

Inevitably, however, a more ardent and outspoken feminism began to make itself heard, challenging the presumption within American society that women were not entitled to full citizenship, owing to an innate fragility of mind and body in comparison with the male of the species. The suffrage movement that had begun as early as the 1840s gathered considerable force in the closing years of the century, particularly after the establishment in 1890 of the National Woman Suffrage Association from the merger of two previously separate organizations, one headed by Susan B. Anthony and Elizabeth Cady Stanton and the other by Lucy Stone. During the next thirty years of escalating protest and struggle, ending with passage in 1920 of the Nineteenth Amendment to the Constitution, giving women the right to vote, increasing numbers of American women self-consciously redefined earlier notions of femininity and ideal womanhood. This "New Woman," whose understanding of her mission in life was alternately celebrated and castigated in the popular press, deplored her countrymen's past failures to recognize the contribution already made by women in traditional roles to the advance of American civilization. She wanted more for herself: more respect for her intelligence and talents and more opportunities to participate in the affairs of the world outside her home. But the sudden determination of so many women to put aside conventional expectations of genteel femininity—understood as docility, delicacy of manner, and the cultivation of refined feelings rather than intellectual pursuits—and to demand a measure of independence in decisions affecting their own lives, aroused widespread apprehension even among many who recognized the legitimacy of the cause. This sense of foreboding was intensified by the perception that American society itself was changing too rapidly, that an entire way of life was threatened by accelerating urbanization, industrialization, and immigration.

Such anxieties actually fueled popular interest in finding ways to reconnect with an earlier, allegedly simpler and less stressful way of life associated with the nation's mostly rural and agrarian beginnings. Few city dwellers, however, were so naïve as to imagine that their lot might actually be improved by heading back to the farm and the grueling physical labor required to wrest a living from the land. Theirs was a more pragmatic but at the same time romantic enthusiasm for the natural world and for a nostalgic version of what came to be described as "country life." Liberty Hyde Bailey observed in 1901 that it was "becoming more and more apparent that the ideal life is that which combines something of the social and intellectual advantages of the city with the inspiration and peaceful joys of the country."[13]

Of course, the development of bucolic residential communities outside major cities was already well under way by the turn of the century. What was new was the increased participation in that movement of middle-class professional and working-class families. With a small plot of land, a yard, and perhaps a garden to care for, these new homeowners swelled the audience to which the literature of house and garden design was now addressed, creating publishing opportunities, as we have seen, for significant numbers of women—both ladies of the old school like Mrs. Schuyler Van Rennselaer and a "New Woman" like Frances Duncan (1877–1972), who in 1907 became the first gardening editor of the country's most influential women's magazine, the *Ladies' Home Journal*.[14]

Frances Duncan's career as garden designer, gardening writer, and novelist furnishes a good example of what it meant for a young professional woman to challenge the accepted order of things in what was, and for a very long time would remain, a man's world. As a girl growing up in New York and then Massachusetts, Duncan had advantages of social status and education similar to those that favored most of the other women who were able to pursue careers related to landscape design. After graduation from a private New England academy, where she was exposed to liberal ideas including the cause of women's rights, she found a position at nineteen with a reputable Long Island, New York, nursery, where she hoped to begin a career in horticulture. During the four years she worked there, Duncan's education broadened in ways she could not have anticipated, principally through the mentorship of an elderly German horticulturist who shared with her his knowledge of plants and encouraged her in an ambitious program of reading European philosophy, history, and political theory. She was forced to leave her job in 1900, after succumbing to a mental and physical collapse brought on, apparently, by a series of tragic events in her personal life. Duncan suffered over the course of the next few years from what was called at the time "nervous prostration"—severe depression, fatigue, and an incapacity for the kind of work that had previously given her so much pleasure. Eventually she found solace and a return to health in the simple rituals of gardening, a discovery that prompted her to begin writing about the art and craft of garden making, particularly its therapeutic effect on mind and body. Before long she had become the much sought after author of technical and historical articles for magazines such as *Atlantic Monthly*, *Century*, and *Country Life in America*, as well as novels that allowed her to explore her ideas about the meanings of gardens and gardening in the lives of men and women.

The pressures of her new career never diminished Duncan's energetic involvement in the suffrage movement, with which she was strongly identified in the minds of her readers and, with more troubling consequences, her employers. Edward Bok, the founder and editor of *Ladies' Home Journal*, who was nevertheless notoriously unsympathetic to the women's rights movement, fired her from her position as garden columnist when she criticized in print an article opposing suffrage for women that had appeared in the magazine. When Duncan finally married at thirty-seven, she was well enough known for her political activism for at least one newspaper account of the wedding to be headed "Suffragist Marries." Later, when the husband who had won her heart through his own political activism proved incapable of supporting their family of three children, she resumed her writing career with a keener sense of financial exigency. She would experience at firsthand, however, the stigma that society still attached to mothers who aspired to professional careers. When she sent the manuscript of a new book to an editor with whom she was acquainted, he returned it with a note citing three reasons for turning it down: "Their names are John, Duncan, and Margery"—the children whose well-being now depended on their mother's income from writing.

A Woman between Two Worlds

The life of Katharine Smith Reynolds and her primary role in the design and creation of Reynolda may appear at first to lack any significant connection to the lives of these few representative women who successfully pursued professional careers through the practice of landscape design, through writing about gardens and landscape, or through some combination of these two activities. Yet historians have recognized the singular importance of Reynolda as a "model" estate,[15] significantly different, in its experimental agricultural agenda and village-centered communal life, from even those few among the great estates of the American country place era to which it bears a superficial resemblance. Reynolda was conceived, planned, and administered by a woman acting as client in her own right rather than in the supportive role of the client's wife. That it might represent one of the most important women's projects of its era—equivalent in importance, for example, to the pioneering achievement of architect Julia Morgan (1872–1957) in designing William Randolph Hearst's San

Simeon estate on California's central coast—seems not to have occurred to historians of American landscape design and planning.[16] Morgan's biographer, commenting that her own subject had been similarly neglected by architectural historians until at least the 1970s, wondered, "How had she managed to hide herself so successfully from history?"[17]

In the case of Katharine Smith Reynolds, that question is easy to answer. There is probably no segment of American society, even today, more anonymous than that consisting of women whose principal identity is that of wife and mother and whose occupations are almost exclusively domestic in nature. Contrasting the personal autonomy that American society equates with manliness to the notion, persisting throughout most of the twentieth century, that women's "proper sphere" was the home, one feminist historian noted wryly that "men never had a 'proper sphere,' since their sphere has been the world and all its activities."[18] However much authority Mrs. Reynolds garnered from her husband's respect for her and his indulgence of her project, however much responsibility she assumed for civic endeavors not just at Reynolda but in the city of Winston-Salem, for most of her life she lived out the conventional expectations of her community for a girl from a respected family. Well brought up, and given the relatively unusual advantage of a college education, she married a wealthy industrialist and became as dutiful a wife and mother as she was a daughter.

The small-town southern culture into which Katharine was born was, after all, even more conservative on questions of how a young woman must behave to preserve her family's good name and her reputation as a lady than was the more liberal and cosmopolitan culture of the North. Nevertheless, the years in which she came to womanhood—the last two decades of the nineteenth century—were precisely those in which the emergence of a new urban and industrial culture, of which her husband's tobacco empire was just one manifestation, held promise of rescuing the South's failed agrarian economy from the stagnation that had lingered since post–Civil War Reconstruction. That new southern culture centered on the world of business and cities was also, inevitably, a seedbed of new social patterns and ideas, including even such heady notions as those proclaimed in the label "New Woman" and in the suffrage movement.

Growing up in the little town of Mount Airy, Katherine Smith (she would later change the spelling of her name to "Katharine") appears to have been one of those bright, intellectually curious, somewhat serious young women for whom leaving home for college proves to be a turning point that sets the course of her future life. Although she was forced to withdraw from the State Normal and Industrial College before completing her degree, Katharine had already been exposed there to something much more momentous than the series of illnesses that may have permanently compromised her physical health. The charismatic educator, minister, and political activist Charles Duncan McIver, and probably others among the faculty of the recently established Normal School he headed, had challenged Katharine to become a "New Woman" through what amounted to a conversion of mind, heart, and soul. The ideal that they held up to students preparing for careers in teaching and in business was that of a woman who claimed new rights and responsibilities for herself, but not in a scandalous or aggressive way, nor by rejecting woman's traditional role as guardian of the well-being of the family. On the contrary, Katharine and her classmates were encouraged to see themselves as called, in the spirit of "noblesse oblige" but also in the spirit of a missionary Christian zeal, to engage with selfless ardor and commitment both the traditional work of women and the careers now opening up for them. By working strenuously to improve the homes, schools, and communities they served, these women graduates would soon constitute a significant social force striving to move the South toward a more humane, enlightened, and progressive future.[19] Perhaps it was the very brevity and excitement of this first, intense college experience that made it so precious a memory for Katharine.

She was sent to another college, Sullins in Virginia, to finish her education in an academic environment more typical of what was believed best for young ladies from good southern families. Her new classmates thought of themselves more as carefree college girls than as "New Women," and looked forward with delicious anticipation to imminent courtship and marriage. Katharine had no trouble accepting the girlish dream of a thrilling romance as prelude to an equally blissful married life. But at the same time, she must have recognized with some apprehension the difference between herself and most of her less serious classmates—a difference subsequently reinforced by her spending the next few years as a single woman. She was twenty-four when she accepted the marriage proposal of Richard Joshua Reynolds, her cousin and a man thirty years her senior.

R. J. Reynolds was far from being an opportune last chance for Katharine Smith. In combining gallantry and an endearing need of her with a reputation for legendary daring in his business deals and a sporting man's personal style, he seemed a strikingly larger-than-life figure. Katharine fell in love with him easily and passionately. But marriage and the childbearing that followed—four children in their first six years together—added physical and emotional stress to the other responsibilities she assumed as mistress of a large household, hostess to the high society of Winston-Salem, and active participant in local charitable and educational causes. The management of so busy and complex a domestic and social life gave Katharine ample opportunity to use her organizational skills, but these daily preoccupations also threatened to distract her from larger ambitions. Not for long, however.

There can be no question that Katharine thought of herself, and was perceived by others, as first and foremost a wife and mother. It would have been quite impossible for a woman in her position to aspire to any occupation that enlisted her intellect and talents in significant work outside her home. The wife of R. J. Reynolds might understandably have felt obliged to abandon any hope of living out the promise of the "New Woman" of the twen-

R. J. Reynolds, c. 1905.

tieth century, had she not been first inspired by the model of the feminine ideal that Charles Duncan McIver had impressed upon his students. McIver had framed the ideal of the "New Woman" in religious and moral terms, so that Katharine, feeling the power of her own gifts but pious as well, could embrace it not as a form of secular liberation but as a sacred calling. The historian Leslie Close, in writing about the difficulties so many women faced in earning respect and credibility in landscape careers up until the 1930s, observed that for many of these pioneering women, "one answer was to create paths of their own."[20] That was obviously the resolution that Katharine Smith Reynolds formed during the early years of her marriage. A woman possessed of "a head for business" need not be forced to choose between the traditional responsibilities of married southern ladies and the mission that McIver urged upon educated women in the "New South" that was being everywhere proclaimed. Katharine would not be caught between these two worlds; she would live in a better world of her own making.

"The Art That Is Life"

There were other currents abroad in the land during the years just before and after the turn of the century to support Katharine in her conviction that the ordinariness, even the banality, that inhered in conventional domestic life and middle-class society need not deprive her of the chance to pour her energies into some great project. Katharine had studied art in college, even taught an art class in Mount Airy during the year after her graduation. As Beatrix Jones Farrand understood, just to think of oneself as an artist is liberating; for Farrand, identifying herself as an artist meant that she was proof against the indifference and contempt of male colleagues. There is an infamous description of Farrand, attributed to Frederick Law Olmsted, as a woman "supposed to be in some way inclined to dabble in landscape architecture."[21] For Katharine, thinking of herself as an artist meant that sacrificing any possibility of a professional career to the demands of home and family need not require that she turn her back on her own sense of who and what she was, and was meant to be.

The early years of the twentieth century—eventful years for Katharine, before and after her marriage in 1905—were a time when art and design were turning dramatically inward to focus on the arts of the home. The magazines and books aimed at young married women interested in fashion and the decorative arts, as Katharine certainly was, were full of enthusiasm for the work and reforming spirit of designers and architects inspired by the ideals of the English Arts and Crafts movement. On both sides of the Atlantic, the movement marked a reaction against what was perceived to be the decadent opulence of Victorian taste, including the inflated neoclassicism of Renaissance Revival and Beaux-Arts styles. While those in the vanguard of the movement might propose very different strategies for promoting simpler, more rational and authentic modern styles, they shared the belief that changes in work and community life brought about by the industrial revolution were responsible for the erosion of quality in consumer goods, in home design and furnishings, and in architecture and the landscape.

One such reformer, the Philadelphia architect William L. Price (1861–1916), helped to found Rose Valley, one of several noteworthy experimental communities of artists and artisans who attempted to put the values of the Arts and Crafts movement to work in actual settlements, usually in rural settings. In addition to the furniture, pottery, and books produced during the eight years of Rose Valley's existence, Price published a journal between 1903 and 1907, *The Artsman*, to which he gave the subtitle *The Art That Is Life*.[22] By affirming an ideal that reconnected ordinary life with the making of art, this simple but highly charged phrase captured the powerful appeal that the American Arts and Crafts movement would have for a woman like Katharine Smith

Artisans cottages, Rose Valley, Moylan, Pa., c. 1906.

Reynolds, who aspired to art but had obligations to home and family that made the pursuit of "high" art and traditional heroic models of the artist impossible for herself. In the years before her marriage, Katharine had delighted in mastering many of the domestic arts practiced by women of her generation; she sewed beautifully and enjoyed painting china. Now she came to understand that her mission as mother and matron, and as an educated woman married to the richest man in Winston-Salem, demanded that she commit her life to a much nobler and more exalted art. Nothing within the domestic environment—no space, no object, no event—was unworthy of being artfully transformed into something beautiful and meaningful.

If this potential elevation of the home—and home*making*, in a literal sense—to a significant form of art suited both Katharine's natural instincts and the circumstances of her life, certain ethical and philosophical strains of Arts and Crafts theory would confirm her sense that she had finally found a way to put into practice the principles instilled by her education and her religious faith. William Morris (1834–1896), who as artist, writer, and entrepreneur was the leading spokesman for the English phase of the movement and was influential in the United States as well, had been so troubled by the difficulties he and his followers encountered in extending the goals and goods of the movement to working-class men and women that he had posed the question, "What business have we with art at all, unless all can share it?"[23] While Morris and some few others took up the cause of reform through socialist political action, most adherents of the Arts and Crafts philosophy were suspicious of national programs and organizations. They dedicated themselves instead to advancing democracy at the local level, either as individuals or within guilds of craftsmen and vibrant small communities of the like-minded, such as Will Price's Rose Valley outside Philadelphia. Town meetings in Rose Valley were modeled on the community gatherings described in Morris's utopian novel *News from Nowhere*.[24]

Price was also one of the founding members in 1883 of the T-

Square Club, which, by serving as a forum for Arts and Crafts ideas through sponsorship of lectures, exhibitions, and publications, helped to foster in the area around Philadelphia one of the most cohesive and dedicated fraternities of artists, designers, craftsmen, and architects anywhere in the country.[25] Although Katharine Reynolds is bound to have learned a good deal of what she knew about this new aesthetic from books and magazines, she was just as much educated in these matters by frequent exposure to Philadelphia. Her husband had so many business, professional, and social connections there that they became very familiar with the city and its environs. She would select Charles Barton Keen (1868–1931), a distinguished graduate of the architectural program at the University of Pennsylvania, and a man thoroughly schooled in the design traditions and aesthetic values of the T-Square Club, as architect of Reynolda. Her principal landscape architect after the initial phase of site development, Thomas Sears

Charles Barton Keen.

Thomas Sears.

(1880–1966), was part of the same Philadelphia circle, and had already earned a reputation as a skilled garden designer when Katharine hired him for a major expansion and elaboration of Reynolda's formal gardens.

In the debate that surfaced within the American Arts and Crafts community on the issue of whether the products of machine technology might be integrated with those employing traditional handicrafts without sacrifice of quality, the Philadelphia School, for which the T-Square Club served as a nexus of dialogue and influence, became strongly identified with the conservative stand. For the most part, this group was unsympathetic toward Frank Lloyd Wright's efforts to persuade the Chicago Society of Arts and Crafts that ways might be found, through collaborations between artists and manufacturers, to apply modern industrial processes to the production of materials and objects meeting the highest artistic standards. By comparison with other centers of Arts and Crafts activities in the Northeast, the Midwest, and California, the Philadelphians remained, according to one historian, "idealistic and insular" in their retreat from the city to a romanticized rural and suburban landscape that represented, to their minds and those of their clients, the last stronghold of a way of life marked by civility and grace, in harmony with the rhythms of the natural world.[26] The residential properties they designed drew on sources in the vernacular building traditions of rural Pennsylvania and Delaware and the English countryside to project an image of continuity with the past, of rootedness in the land and the good life lived close to nature.

In this respect as well, the designers Katharine found in Philadelphia were a good match for her own taste and sensibilities. Especially after the birth of her children, she felt strongly attracted to country life, with its promise of cleaner air, purer water, and more opportunities for healthful physical exercise outdoors, to say nothing of the spiritual and emotional satisfactions of a life lived in beautiful natural surroundings. While these advantages also motivated countless numbers of her countrymen to move out of the city to greener suburban and rural enclaves, they had added importance for Katharine because of the lingering effects on her own health of the illness she had suffered late in her adolescence. Moreover, she had seen for herself, while traveling with her husband in rural England and Scotland during their European honeymoon, just how seductively peaceful and charming were those scenic farms and villages that had inspired the picturesque landscapes so favored by the Philadelphia School.

From the beginning Katharine understood her project as a complex program of land development, one that everyone but her husband would assume to be entirely unsuited to the capacities— much less the proper occupations—of a southern matron. The farm and its successful operations came first in her planning, followed by the landscape of the "home place,"[27] an area surrounding the main house that included expansive lawns, a small lake, and woodlands, as well as an adjacent village of workers' homes and gardens, schools, a church, workshops, farm buildings, and a greenhouse complex with formal gardens. Yet although the estate might in certain respects resemble others of the country place era, Reynolda was an experimental farm and community not just from an agricultural, technological, or architectural perspective, but in the philosophy and goals that inspired its creation. Katharine's vision represented a unique confluence of progressive and populist ideology with a distinctively southern understanding of community as a people formed by a common history, religious traditions, and folkways who flourished best when "rooted," to borrow the words of William Butler Yeats, "in one dear perpetual place."[28] Thus the real meaning of the landscape of Reynolda had less to do with its beauty or modernity than with the values and moral force with which a gifted and ambitious New Woman of the New South energetically invested it during her lifetime. Reynolda should represent exceptional opportunities for all whose lives it touched—a welcoming and supportive home and workplace where living well counted for just as much as living virtuously, and the promise of a better future just as much as the storied past.

Katharine's strategy in achieving these ends was to apply to a working farm and a community of ordinary people the Arts and Crafts ideal of elevating and transforming daily life by approaching its every aspect as essentially a work of design. Art had been her vocation; Reynolda would become at once her mission and masterpiece—analogous, in its human and temporal dimensions, to performance art rather than a material object. Her search for designers capable of capturing in physical form the intangible environmental qualities that she wanted the estate to embody generated a creative process in which she played a defining role, just as she did in taking responsibility for the complex and productive interactions within the community and between the community and other groups and institutions.

Like women of later generations who would struggle to balance the multiple demands of their domestic and working lives, Katharine Reynolds believed that she could "have it all," while maintaining the highest standards in every detail. Her untimely death threatened not only the survival of the estate as a farm, home, and community, but eventually the loss of public awareness of the social and cultural significance of the project as originally conceived. Nevertheless, in spite of the vagaries of time and changing circumstances, enough memories, records, and original architecture and landscape have survived to frame a narrative of Reynolda's beginnings, as vision and as place, that illuminates a remarkable continuity between past and present, as if Katharine's indomitable will and spirit were still at work.

ONE

Kate Smith of Mount Airy

ANYONE BORN AND RAISED IN THE HEARTLAND OF THE American South during the hundred-year period between the end of the Civil War and passage of the Civil Rights Act in 1964 was almost inevitably blessed, or burdened, with a strong sense of regional identity. For many, in fact, awareness of being southern took precedence even over the sense of oneself as American. To an extent that those from other regions seldom fully appreciate, the cataclysm of that distant war and its consequences shaped common perceptions not just of the historic past, but of a present lived in the shadow of that past. More than a century after the event, many white southerners remained surprisingly defensive about the causes for which the war had been fought in the first place.

A local history of Surry County, North Carolina, produced for the national Bicentennial celebration in 1975, argued, for example, that delegates from Surry and elsewhere in the South who signed the United States Constitution in 1787 were confident that individual states had reserved their right to withdraw from the Union if they felt compelled to do so at some future time. Enlightened southerners, according to this account, recognized that slavery was "a moral and political evil," as Robert E. Lee himself had said, but they "wanted a chance (without the interference of the northern states) to work out a system to abolish slavery." Instead, "the grandsons and great-grandsons of those who fought to free their country from Mother England" were forced to fight another war to preserve rights already achieved in the earlier struggle.[1]

Katharine Smith's father, Zachary Taylor Smith, figures in the same narrative. A Virginian by birth, this "descendent of three presidents" is said to have joined the Confederate army as a drummer boy at fourteen, although more reliable records indicate that he was at least seventeen when he enlisted.[2] He was subsequently captured, then imprisoned at a federal fort in Maryland for the duration of the war. We are told that some years later Smith made his way to Surry County, bought a farm just north of Mount Airy, and in 1879 married a young woman of the town, Mary Susan

Zachary Taylor Smith.

Jackson. "Mr. Zack" is described as having remained an "unreconstructed Rebel," who faithfully attended reunions of Confederate veterans until his death at ninety-one. It seems likely that the six Smith children grew up in a household in which their father's participation in the late great cause was a source of pride that lent color to all their lives.

It was also a symbolic source of meaning, and of values passed from one generation to the next. For families like the Smiths, the conviction that secession and war had been forced upon the South by intractable federal policies helped to preserve self-esteem in the face of defeat, occupation, and other humiliations associated with postbellum Reconstruction. Moreover, refusal to accept moral culpability for the war's unimaginable costs in human life, physical devastation, and economic ruin allowed for continued devotion to the South as the authentic *patria*—the region that was to have become a republic in its own right—under the tattered flag of "southern honor."

United Daughters of the Confederacy parade, Mount Airy.

That code, based on a cultural consensus that ran deeper in white society than divisions of ethnicity, class, or ways of living, defined specific ideals of southern manliness and the commensurate, selflessly supportive responsibilities of southern women. Not just a fierce valor but bristling anger in response to real or perceived insults and swift action to avenge any offense were taken to be signs of a wholesome virility in boy and man. Women and girls, at least those of the middle and upper classes, were ideally fair, physically and mentally fragile by nature, but naturally virtuous; their need, like that of children, for masculine support and protection inspired men to tender devotion and heroic deeds.[3]

The striking similarity between these gender roles and those associated with the chivalric code of the Middle Ages is not coincidental. A substantial historical literature produced over the course of the last century attests to the influence of western European feudal culture and mores on the antebellum South, especially as southerners viewed that world through the lens of nineteenth-century romantic fiction. Moreover, while protecting members of his family and their interests was a man's first duty, bonds of family attachment extended easily in the South to a close-knit kinship network, to a historic community, and finally to the region itself. They constituted, in a sense, a more primal covenant than that of law in governing the relations between the public and private social orders, between state and family. We hear them invoked in the rhetoric of an Alabama delegate to the 1860 Democratic convention as he warned against the threat to the South of the impending war: "Ours is the property invaded; ours are the institutions which are at stake; ours is the peace that is to be destroyed; ours is the honor at stake—the honor of children, the honor of families, the lives, perhaps, of all."[4]

Nevertheless, by the time the Smiths' first child, Mary Katharine, was born on the seventeenth day of November in 1880, prophetic voices within the region were beginning to suggest that southern honor was not well served by the smoldering legacy of self-righteous resentment and hatred of Yankees. These critics were pragmatists, less interested in revisiting futile debates about guilt or innocence than in making their fellow southerners aware that if the region were ever to be restored to prosperity, a change in attitude and new economic and social strategies were demanded. The best-known propagandist for this idea of a "New South" was Henry W. Grady, who, after assuming editorship of the *Atlanta Constitution* in 1879, challenged southerners to bring an end to "a subjection more grievous" than any the war had inflicted. "The farmers may farm as wisely as they please, but as long as we manufacture nothing, and rely on the shops and mills and factories of other sections for everything we use, our section must remain dependent and poor."[5] Grady and others attracted to his cause advocated rapid industrial development and a more diversified agricultural economy for the South, and accommodation and competition with northern interests rather than defiant isolation. They steadfastly maintained, however, that such changes did not threaten the traditional culture of the region, including racial segregation. "The new South," Grady assured his readers, "is simply the old South under new conditions."[6]

A Daughter of the New South

In spite of the remoteness of Mount Airy from the noise and bustle of a rapidly growing city like Atlanta, the little town in the northwest Piedmont of North Carolina, nestled among the foothills of the Blue Ridge Mountains, was not untouched by the changes that proponents of the New South ideology had set in motion. Surry County, which shares a border on the north with Virginia, had been settled after the Revolutionary War mostly by Virginians moving south in search of land to farm, just as Zachary Smith would do after the Civil War. The agricultural way of life that developed in that part of North Carolina was very different in character from the plantation culture that predominated along the southeastern seaboard. Farmers raised tobacco and cotton, but not on the scale of large eastern plantations producing for an international market. In areas such as Surry County, farms were small, most of the work was done by family members rather than by slaves, and almost everything needed to sustain life was produced independently. Corn was a more important crop than wheat or cotton, since it furnished food, fodder, and material for mats, mattresses, brooms, and endless other useful items—a pipe or a doll or a jug of whiskey. Cows, hogs, chickens, sheep, horses and mules, orchards, fields and gardens, woodlands and wood-lots—and all the stables, sheds, cribs, pens, springhouses, and well houses needed to maintain them—made up the landscape of homestead and farm. Tobacco was usually the only cash crop; chickens and eggs could be bartered for goods at a general store. Rich or poor, people lived quite simply.[7]

The emancipation of slaves had a much less dramatic effect on rural Piedmont economies than other changes that were under way in the two decades that followed the end of hostilities. As the South's railroad system was rebuilt and expanded, many settlements along rail corridors were rapidly transformed into market towns. Entrepreneurs investing in cotton gins and tobacco warehouses actively encouraged local farmers to expand the acreage devoted to commercial crops. Before long, all sorts of new businesses were opening along Main Street, catering to the needs of families with cash in their pockets on market days and the swelling numbers of people moving in from farms to live and work in towns. In 1850 Mount Airy had been a sleepy village of four hundred souls. Thirty-five years later the town incorporated, welcoming soon after the arrival of the Cape Fear and Yadkin Valley Railroad, and by the time Katharine Smith turned twelve in 1892, it boasted a population of close to three thousand.[8]

Despite its remoteness, the town that Katharine grew up in had a more cosmopolitan atmosphere than did most rural areas of the South in that era. Even before the arrival of the railroad, Mount Airy's proximity to a major wagon road had brought a stream of traders and travelers through town as life returned to

Main Street, Mount Airy, postcard, 1910.

normal after the upheaval of the war years. As these visitors spread word of its scenic location, cool mountain air, nearby sources of health-giving mineral waters, and genial atmosphere, hotels and boardinghouses opened their doors to growing numbers of vacationers, and Mount Airy prospered as a summer resort. Many came from the "low counties" of the Carolina coast and Georgia, hoping to escape not just the sweltering heat but the still prevalent and mysterious seasonal fevers of those places. A guest in the 1890s at the best known of Mount Airy's hostelries, the Blue Ridge Inn, recorded his pleasure at discovering the "unsurpassable" view from the dome of the three-story structure, a panorama of "picturesque" forested landscape embracing a town of "magnificent shade trees, elegant residences, well kept lawns, towering spires, and splendid business blocks."[9] He overlooked, perhaps as an intrusion, the presence on the same horizon of a major local industry, the granite quarry east of town, which, having begun production in 1890, furnished handsome stone blocks not just for churches, banks, and fine homes in Mount Airy but for projects in distant cities as well.

Although the Smiths lived for most of Katharine's childhood on the edge of town, her father's business interests included both

The Smith family home, Mount Airy.

rural farmland and downtown real estate. There were many southern families like theirs, a generation of men and women raised on farms, as Katharine's parents had been, who became middle-class capitalists living in towns. And for all that Mount Airy might remain in many respects a backwater of unpaved streets and primitive sanitation, as a town whose business it was to attract and entertain people from faraway places, it did not escape the influence of a national urban culture reaching its citizens through the buzz of conversation on its streets and in hotel lobbies and dining rooms, through newspapers and magazines, and through expanding commercial enterprises. Traveling stock companies came for week-long engagements at Galloway's Opera House, and ladies "robed in rich and elegant gowns" and gentlemen in "patent leathers and 'spike tails'" danced to the music of Mr. Pascucci's orchestra at the opening "german" of the season, a cotillion at the Blue Ridge Inn.[10]

None of these signs of returning affluence as the century drew to a close were understood by southerners to mean that they should now be content to think of themselves as part of "Yankeedom." On the contrary, every indication of regional economic recovery—even in the teeth of recurring episodes of instability affecting both North and South—was celebrated as proof that

Henry Grady's "New South" ideology was working, that the battle for southern autonomy was not over but would finally be won peacefully. The editor of the *Raleigh News and Observer* had laid out the strategy years earlier in language less grand than Grady's; he exhorted southerners to "make money" in order to "force from the North that recognition of our worth and dignity to which that people will always be blind unless they can see it through the medium of . . . material strength."[11] In a sense, the ideal of southern manhood represented by the rebel "cavalier"—the crafty hunter, the relentless adversary, quick to take umbrage at the slightest insult to his family's honor—had been only slightly domesticated and dressed for a new role in a new war, that of the equally shrewd and daring man of affairs, succeeding in the cutthroat world of business against all odds, and redeeming the pride of his race and region.

Zachary Smith, that "unreconstructed Rebel," might have fancied himself such a man. But just as his children basked in the reflected glory of their father's exploits in war, Smith took personal pride in the larger-than-life success of his lifelong friend and younger first cousin, Richard Joshua Reynolds. Reynolds had used what he learned through his father's tobacco farming and subsequent manufacturing of tobacco products in Patrick County, Virginia, to start his own firm in the North Carolina city of Winston in 1875. Within barely ten years he had amassed a sizable fortune and a reputation to match, sufficient for the editor of the *Winston Sentinel* to hail this public-spirited town father even then as a self-made man, owing his success neither to inheritance nor to luck but to "hard work and sound practical judgment" and an uncanny instinct, "like a skillful physician with his hand upon a patient's wrist," for figuring out what clever innovation in a tobacco product might appeal to popular taste.[12] By the 1890s, R. J. Reynolds was a big enough player to try to block the railroad trust of J. P. Morgan from taking over the Richmond and Danville Railway, an unsuccessful effort that nevertheless won him the praise of still another editor as "a friend of the people who had not hesitated to put up a financial fight against the wealthiest financier of the nation."[13]

Although he had been too young to join his brother Abram in fighting for the Confederacy, cousin Dick cut as glamorous a figure of southern manhood as did Katharine's handsome father. He was tall and robust, tirelessly energetic and outgoing, a sportsman and "man about town" whose chief extravagance was fine horses. Townsfolk in Winston took pride in their belief that Reynolds owned "the fleetest span of matched mares in the South, if not in the United States," which "with Dick behind them to give the Patrick whoop on some good track . . . would make you think that a full grown Texas tornado had broke out in your immediate vicinity."[14] Yet for all the gusto with which this man of action engaged both work and pleasure, Reynolds had other traits that earned him the respect of his neighbors as a traditional man of honor, well schooled in the values of southern gentility. He was conspicuously generous, hardworking, and fair, but perhaps his greatest virtue in the public's eye was his loyalty to family and friends, and particularly his devotion to his widowed mother. A bachelor who sacrificed marriage at the usual age to the demands

The Reynolds home, Fifth Street, Winston, 1912.

Katharine Smith,
about age ten.

of building a business empire, Reynolds lived in a rambling Queen Anne–style mansion in downtown Winston with his mother, his younger brother Will, whom he employed in his factory, and Will's wife, Kate.

A story has come down in the Reynolds and Smith families about the gift of a gold bracelet from Dick to his cousin Kate Smith when she was a child of ten.[15] It came with a promise—the kind of promise little girls delight in receiving from a favorite older male relative or family friend—that when she had grown into a lady he would marry her. Katharine appears to be about ten years old in the earliest surviving photograph of her, which shows a sweetly pretty child with large eyes and a gaze of precocious solemnity not unusual in nineteenth-century photos of children, but perhaps understandable in her case. By that time she was the eldest of four living children, with her mother probably already expecting a baby to come in 1891. The Smith's second child, a boy born two years after Katharine, had died when she was seven. The loss of her nearest sibling must have been a traumatic experience for a sensitive little girl, a firstborn who seems to have manifested from an early age the qualities associated with that place in a large family. When Katharine completed her secondary schooling at seventeen, the principal of the Mount Airy school she attended wrote a letter recommending her admission to the State Normal School that had opened a few years previously in Greensboro. "She is a hardworking, painstaking student, who never sought to evade any duty or task," he declared. "Possessing a splendid intellect, she does everything that she undertakes with credit to herself and a great satisfaction to her teachers. . . . She is further advanced and more thorough than any student heretofore sent from Surry County to your institution."[16]

It is hardly surprising that this bright and earnest young woman, studious by nature, should aspire to be a teacher herself, and Katharine was enough the apple of her father's eye to win his approval of a college education, even though it meant leaving the familiar world of home and Mount Airy. At a time when educational opportunities at every level and access to all but a few professions were severely limited for women in most parts of the South—the first graded school system in Mount Airy was not established until 1895—her parents' decision to provide college training for their daughters as well as their sons represented an unusually enlightened commitment.

Crusaders for Educational Reform

Their attitude was likely to have been influenced in some measure by a progressive movement that had made the cause of improved education an urgent political issue in North Carolina, beginning early in the 1880s after national census figures showed the state to have the highest rate of illiteracy in the entire South. Nationally, about 9 percent of the white population was unable to read or write; in North Carolina, the figure was closer to 33 percent. The reformers saw free public education as an essential prerequisite for the economic, social, and cultural renaissance envisioned by promoters of the "New South." If the entrenched poverty of the region was to be overcome by expanding industry and diversifying agriculture, first-rate systems of public education, including colleges and universities, were needed to provide the next generation of professional and working people with the knowledge and skills required by the new economy and their responsibilities as citizens of a democratic society.

One of the most eloquent spokesman for these imperatives was the journalist and author Walter Hines Page, founder and editor of the weekly *State Chronicle*, published in the North Carolina capital at Raleigh, who subsequently achieved national eminence as editor of *Forum* and the *Atlantic Monthly*, then as U.S. ambassador to the Court of St. James's. Page castigated conservative voices in the state that steadfastly resisted any government initiative, to be supported by taxes, aimed at improving the lives of ordinary people, large numbers of whom were leaving North Carolina in search of better opportunities elsewhere. This coalition of politicians, clergy of the more "primitive" orthodoxies, and elitists indifferent to the public good—in Page's words, "the presumptuous powers of ignorance, heredity, decayed respectability and stagnation that control public action and public expression"—was responsible for the hopelessness and suffering of the poor surrounding them on every side.[17] In a famous address that struck a responsive chord not just across the South but in the country at large, galvanizing the crusade for democratic access to education, Page urged southerners to stop clinging to romantic notions of their history and traditions, for they had in fact been "dominated by a little aristocracy, which, in its social and economic character, made a failure and left a stubborn crop of wrong social notions behind—especially about education."[18] He was speaking on that occasion to the graduating class at the State Normal and Industrial School for Women in June 1897, less than a month before

Katharine Smith sent off her application requesting admission in the fall of that year.

Page had been invited to the campus by another native son of North Carolina, his friend and ardent supporter Charles Duncan McIver, founder and first president of the Normal School. McIver, like Page, was something of a firebrand, a descendent of Scots who had settled in the coastal Cape Fear region early in the nineteenth century, a Presbyterian, and an 1881 honors graduate of the University of North Carolina. He, too, believed that education was the "supreme issue with which the South must cope."[19] He had begun while still in his twenties to earn the respect of more senior educators in the reform movement for his innovative teaching in private and public schools in Durham and Winston. Page believed that McIver was in fact "concocting a revolution"

Charles Duncan McIver.

once his interests began to focus in particular on the state's appalling failure to provide adequate opportunities for women—not just to be educated, but to become teachers. McIver pointed to the irony that not only white men but both black men and black women had significantly more opportunities for higher education at southern institutions than did a young woman such as his own sister—owing to endowments made by northern philanthropists to private institutions and the willingness of some state legislatures, even in North Carolina, to provide schooling for blacks of both sexes.[20]

While it made sense that McIver would recognize the absurdity of a system in which very few white women were teaching even at the elementary-school level, his marriage to a woman who was truly remarkable for her time, an ardent feminist and schoolteacher, certainly helped to focus his career on a cause to which both he and his wife might commit their lives. His own diary as well as surviving correspondence between Charles and his brother Will suggest not simply that "Charlie" had been something of a ladies' man during and immediately after his college years, but that he genuinely enjoyed the company and conversation of women. His mother was a smart, capable, and pretty woman, stylish and "merry as a lark," but also gentle and caring. Lula Martin must have been like her in ways that attracted Charles. She was certainly pretty, although Will once remarked of his brother that "it is not so much beauty as novelty in women that attracts him." In Lula, Charles discovered something more than novelty. She was a young woman possessing a brilliant and original mind, a heart as loving as his mother's, and a determination to make the world a better place that equaled his own.[21]

Lula Martin was a strikingly unconventional southern woman. Her father was a doctor, her mother had attended an elite private secondary school, and Lula had grown up in a house filled with books and with literary and scientific journals, which she read precociously. When she was eleven, her parents allowed her to journey alone from their home on the Missouri plains to the

Moravian settlement of Salem, adjacent to Winston, where she had been born, to live with relatives and attend school while awaiting her parents' return to North Carolina.[22] At Salem Academy the girl's character was formed by a religious tradition that professed equality between the separate spheres of men and women. Ambitious and confident of her own intellectual gifts, Lula was quite unprepared for the disappointment that came with the realization that, because of her sex, she would be forced to abandon her dream of becoming a doctor like her father. When at some point in her adolescence she also learned that her church had once permitted a group of Moravian pioneers on the frontier to choose wives for themselves by casting lots, she announced to her parents that she intended to change her religious affiliation, and thereupon became a Methodist. Little did she know that her future husband's staunchly Presbyterian family would find that choice the only serious impediment to acceptance of their son's decision to marry the charming first-grade teacher he had met in Winston. They were ultimately won over by Lula's charm and Charles's determination to wed this "most sensible" of women. His parents may have been somewhat discomfited, however, to learn of the bride's intention, which their son respected, to delete the promise to obey from her wedding vows and never to wear a wedding ring, since to do so represented, to her mind, a husband's possession of his wife as a kind of property.[23]

The marriage took place in July 1885; Charles was twenty-four, Lula barely twenty-one. During the months that followed, they plunged into the work of exploring ways to train teachers for the North Carolina schools. Charles seemed literally to discover his own voice in this period, since with Lula's help he overcame an early fear of public speaking in his enthusiasm for the mission that increasingly occupied his mind and his formidable energies. His frequent public lectures were less eloquent than fervid, but at the same time genial and warmly persuasive, interspersed with anecdotal stories and humor. He succeeded in establishing a preparatory course for teachers at the Winston Graded School that fall, and the following spring was elected vice president of the state's Teachers' Assembly. At a meeting of that group soon after, McIver won over to his position on the absolute priority of educating women, particularly as teachers, a friend from his college days at the University of North Carolina, Edward Alderman, who subsequently became identified with him in the struggle. Alderman would later recall that the idea of a state normal school for women was "born in the brain of Charles McIver": "The whole scheme forced itself upon him out of the dust of injustice and negligence right before our eyes. . . . Together we drew up the memorial to the Legislature in its behalf, and I remember the day in 1886 that he, as chairman . . . presented this matter to the Committee on Education. We knew that it was doomed, but came away elated and somewhat excited over our first contact with legislative responsibility."[24]

The McIvers were indefatigably committed and optimistic even when setbacks such as these occurred. Moreover, Charles had received an attractive offer earlier that year to direct the literature program at an elite private school for girls in Raleigh, the Peace Institute, so he and Lula had moved to the capital after the

Charles and Lula Martin McIver with their children.

birth of their first child, a daughter. They clearly relished their new proximity to the legislature, whose members could be lobbied on behalf of the normal school proposal. Indeed, their home soon became locally famous for gatherings that combined gracious hospitality, good conversation, and frequent lively debate on the subject closest to the hearts of both McIvers.

Charles found additional work and support for his growing family—a son arrived in 1887—by teaching in a program of summer normal schools offered in cities around the state, four at first, then eight, modeled on a program developed ten years earlier at the University of North Carolina. Since even the expanded program proved inadequate to meet the needs of those living too far from the selected locations, the state Board of Education came up with a new plan, a "Campaign for Education" ratified by an act of the legislature on March 11, 1889. The act abolished existing programs and stipulated that two full-time educators should be hired, to be responsible for undertaking an assessment of the quality of education and conducting week-long summer educational institutes in all ninety-two counties of the state. McIver and Alderman, who was then superintendent of public schools in Goldsboro, were appointed to this herculean task.

The separate reports that the two men presented at the end of their first year of travel and teaching as County Institute "Conductors" painted a dismal picture of public education in North Carolina. There was a crippling lack of such basic educational resources as textbooks and adequate funding for salaries, but even worse was the lack of preparation or experience among the teachers themselves, two-thirds of whom were male. There were exceptions, of course, those few fine teachers discovered "generally among the women."[25] The reports, whose findings were widely published not just in the state but in newspapers and magazines north and south, gave a voice to hundreds of untrained, underpaid, and overworked teachers laboring against formidable odds, many in remote rural towns. Suddenly, according to one commentator, "the school teacher had come on the stage as a new factor in creating a militant public sentiment in favor of radical improvement in the public schools."[26]

Although Alderman and McIver had very different oratorical styles, both men attracted large audiences when they arrived in a town to teach an institute course and offer lectures to any group willing to listen: local educators, county commissioners, farmers' groups, and at Saturday rallies the general public. A friend of both men observed that after hearing Alderman people would exclaim, "What a wonderful address!" but after hearing McIver, who spoke the language of the common man, they were more likely to say, "What can we do to help Professor McIver?" In spite of ingrained opposition to the notion that private wealth should be taxed to educate those unable to pay for it themselves—education, after all, was useful in distinguishing among the classes—he was able to persuade North Carolinians that no man of conscience could any longer refuse support of an expanded and improved system of public education. The historian Dumas Malone would later describe McIver as the "most beloved" of the educational crusaders of his generation.[27] Since Mount Airy was the county seat of Surry, perhaps one or both of Katharine Smith's parents had a chance to hear McIver hold up to his audience the ideal of the teacher as the most important public official in any community, "the seed corn of civilization, and none but the best are good enough to use."[28]

During these years of arduous work, McIver, Alderman, and growing numbers of their supporters continued to lobby the legislature for passage of the act that would establish the Normal and Industrial School in Greensboro. Success came early in 1891 with ratification of the bill "to give young white women such education as should fit them for teaching, and to give instruction in drawing, telegraphy, typewriting, stenography, and such other industrial arts as might be suitable to their sex and conducive to their support and usefulness."[29] The act funded establishment of the school, provided free tuition for any student preparing to teach, and required that faculty of the school would continue the pro-

N.C. State Normal and Industrial College, Greensboro, postcard, 1912.

Normal College Avenue and College Buildings, Greensboro, N. C. 21422I

gram that offered summer teaching institutes in North Carolina counties, but for a term of eight weeks rather than just one. The Normal School, with Charles McIver as president, was ready to receive its first students in late September of the following year. Ed Alderman taught there that first year, then moved on to the University of North Carolina, where he was appointed president of the university in 1895.[30]

Life at "The Normal"

Throughout these years of exhausting travel, lobbying, teaching, and public speaking, Lula Martin McIver had not abandoned herself entirely to the demands of managing a household with two small children. Intellectual interests continued to define her at least as much as the preoccupations of domestic life, while her capacity for long hours and hard work matched her husband's. Moreover, the relationship between the two was so close and tender that Charles often pleaded with her to join him on institute trips, and frequently urged her participation in the teaching as well. To make that possible under his contract, he had written to the state superintendent of schools that "what I need is somebody to give me a breathing spell occasionally between lectures and to give variety to my work. Mrs. McIver can do both of these things, and besides, can present one or two subjects better than I can."[31] Lula had also taught classes at Peace Institute, and before long her experience and growing professional reputation earned her an offer of full-time employment, which she accepted, as "Lady Principal" of the Presbyterian Female Institute in Charlotte, beginning in the fall of 1890. Although his institute work made it necessary for Charles to be away from his family most of the time, the McIvers made Charlotte their home until taking up their new life together in the president's house on the grounds of the Normal School in Greensboro.[32] Both must have felt the heady sense of having realized their destiny as they threw themselves into the exhausting labors of getting the school and their own home ready in time for the start of the first academic year. Having anticipated an initial student body of 125 young women, they were forced to crowd dormitory rooms—and beds—to accommodate the 176 who had been admitted.[33] Years later, Lula would regale listeners with the story of her adventures on the momentous October day of the official opening. Charles had asked her, since he was otherwise occupied on that hectic morning, to show a visiting newspaperman around the campus. When the horse pulling their buggy bolted, Lula got out and attempted to calm the animal, in the course of which she suffered severe bruising of her feet. Ever the valiant woman of Scripture, she continued the tour before heading back home for ice and a brief rest. But even before the campus ceremonies were over, word came from her father, who was caring for the children during this busy time, that both were seriously ill. Lula calmly proceeded, in spite of her pain and fresh anxiety, to host a luncheon for visiting dignitaries. In the evening, she took the night train to Winston. When the train jumped the tracks a mile or more from its destination, the exhausted woman joined two men who decided to go ahead on foot—in her case, hobbling along. She made it to her father's house, where she nursed the children back to health over the course of several days, soaking her battered feet as often as she could in a basin of ice set between their beds.[34]

There is more to learn from this tale than an appreciation of Lula McIver's womanly fortitude. The fact that her pluck and independence surpassed what was normally expected of a southern lady—literally "taking the reins" when there was a gentleman at hand, for example—may be seen as a portent of a radically different ideal of feminine behavior that was being launched on the campus of "the Normal," as the school came to be called. The McIvers and Ed Alderman undoubtedly had spent hours deliberating about the kind of faculty they hoped to bring together, and in spite of budgetary constraints they had done a remarkable job. Most were highly dedicated single women with degrees from prestigious colleges and universities. One of the science professors had an undergraduate degree from the Massachusetts Institute of Technology and a doctorate from a German university. Another MIT graduate, who also served as school physician, had her medical degree from the Women's Medical College of New York Infirmary. There were two Wellesley College alumnae, and many of the women had spent summers doing graduate work at such major universities as Chicago, Columbia, Cornell, Harvard, and California at Berkeley. As a group they were conspicuously well traveled and cosmopolitan.[35] And to a woman, they were dedicated feminists, although they might not use that term.

That said, it is important to understand that another aspect of Lula's challenging exploits on the Normal School's opening day may shed light on the special nature of the feminism that she and Charles espoused. Notwithstanding her manifold responsibilities, Lula was the wife of the college president, and as such she graciously assumed the traditional role of helpmate in order to allow her husband to preside over the more important duties that came with his office. She was also the consummate caregiver, heedlessly sacrificing herself to protect his peace of mind and her children's well-being. Charles, keenly sensitive to the difference in status between them, apologized to his wife for the "galling" dependence and vulnerability that seemed inevitable in married life, particularly after children had arrived on the scene. Nevertheless, in campaigning for the cause of women's education, he had repeatedly argued that in the classroom as in the home, their sex was the "natural teacher of the race." This confidence that women enjoyed some kind of biological predisposition to teach the young gave rise to a still more exalted elevation of the role of wife and mother as "high priestess in humanity's temple."[36]

But there was as much country-boy pragmatism as high-minded liberalism reflected in the rhetoric of his favorite, oft-quoted aphorism: "Educate a man and you educate an individual; educate a woman and you educate a family." Perhaps the most brilliant stroke of reformers such as Page and McIver had been to frame the movement to establish public educational institutions for white women as nothing more than a timely and necessary expression of values that southerners were presumed to respect, values based on the innate need of "the weaker sex" for the help and protection of their menfolk. Moreover, McIver continually reminded male voters, if they answered the call to behave honorably by supporting his cause on behalf of their own sisters and daughters, they could take added satisfaction from knowing that they had simultaneously helped to resolve one of the South's most humiliating social issues, its poorly educated workforce. For the most intractable problem facing the South, he insisted again and again, was not racial in nature. Instead, "for whites and blacks, rich and poor, cultured and illiterate, the question of questions in the Southern states is 'How shall the great mass of people . . . be educated?'"[37] In their turn, the promising young women who availed themselves of the opportunity for an education funded mostly through the largesse of the citizens of North Carolina were bound by equally urgent, reciprocal moral obligations. Entering the Normal was like nothing so much as joining the army or becoming a missionary; in fact, McIver and his enthusiastically feminist faculty favored metaphors borrowed from military combat and evangelical religious crusades to describe the great civilizing work to which each student must now pledge her life.

This politic strategy, by emphasizing continuity between the vocational preparation to be provided at the Normal School and those mythic idealizations of womanhood particularly favored by southerners, served to shelter the spark of genuine revolution that the administration and faculty hoped to ignite in the heart of every young woman under their care. The girls' parents had en-

Members of the Normal College faculty, from The Carolinian, *1909.*

trusted them to the Normal with the expectation that the school would function—as any college for women, north or south, would be expected to do at that time—in loco parentis, responsible for nurturing the physical, emotional, and spiritual needs of the students as much as their intellectual development. It is likely that very few parents sending a daughter to Greensboro to be trained as a teacher, including the Smith family of Mount Airy, fully understood how different this institution was, not just from any other in the state but from almost any of the other colleges for women in the entire South. Most of these were little other than finishing schools, offering a curriculum no more rigorous than what was required to produce the appearance of refinement, poise, and cultivation in a young woman. Academic programs typically favored such subjects as literature, art, music, the Bible, and nature study, with generous allotments of time left for churchgoing, social events, and club activities.

In some respects, life at the Normal School might appear at first to have been not very different, at least in atmosphere, from the cheerful and homelike environment of the typical private women's colleges in the South. The formidably proper Miss Kirkland, whose social credentials the trustees had depended on—correctly, as it turned out—to attract a desirable percentage of students from middle- and upper-class families, was in charge of inculcating ladylike decorum in such details of self-presentation as speech, posture, dress, and table manners. While it was customary for male faculty, mostly married, to live off campus, single women lived in the same dormitory as the students. Nor did these faculty women dine together as a group; instead, each presided at a student table, joining the conversation and no doubt directing it to some extent as well. They not only supervised but also participated in many extracurricular activities, and students were assured of frequent opportunities for conversation with any individual teacher, either on one of the required daily afternoon walks or by meeting with her on Sunday evenings, a time set aside for private chats about any matter of concern, academic or per-

Dorm rooms at Normal, from The Carolinian, *1909.*

sonal. It is hardly surprising that the relationship between faculty and students was close and caring.[38] The McIvers, whose gift for warm and generous hospitality was well known, set the tone for the entire school, which was that of a small community of friends—administration, faculty, and students together—bound to one another by strong ties of affection and respect.

Another way in which the school fulfilled parental expectations was in its assumption of a Christian identity among its students. Both the Baptist and Methodist churches in North

Sue May Kirkland, charter faculty member, from The Carolinian, *1909.*

Carolina had been outspoken adversaries of any state-supported educational institutions beyond the grade-school level, on the principle that they represented unfair competition with private, specifically denominational, schools and colleges. There was also the sense that, since any proper education ought to be grounded in the cultivation of religious faith, nonsectarian public institutions threatened the constitutional separation of church and state. A number of other denominations joined the bitter fight against continued appropriations to the Normal School, even after it had begun operating successfully. McIver, ever that "prince of persuaders," did a masterly job in allaying the fears of this powerful coalition, chiefly by pointing out that more than 80 percent of the students at the Normal could not have afforded tuition at a private college.[39] But he also bravely challenged as "outmoded" the insistence of church groups that religious formation was intrinsically the chief end of education.[40] Notwithstanding this liberal and humanist posture, however, the fact that Charles McIver's personal style was so like that of a Protestant preacher—and he and Lula were, after all, devout Christians—must have reassured the public that a nonsectarian institution with McIver at its helm would be a perfectly suitable environment for any young woman. Even when he did battle with distinguished churchmen, the parents of prospective students trusted him.

And religion *was* an important part of life at the officially non-sectarian Normal School. The main building housed a chapel in which morning prayer services were held each day, usually with President McIver presiding. He would read sonorously from Scripture, frequently choosing as his text either Christ's Sermon on the Mount—"Ye are the salt of the earth. . . . Ye are the light of the world"—or the thirteenth chapter of Saint Paul's First Letter to the Corinthians, both of which exhort the faithful to selfless and loving service to one's fellow man. Then there would be a brisk, inspiring, but always down-to-earth homily pointing out the ways in which such simple courtesies as promptness and diligence in work were expressions of Pauline charity.[41] He quoted five lines of a favorite poem so often that every graduate of the Normal School from the McIver years carried them in her memory for the rest of her life:

> *The man who seeks one thing in life and but one*
> *May hope to achieve it before life is done;*
> *But he who seeks all things, wherever he goes*
> *Only reaps from the hopes which around him he sows,*
> *A harvest of barren regrets.*[42]

Although the language may appear sexist by today's standards, students of the Normal School knew that both McIvers, husband and wife, had made the lesson of these lines a rule of life. They had embraced in their youth one great work—to open up educational opportunities for the women of North Carolina—and had steadfastly concentrated all their energies on achieving it. Now

they were seeing their years of struggle and sacrifice begin to bear fruit in the lives of the young women of the Normal School, whom they inspired to commit their own lives unselfishly to teaching others.

One of the most important of the extracurricular activities in which the student body participated, as well as a number of women faculty, staff, and spouses of male faculty, was the Young Women's Christian Association. Although the YWCA would later become a leading force for social reform in the South, demanding an end to racial segregation long before legal sanctions became a reality, in the early years of the Normal School its members concentrated on prayer, personal conversion, and response to the gospel injunction to "go forth and teach all nations."[43] The missionary zeal so characteristic of the McIvers, however, had effectively translated the religious conviction of being "elected" or "called" into a secular vocation, if one just as surely aimed at accomplishing some worthwhile purpose in a world that needed to be reminded of Christian values. This expanded understanding of what it might mean to "take up the

Normal College YWCA Cabinet, from The Carolinian, *1909.*

Lord's work of salvation" made the activities of the YWCA on the Normal School's campus rather different from those of more conventional chapters, whose members concentrated on explicitly religious projects.

When a graduating senior wrote an essay for the school magazine titled "The Duty of the Class of '97 to the State," in which she proclaimed that she and her classmates would now turn their hands to "the work which God has given us to do," which was to lead "a great awakening among the people,"[44] she was borrowing the name that historians had given to the series of religious revivals that swept across the American colonies in the middle of the eighteenth century. The "Great Awakening" is credited with having unleashed a democratic spirit that eventually linked mass doctrinal dissent from established churches to the revolutionary movement to overthrow British rule. In the South, Baptists, Methodists, and Presbyterians had gathered strength and numbers from the success of evangelical preaching by itinerant ministers. The claim of these unorthodox messengers of the gospel was that true conversion of the sinful heart was not a gradual process but "an absolute, immediate, instantaneous work—darted in upon us like a flash of lightning . . . changing the whole man into a new creature in the twinkling of an eye."[45] This Pentecostal emphasis, anticipating a charismatic experience of being "born again," survived well into the nineteenth century and beyond, forming the central core of a religious sensibility still strongly identified with the American South.

It is hardly surprising that having been formed within this "dissenting" tradition, Charles McIver and others among the crusaders for southern educational reform unselfconsciously adapted its language and persuasive strategies to new political purposes. But Lula Martin McIver and the northern women hired as teachers for the Normal School were also passionately committed converts to the still revolutionary notion of women's inherent intellectual and social equality with men. Under the veneer of ladylike propriety encouraged in the students of the Normal

School as a desirable aspect of their professional formation, the real educational objective was to nurture in each young woman's mind and heart an entirely new self-awareness. Once converted to ideas that their own parents and the larger society of the South would find radically subversive, these "born again" graduates, married or single, were expected to take an active part in the arena of public life, until now the exclusive preserve of men. Moreover, if they were to lead the battle for better schools throughout the state, they must possess the self-confidence of the truly expert, McIver warned, "familiar with all the details of taxation and school revenue. . . . able to address an audience . . . and

The Cats, from The Carolinian, *1909.*

Field hockey at Normal, 1909.

"To Sunny Fields Beyond," landscape at Normal, *from* The Carolinian, *1909.*

give them a business statement in regard to the public schools of the community."[46] If the administration and faculty prided themselves on the high standards of the academic and professional programs at the Normal School, so did their students. Most of them, the daughters of small farmers and shopkeepers, had a thrilling sense of having entered a marvelous new world. Here, caring, articulate, intellectually stimulating men and women, different from any they had known before, made them feel important, needed by a great cause, and ripe with promise of an exciting future as women of the New South.

Kate Becomes Katharine

This is the world that Kate Smith of Mount Airy entered in the fall of 1897, having written to President McIver in her letter of application that she had decided upon investigation that the Normal School promised to provide the best education available to women anywhere in the state.[47] She also asked to receive the waiver of tuition provided to students who intended to pursue a teaching career. Although we know few particulars of Katharine's daily life over the course of the three years during which she attended the Normal, there can be no doubt, based on the evidence of the interests and commitments closest to her heart in later life as well as the documented quality of the school's learning environment, that her experience was profoundly transformative. In fact, in considering the dramatic effect of this education on the personality and character of the woman she was to become, one is tempted to use the same language of ecstatic religious conversion that fell so easily from the lips of her teachers and mentors. The bright, sensitive seventeen-year-old who left home to enter the Normal in 1897 had signed her original application form "Kathrine Smith" and her supporting letter "Kate Smith." Later correspondence between her and Charles McIver is signed "Katherine," and still later she begins to use the spelling of her name that she would keep for the rest of her life, Katharine.[48] What new sense of who she was—or wanted to be—does this renaming, as it were, represent? Katharine's residency at the Normal School was substantially interrupted several times by illness—her own or that of family members, as well as a tragic outbreak of typhoid at the school. Early in her freshman year she contracted measles, a childhood disease often more serious in adolescence.[49] Two years later, at the start of her junior year in the fall of 1899, she was among the first of more than sixty students succumbing to a malaria epidemic that devastated several counties of North Carolina. The decision to send Katharine home to recover probably saved her from exposure to the even more deadly typhoid fever that erupted at the school over the course of the following weeks, forcing its closing for two months early in 1900. During this period a panel of scientists and engineers hired by the trustees determined that the main well from which the school drew its water was contaminated by the typhoid bacillus. Fifty-five students had been infected, fourteen of whom died.[50]

McIver's enemies among the churchmen and conservatives who had failed to prevent the state's continued support of the Normal School now seized the opportunity to place blame for the epidemic and its consequences on his administration. They won support among a few of the students' families. For example, a letter published in the *Raleigh News and Observer* from a doctor whose sister had died asked: "Why was it these young ladies were huddled in a pest hole? If it be criminal indifference and neglect it is nothing short of murder. If it be incompetence it is surely a scandal."[51] This was without doubt a sad time for Charles and Lula, for their faculty—especially Anna Gove, the resident physician—and for the students who admired and loved them. Lula, who regretted not having become a doctor herself, took particular pride in her scrupulous attention to matters of health and sanitation, having frequently led teams of students and teachers in strenuous cleaning operations at the rural schools they visited during the summer institutes.[52] But a sense of helplessness in preventing or effectively treating contagious and deadly disease was all too familiar to nineteenth-century Americans. What must it have been like for the students themselves to lose fourteen members of their close-knit community?

Katharine, who had experienced the loss of her five-year-old brother when she was just seven, must have considered the possibility of her own imminent death during the throes of her malarial fever. Fortunately, however, the Smiths were apparently among the much larger group of North Carolinians, including most of the parents, who did not hold the McIver administration responsible for this terrible occurrence. Katharine returned to school when classes resumed in February 1900, although she may have had to continue making up coursework during the academic year that began that fall.

Something happened in the extended interval between what would have been her junior and senior years, however, to prevent Katharine from finishing her education at the Normal. Instead, she was sent in the fall of 1901 to begin a fifth year of college enrollment at a private school, Sullins College in Bristol, Virginia, where her younger sister Maxie was a sophomore. Their cousin Dick's sister Lucy had graduated from Sullins many years earlier, so there were family ties to the institution and kinfolk living in the area. Since Katharine had been one of that small percentage of students at the Normal whose families were not financially dependent on the tuition waiver that she received as a teacher in training, Zachary Smith had no difficulty assuming the expense of enrolling his two eldest daughters at Sullins. One explanation for Katharine's transfer, and perhaps the one actually tendered to anyone who inquired, was her parents' concern for her health after the typhoid crisis in 1899. Yet she had gone back to the Normal to continue her interrupted junior year in 1900, not moving to Sullins until well over a year later.

There is a good possibility, however, that during this period the physical frailty that plagued Katharine's adult life may have begun to manifest itself, although it seems not to have been related to the bouts of measles and malaria she had survived while a student at the Normal. Katharine had a weakened heart, which, while not serious enough to make her an invalid, was bound to have been a matter of concern to her parents. The symptoms that emerge in later descriptions suggest that at some time in her youth she must have developed rheumatic fever following a streptococcal infection, which in those days would have looked like any other high fever accompanied by aching joints. Now we take for granted the use of modern antibiotics to prevent the physical damage to the heart that occurs when streptococcal bacteria invade its valves; that remedy, of course, was not yet available. Whatever the case, Katharine suffered from a chronic heart condition that her family associated with an adolescent illness.

All the same, it is tempting to speculate that some other motivation may have prompted—or at least reinforced—the decision that Katharine should not complete her education at the Normal School. It seems unlikely that Katharine herself favored transferring to a new school for her last year, to enter a graduating class consisting mostly of students who had been together during the previous three years. Katharine was clearly tied to the Normal by strong emotional bonds, for she stayed in touch with the McIvers and other faculty, and essentially put into practice over the course of her life the mission that she had first embraced under their influence. Perhaps her parents had some misgivings about a perceived transformation of their Kate under the influence of McIver and that impressive group of unmarried, highly motivated professional women, avowed feminists, he had hired as faculty. What new ideas filled her head and spilled out in conversation during the weeks she lived at home? Talk of women's suffrage and racial equality were already in the air at the Normal School, although McIver was personally determined that these controversial questions should not surface to distract the public from the goal of women's higher education, which in his view was the most practical avenue through which genuine social and sexual equality might ultimately be achieved.[53] Moreover, developing ease and skill in public speaking and debate was an important part of student formation at the Normal School. Were Katharine's parents occasionally disturbed by what seemed to them an excess of fervor for a variety of causes, some of them sounding rather radical? Their daughter was poised and physically attractive, but also fiercely intelligent, with intense feelings about things that mattered not at all to most girls her age. What eligible man would be inclined to court such an outspoken and militant young woman? Even more troubling, was there any danger that Katharine might choose to be a spinster, like the faculty women of the Normal School?

Now "Ruler of Hearts"

It is impossible to know, of course, whether reflections of this kind contributed either consciously or subconsciously to her parents' decision to have Katharine complete her education at Sullins. What is certain is that the environment at her new school could not have been more different from that of the Normal. The trustees of the Normal School, as well as McIver and his faculty, understood from the inception of their enterprise that however

The Normal girl, from The Carolinian, 1909.

The Sullins girl, from The Omega, 1902.

Sullins College

for

Young Ladies.

MRS. JAMESON voices our design in the following words: "The true purpose of education is to cherish and unfold the seed of immortality already sown within us; to develop to their fullest extent the capacities of every kind with which the God who made us has endowed us."

much their students would be encouraged to reject the traditional restriction of women's "proper sphere" to home, family, and church, these young women must at the same time acquire the manners—the confidence, grace, and gentility—expected of a southern lady. Without that cachet, it would be impossible for them to enter the public sphere as influential leaders of their community, which was the whole point of their education. So the faculty took pains, in and out of the classroom, to expose students to social situations, including dances and teas, as well as concerts, plays, and literary debates, that would help them to overcome any of the shyness or awkwardness common to adolescence and to develop, as had the women who were their mentors, a pleasing and effective personal style.

There was never any question, however, that the cultivation of mind and moral fiber counted for more than manners. The young women of the Normal School were being trained as "soldiers" in the battle to liberate the South from the poverty and ignorance that were the consequence of the region's long neglect of public education. Not surprisingly, there is evidence that the students frequently felt a measure of anxiety about being in the vanguard of a movement to redefine the ideal of southern womanhood, since there was no way to know what sacrifices might be demanded of them in the future.[54] At Sullins, by contrast, education was seen as a desirable enhancement of a young lady's preparation for marrying well and assuming her traditional responsibilities as wife, mother, and mistress of a household. Still, the college was apparently not entirely untouched by the idea of the "New Woman" in a new century. Katharine Smith may even have had something to do with choosing the topics to be argued by the Sullins debating team, which she joined after her arrival on campus. Topics that year included "Resolved, that women should be admitted to American universities on equal terms with men"; "Resolved, that a college education helps a woman in her home life"; and "Resolved, that it is better to be an old maid than an unhappy married woman." The last of these was won by the team defending the resolution; Katharine's sister Maxie was on the opposite, losing side.

It was the custom at Sullins to award the positions of class officers based on academic rank. Since she was a transfer student, Katharine's class rank would have been subject to interpretation of her academic record, so it could hardly be expected that the "new girl" would be made president or vice president of the graduating class. It says something for her academic credentials, however, that she was appointed class treasurer. She was also elected president of the literary society, president of the Young Women's Missionary Society, and editor in chief of *The Omega*, the 1902

Katharine Smith (center) and her Fairesonian sisters, from The Omega, *1902.*

"Most College-Spirited Girl," from The Omega, 1902.

Sullins College yearbook.[55] How shall we interpret the superlatives she garnered—"Faculty Favorite" and "Most College-Spirited Girl"—in the voting among graduating seniors? The eldest child in a family is often inclined to be a "pleaser," modeling first the behavior of parents, then that of other adults in authority, and Katharine obviously fit that profile. It is harder to know for sure what it meant for this newcomer to have had the most "college spirit" of anyone in her class, although we must not assume that the title proves that Katharine had just as much enthusiasm for the education offered at Sullins as she did for that of the Normal School. More likely, her leadership role reflected exactly those values of zealous work on behalf of improving one's community with which she had been imbued at the Normal. Her "college spirit" at Sullins may have expressed itself as a voice urging change and energetic commitment to worthy projects; she was, after all, the president of the Missionary Society. Clearly, she struck her peers as an exceptionally high-spirited and articulate person, a natural leader.

They may also have liked the fact that in spite of Katharine's air of maturity and the studiousness that always pleased her teachers, she made friends easily and entered into the frivolous and playful activities of her new school with no apparent reservations. Many of these entertainments took advantage of the proximity of the Sullins campus to Kings College for men, which figures so prominently in the yearbook Katharine edited that it is impossible to escape the perception that a preoccupation with courtship and marriage among the Sullins student body took precedence over academic interests. There is a lengthy article in the form of "Model Love Letters of a Kings College Boy and a Sullins Girl" and a roster of Kings College "Gallants" voted on by Sullins seniors: "Most Popular Man," "Handsomest," "Jolliest," "Most Practical," "Most Susceptible," "Greatest Flirt," "Most Intellectual," "Manliest," "Cutest," "Best Talker," "Most Dignified," and (significantly last?) "Smartest." Katharine Smith's name appears among the "Rulers of Hearts" within the membership of the Diamond Ring Club, and she chose "When We Are Married" as her favorite song. Club members were not required to be engaged, but perhaps Katharine's parents were reassured by this declaration of their daughter's obvious intention to marry.

The yearbook also includes, presumably on the basis of their literary interest as travel narratives, two letters sent by a graduate of Sullins to one of her former teachers describing a trip taken in the summer of 1900 to the British Isles. There is a passage in one letter that reminds us of the extraordinary popularity among nineteenth-century southerners of Sir Walter Scott's poems and his Waverley novels:

> From Edinburgh we went to Aberfoyle, a small village in the Highlands, and found ourselves in the district once held in terror by Rob Roy and his band of Highlanders.

Aberfoyle is beautifully situated, being surrounded on all sides by mountains covered with heather . . . and the valley is dotted here and there with small lakes, the prettiest of which is Loch Katrine. Scott tells us in his "Lady of the Lake," that on a small island in the middle of the lake, lived Ellen Douglas and her father.[56]

The correspondent then describes the trip across Loch Katrine in a boat named *Sir Walter Scott*. As part of her duties as editor, Katharine no doubt read this letter many times. It seems, in fact, to have inspired a resolution in her mind, a determination that she, too, would one day have such an experience of those distant and romantic places she had loved reading about during her growing-up years. She imagined more than just seeing them; she wanted, somehow, to make them her own, just as those who love a book may long to live inside its story, to be there, in that wondrous place.

Leaving Home

The most formal of the photographs of Katharine included in the Sullins yearbook shows a serenely beautiful young woman, although her gaze has the same haunting suggestion of melancholy that appears in her childhood portrait. Her neck and shoulders, framed by the intricate detailing of her bodice, seem fine-boned and delicate in contrast to her strong facial features—the dark eyes, full brows, wide lips—and her dark hair like a coronet. There is nothing delicate, however, about the size or the set of Katharine's jaw. In family photos taken throughout her later life, the angle of the shot would occasionally exaggerate the cut of her jaw in a way that coarsens the image of sweetness, even of vulnerability, projected here.

Perhaps it is not so much melancholy as worry that shadows Katharine's expression in the photograph. For all its harmless

Portrait of Katharine Smith, from The Omega, *1902.*

collegiate high jinks, spending her last year at Sullins had exposed her to social pressures that would have scandalized the administration and faculty of the Normal School. Charles McIver never denigrated a woman's choice of marriage and family over life as a single woman pursuing a career, so long as she put her education to work not just in raising her children but in assuming an active civic life in service to her community, her state, and the region. But a man whose own wife refused to wear a wedding ring might not have been pleased to learn that Katharine had joined the Diamond Ring Club. She may have been uneasily aware that, at least on the surface, she had betrayed a vision of feminine independence that she knew to be valid and good, and right for her.

She must also have spent a lot of time, once she and Maxie had returned to Mount Airy after Katharine's graduation from Sullins in June 1902, thinking about what course her life would take next. The family had moved a few years earlier into a sprawling nine-bedroom house on a ten-acre site in town.[57] In addition to Katharine and Maxie, there were the Smith boys, Zachary Madison (called "Matt") and Gene, who were then fifteen and thirteen, and the little sisters, Irene and Ruth, ten and three years old. Although Katharine's bachelor's degree from Sullins indicates that she majored in English literature, another photograph in the yearbook places her among the art students, and she had taken art courses at the Normal as well. Family tradition holds, in fact, that art was Katharine's primary career interest, and she did teach an art class in Mount Airy for a brief period after her graduation.[58] These were private lessons, probably given in some quiet corner of that bustling house; there is nothing to suggest that she obtained a formal teaching position in Mount Airy during the school year that began in the fall of 1902. We do know that by December, Katharine had apparently entered into a new relationship with her father's friend and first cousin once removed, Dick Reynolds.[59]

He was a man of her parents' generation, not her own; his mother and Katharine's grandmother were sisters. He was just three years younger than her father, five years older than her mother, and thirty years older than Katharine herself. He was even ten years older than the revered president of the Normal School, Charles Duncan McIver. By then in his fifties, "Cousin Dick" had already exceeded the average life span of American men at the turn of the century. But at twenty-two, Katharine Smith must have felt the first stirrings of a different and deeper affection for this aging bachelor kinsman. He was a man of the world in every sense, an industrialist fabled for daring business acumen whose tobacco brands were being marketed across the country and halfway around the world, and as the largest employer in North Carolina, well on his way to becoming a millionaire. He was also, fervently, a man of the South, proud of his heritage and committed to making the "New South" dream of regional recovery and prosperity a reality.

There were other ways in which R. J. Reynolds may have reminded Katharine of her mentor Charles McIver, in spite of their belonging to very different worlds. Like McIver, Reynolds possessed the common touch; nothing about him was slick or pretentious. Although he had the benefit of a decent education and came from a family in which the refinements that wealth makes possible were highly valued, some aura still clung to him of those rough-and-ready men of the soil, the generations of yeoman tobacco farmers from whom he was descended.[60] He was awkward in speech, suffering from a stammer, yet people of every class responded to his plain speaking, high spirits, and even raucous good humor just as McIver's audiences responded to him, liking the man for himself. And in his own way, Katharine's cousin Dick projected an intensity not unlike McIver's, and not unlike her own. Best of all, he clearly recognized that she had grown into a beautiful woman who was a match, in her intelligence and fire, for any man. He was no stripling boy, to be put off by a woman who could think for herself and hold her own in conversation, who loved literature and art and had a mission to change the world.

After the mother to whom he was devoted died in the spring of 1903, Dick invited Katharine and another young cousin with whom she was close to accompany him on a business trip to New York City. Perhaps he was moving cautiously ahead on a project already conceived in his mind. The trip represented an opportunity for Katharine to see this cousin she had known from childhood in a more cosmopolitan setting, one in which he was a commanding presence; surely he hoped not simply to dazzle her but to let her bask in his tender care of her and her cousin. He wrote her soon after their return that "your proving a favorite with the older people is a good indication that I judged you correctly, as one of the few that is so constituted or has the capability of enjoying whatever you may do that will make yourself most useful during life."[61] However stilted the prose, the sentiment is clear, and captures Katharine's spirit.

Wasting no time, he next offered to employ Katharine as a secretary in his Winston office. She had acquired during her college years the necessary basic skills in typing and stenography, while her gift for graceful composition promised to make her a valuable resource for an executive for whom writing would always be a challenge, as was true for Dick. She accepted his offer and within the month had packed and left home, moved to Winston, and begun work at the R. J. Reynolds Tobacco Company. We have to imagine how exciting it would have been for her to begin this great adventure, setting out into the world to live as a working woman in the thriving industrial "Twin Cities" of Winston and Salem, with their population of eighteen thousand, their department stores, streetcar lines, handsome homes, churches, parks, and public buildings, to say nothing of the trains that left every day for Washington, D.C., and New York City. The only thing we know of her experience during that first year is that Katharine won the remarkably extravagant thousand-dollar prize in a competition within the firm for the best advertising copy celebrating the quality of R. J. Reynolds tobacco products.[62]

Another week-long spring holiday in New York, this time in the company of Dick's sister Lucy and her husband, Robert Critz, followed in 1904. By this time the suitable mourning period following his mother's death had come to a close, and Dick was free to offer Katharine, "Ruler of Hearts," the kind of courtship that fulfilled the romantic expectations she had shared with her classmates at Sullins. He spoke to her father, then proposed to Katharine formally, in writing, and she replied the same way, agreeing to be his wife. Their engagement took place on the third day of October 1904, just short of her twenty-fourth birthday. Dick Reynolds was the most eligible bachelor in Winston, perhaps in all of North Carolina, with a reputation as a man about town, a sporting man who liked cards, gambling, strong drink, and the company of women. Katharine's natural maturity and poise

did not belie the fact that she was still quite young and innocent; she played the ingenue to his charming roué. But he was passionately in love with her, and wrote to reassure her as their wedding date drew near: "I feel that no one on earth is blessed with a more noble, earnest, and sincere, lovely, sweet or better wife than I will have in you. I love you and respect you so much more than I ever did anyone else, that I really feel I never knew what true love was;

View toward the south and a street scene, Winston, 1905.

it must be God's blessing in having me to wait for you and receive more happiness than earlier marriage would have given me."[63]

The wedding took place, in what may have struck some guests as "New Woman" style, in the parlor of her parents' home in Mount Airy at eight in the morning on what is likely to have been at best a brisk and chilly February day. The couple had a train to catch, the train that would get them to New York in time to board the ocean liner that would take them off on a four-month-long European honeymoon. This was the trip that Katharine had dreamed of ever since she had edited the travel letters of a Sullins alumna for her college yearbook. But now she would make her journey—the start of a life's journey to which she felt she had been called by God—on the arm of the kinsman who was now her spouse.

TWO

A Mission for Mrs. Reynolds

DICK REYNOLDS SPARED NO EXPENSE IN ENSURING THAT Katharine's European tour would be as luxurious as it was thrilling for a young woman who had as yet seen very little of the world and had long dreamed of traveling. Even the decision to allow himself extended time away from his business suggests how much this hands-on entrepreneur wished to savor his happiness. Perhaps Dick sensed, too, that their four-month honeymoon presented what would be a rare opportunity to have only each other for company, since once back home they would be obliged to resume a bustling life in society and within a large and intimate extended family. A surviving handwritten list of hotels in which the couple either planned to stay or did stay provides at least a partial glimpse of the stops their itinerary may have included: London, Paris, Monte Carlo, Genoa, Florence, Rome, Milan, Basel, Frankfurt, Berlin, Dresden, Vienna.[1] We can imagine the Reynoldses touring these places, dining well, shopping, and strolling along handsome boulevards and through parks, attending concerts and theatrical performances, visiting museums and galleries, altogether delighting, as Katharine wrote her mother from Venice, in their shared discovery of Europe's cosmopolitan culture.[2] We know that they purchased works of art on the trip, that Katharine had two exquisite "afternoon or reception gowns" made in Paris by a couturier particularly favored by wealthy Americans, and that they each had a portrait taken in the photographic studio of Eugène Pirou on the rue Royale.[3]

For two centuries, the tradition of a "Grand Tour" such as this was considered an essential complement to the formal education of young men of the upper classes. By the time Katharine

Katharine Smith Reynolds, honeymoon photo, 1905.

and R. J. Reynolds arrived in Europe, however, the industrial revolution in England and America had already reconfigured traditional economic and social systems based primarily on land and lineage. The new capitalists on both sides of the Atlantic had learned to use their financial fortunes to leverage access to political power and social status, just as earlier, more homogeneous ruling classes had done, a process sardonically captured in the epithet "robber barons." Perhaps it was natural, too, for

R. J. Reynolds,
honeymoon photo,
1905.

American princes of industry to seek to emulate, in their homes and lifestyles, historic models associated with the European aristocracy, even when doing so earned the scorn of social critics such as Thorstein Veblen, whose scathing *Theory of the Leisure Class* appeared in 1899,[4] or the expatriate literary titan Henry James. Just a year before the Reynoldses' honeymoon trip, James had been appalled, while revisiting the United States after twenty years abroad, to see the "distressful, inevitable waste" exhibited by the "white elephants. . . . all house and no garden," of the millionaires' enclave in Newport, Rhode Island.[5]

Even the term "American Renaissance," often used to describe the period dating from the centennial year of 1876 through the end of the First World War in 1917, reflects the importance of European sources not just for the visual arts, architecture, and interior and landscape design, but for urban design as well, particularly after the huge popular success of the neoclassical "White City" designed by a team of the country's leading architectural firms for the 1893 World's Columbian Exposition in Chicago. Americans increasingly wanted their own towns and cities to reflect the same elegance and grandeur, the same suggestion of continuity with a heroic and refined historic culture that was everywhere evident in the capitals of Europe. The painter John La Farge summed up the mood of national optimism that flourished in this country during the presidential administration of Theodore Roosevelt (1901–9) when he hailed the recent establishment of the American Academy in Rome to educate American scholars, architects, and artists in classical and Renaissance traditions. It was, he said, "in itself a statement that we too are rivals of all that has been done, and intend to rival all that shall be done, and we can then feel that the old cycle is closed and that a new one has begun."[6]

Katharine and Dick must surely have shared in this exhilarating anticipation that the new century unfolding before them as they began their married life together would see a great flourishing of American prosperity and cultural achievements. Newspa-

View from the Manufactures Building, World's Fair, Chicago, from The Magic City *(1894).*

"The Civic Center That Denver Is About to Realize" by Charles Mulford Robinson, from Los Angeles, California: The City Beautiful *(1909).*

pers and magazines were filled with articles about the "City Beautiful" movement, given its name and guiding philosophy by the pioneering journalist and author Charles Mulford Robinson (1869–1917) and inspired by his experience of the Chicago fair. Early in his career Robinson had proposed in a three-part series in the *Atlantic Monthly* that an improved urban life in America required substantial progress in three key areas: philanthropy, education, and aesthetic standards. More articles and two best-selling books followed, detailing practical strategies for realizing improvements to communities from village to metropolis. By 1904, when the second edition of his *Modern Civic Art, or the City Made*

Beautiful was published, more than 1,200 societies had been founded in the United States to spearhead the development of local planning activities.[7] Katharine, an avid reader of books and magazines, no doubt linked what she knew of the American movement with all that she and her husband admired in the cities they were visiting. Directly or indirectly, her thinking about her own community would be formed by the ideals and methods so persuasively advocated by Robinson and others. Philanthropy, increased educational opportunities, and the improvement of public and private environments would become the linchpins of her own life's work.

Like most new brides, Katharine would also have begun even before the wedding to think about the homemaking responsibilities she would soon take on. She knew that she would be moving into the house that Dick and his mother, as well as his brother and sister-in-law, had occupied for more than ten years, and which her husband had purchased from his brother less than a year before.[8] Every day of her honeymoon must have reminded Katharine that her husband's wealth, relative to that of her own family, would change her life in profound ways. At twenty-four, how else could she imagine the possibilities except as freedom to indulge her artistic inclinations in any direction she chose, but most particularly in the domestic environment that she would create for her husband and the children they hoped to have?

Given these four months spent savoring the life of the *haut monde*, one might expect that this youthful bride—whose only experience of travel outside the South had been her two brief trips to New York with Dick before their engagement—dreamed of one day surrounding herself with the same accoutrements of aristocratic European style favored by American millionaires when they built and furnished their houses. The emerging architectural modernism of such pioneers as Louis Sullivan and Frank Lloyd Wright in Chicago and the firm of Greene and Greene on the West Coast still had very little impact on the prevailing preference of America's industrial aristocracy for the styles that formed the canon of the French Académie des Beaux-Arts. Indeed, the first American architect trained at the Paris academy, Richard Morris Hunt, had designed for George W. Vanderbilt's Biltmore estate in western North Carolina, about two hundred miles from where Katharine grew up, one of the country's most grandiose examples of this fashion. Hunt's 250-room chateau-style mansion borrowed closely from sixteenth- and seventeenth-century models such as the royal chateaux of Blois, Chambord, and Chenonceaux. The landscape plan for the house and gardens, set within a 125,000-acre complex of farms, forests, and supporting facilities, had been the work of Frederick Law Olmsted.

Although her husband's considerable wealth was of a different order from the fortune amassed by the shipping and railroad tycoon Commodore Cornelius Vanderbilt, grandfather of George Vanderbilt, Katharine might easily have been attracted, as so

Biltmore Estate (1887–1895), house on the lake, lantern slide.

many were, to an aesthetic that deliberately conjured up the aura of "old money" rather than new. In a classic study of the ideology and mores of the American South, the historian Wilbur J. Cash named R. J. Reynolds as one of the very few southern businessmen whose ingenuity had helped them to become, by the turn of the century, "rich by any standard save those of the richest Yankees."[9] Katharine and her husband were probably as bitterly self-conscious as most southerners about the lingering poverty and cultural disadvantages that plagued their region, seeming to justify northern preconceptions of southern inferiority. Yet Dick Reynolds, whom Cash described as having "come to his destined fief, Winston, in true Dick Whittington style, perched atop a tobacco wagon,"[10] projected, in spite of his rural origins and awkwardness in speech, a hearty self-confidence. But because Katharine was so much younger than he, and more serious by nature, she may have felt their southernness, if not as a burden, at least as a responsibility always to consider carefully the impression that any words or actions of hers might convey to outsiders.

That sensitivity about southern culture would not, however, make her fearful of trusting her own instincts. However circumscribed her experience had been until then, her capacity for leadership had been confirmed by her schoolmates, and her intelligence and common sense by having been chosen by no less a man than R. J. Reynolds to be his wife. Katharine would relish the feast of learning that European travel offered her, and all that she saw and learned would nourish her own thinking and planning in years to come. She would make something of it, but not by drawing upon traditional styles meant to impress the world with their grandeur and sophistication. Her husband was admired for his lack of pretension; Katharine, too, would want their life together to reflect the values of simplicity and service to others, to her state, and to the South instilled in her by Charles McIver and her teachers at the Normal School.

In the Reynolda Archives there is an undated pamphlet describing Dove Cottage, the poet William Wordsworth's rustic home in the village of Grasmere in the mountainous Lake District of northern England. This was an immensely popular destination for American tourists in the nineteenth and early twentieth centuries, and it is very likely that Katharine and Dick visited there after their boat docked in Liverpool and before heading on to London.[11] A stop at Wordsworth's cottage had been one of the high points recounted in the travel narrative published in the Sullins College yearbook when Katharine served as editor. That letter, so different in character from anything else appearing in the book, seems to have made a lasting impression on her. Moreover, since she had graduated as a "Mistress of Literature," Wordsworth's life and work would have been familiar to her, perhaps piquing her interest in visiting the famously picturesque district that had provided inspiration to a host of literary and artistic figures.

"Dove Cottage" and "Grasmere," from Through Wordsworth Country *(1890).*

"A Leafy Bower: Rydal," from Through Wordsworth Country *(1890).*

At Grasmere, Wordsworth had lived an idyll of creative work and conversation with his sister Dorothy during his most productive years, 1799–1808. Dove Cottage and its village thus came to mean more to him than merely a useful and pleasant retreat from the distractions of the city; it symbolized the life of intimacy with the natural world that he had known as a child and later believed had formed his moral consciousness as well as his poetic sensibility. The poet lived for a time in France when that country's revolution still seemed to hold promise of creating a society based on freedom, equality, and brotherhood. Returning to England, he had been horrified by the frenetic pace and clangor of London's streets; he saw that the same mindless waste and greed powered the engines of England's mills and mines. Shocked by the indifference to human suffering, the sacrifice of childhood in brutal labor, and the despoiling of the rural landscape, he felt himself called, like Milton, "whose soul was like a star and dwelt apart,"[12] to awaken his countrymen to the need for massive social reform and a return to the rural virtues of an earlier time. Grasmere was a refuge, a place where the old way of life and its values still persisted. In a poem written early in the year after his arrival at Dove Cottage, Wordsworth celebrated the tranquil life of the village as a model of how "all the vales of the earth" should be in the future, when the same contentment he had discovered there would be recognized as the right of "all mankind":

> 'Tis (but I cannot name it) 'tis the sense
> Of majesty and beauty and repose,
> A blended holiness of earth and sky,
> Something that makes this individual spot,
> This small abiding-place of many men,
> A termination and a last retreat,
> A centre, come from wheresoe'er you will,
> A whole without dependence or defect,
> Made for itself and happy in itself—
> Perfect contentment, unity entire.[13]

Wordsworth's was a romantic and utopian vision but also an eccentric one, since he proposed that ordinary life, "the very world which is the world / Of all of us," might be transformed into a paradise of ecstatic communion—with the earth in all its wonder and beauty, and with one's fellow man.[14] Universal happiness would finally be achieved, he believed, when every living soul discovered that it is best attained as "a simple produce of the common day."[15]

We cannot know for certain that the pamphlet describing Dove Cottage was a souvenir of Katharine's honeymoon. Wordsworth's vision may nevertheless have influenced her musing on the many ways in which the place one inhabits can expand or limit the possibilities for a particular kind of life. This period of travel in Europe, this steady progress through a series of memorable rural and urban landscapes, must have filled her mind with a host of confusing images of what the future might hold for Dick and for her. What should be the "landscape" of their life together?

At this point, Katharine's landscape tastes had been formed largely by having absorbed, through her reading, popular philosophical notions of the relationship between nature and human

"Where Nature Teaches. Peabody Park," from The Carolinian, *1909.*

experience deriving from both nineteenth-century Romanticism and the American Transcendentalism of such authors as Ralph Waldo Emerson and Henry David Thoreau. She would also have known well the southern poet and author Sydney Lanier (1842–1881), whose work enjoyed a considerable national reputation at the turn of the century. Like Wordsworth, Lanier despaired of the costs to nature and community exacted in modern society by the demon "Trade." In an earlier America, the poet lamented,

> . . . man found neighbors in great hills and trees
> And streams and clouds and suns and birds and bees,
> And throbbed with neighbor-love in loving these.
> But oh, the poor! the poor! the poor!
> That stand by the inward-opening door
> Trade's hand doth tighten ever more,
> And sound their monstrous foul-air sigh
> For the outward hills of liberty,
> Where nature spreads her wild blue sky
> For art to make into Melody![16]

Katharine knew at firsthand the "foul air" of tobacco factories, and the contrast between the grimy city streets of Winston and the picturesque natural beauty and clean breezes of the mountain town where she had grown up. She would have been aware, too, that the impulse toward the creation of great urban parks across America during the preceding half-century was largely remedial, aimed at counteracting what were presumed at the time to be the inherent physical and psychological disadvantages of city life, especially for poor and working-class families. Hence the passion with which Frederick Law Olmsted, whose death just two years earlier the entire nation had mourned, led the crusade to develop broad "greenswards" and woodland walks in urban parks, and to design suburban communities whose inhabitants would be sheltered within a serene pastoral landscape.

This model of landscapes designed to replicate preindustrial rural scenery was appealing to many Americans, including the foremost liberal advocates for social reform, of whom Olmsted was one. It seemed well suited to embody a religious awareness that Romanticism and Transcendentalism had both espoused, namely, the indwelling of the divine in nature, God made manifest in Lanier's hills and streams.

While traveling through the English countryside on her honeymoon, Katharine saw for herself the rural landscape of pasture, field, woodland, and village that the poets praised, the painters painted, and Olmsted had first come to know as a travel correspondent for the *New York Herald*, writing a series of articles later published as a book, *Walks and Talks of an American Farmer in England*.[17] Everything in Katharine's own nature and in her upbring-

Frontispiece to Walks and Talks of an American Farmer in England *(1852)*.

"Old Timber Farm-House," from Walks and Talks of an American Farmer in England *(1852).*

ing would have prepared her to admire this landscape as Olmsted had, and to take inspiration from it, in her own way, and in her own time.

Mrs. Reynolds of Winston

The couple arrived back in Winston at the end of June, settling into domestic life in the big house on West Fifth Street. Dick's brother Will and his wife had found other quarters nearby. A number of Reynolds relations, in fact, would move into the neighborhood over the next few years. Any bride might expect a good deal of visiting back and forth in this situation, but Katharine almost immediately found herself, as the wife of Winston's wealthiest citizen, thrust into an even more public role as one of the city's preeminent society matrons. Not just every social gathering, large or small, over which she presided, but the visitors she received for brief or extended stays, the trips she and her husband took, and the causes either or both espoused were important news, duly noted in the local papers. These accounts document a pace and a scale of social activities that must in itself have represented a challenging learning experience for Katharine, beginning that first summer. By then, too, she was expecting her first child, to be born the following spring. Even with household help, planning "one of the most delightful affairs of the season's many social functions"—a September hayride and al fresco dinner honoring her sister Maxie, who had been her guest for several weeks—must have been daunting, especially in the whirl of all the other entertaining she had been doing. According to one account, "six wagon loads of jolly people left the Reynolds' home . . . at 6:30 and drove out to Nissen Park, where a most delicious two-course supper was arranged under the trees. It was a most picturesque sight, the long tables spread with every dainty and the grounds illuminated with hundreds of tiny electric lights, making as radiant and attractive a scene as one could wish to see."[18]

Since respectable married southern ladies were not employed outside their homes, the women of Katharine's circle occupied their leisure hours during the day with gatherings at one another's houses for luncheon and an afternoon of games; "progressive bridge whist" was the most popular, although euchre, anagrams, and dominoes were other common pastimes. There were also frequent opportunities for Katharine to accompany her husband on one of his many business trips to New York, Philadelphia, Richmond, or Baltimore. After their son was born in April—a nine-pound boy named for his proud father—the Reynoldses continued to entertain lavishly, and now regularly planned family summer vacations away from the city at places to which Dick could commute for visits. Katharine's happiness in marriage and motherhood overflows in playful postcards sent to her family, written and signed in her baby's name, "R. J. Jr." (just as her husband is always "Mr. Reynolds" in her correspondence, and undoubtedly in her conversation as well).

She must have felt at times, however, that the many ways in which her life had changed in the space of little more than a year were distracting, even exhausting. Katharine was a natural manager; she had plenty to manage now, and undoubtedly took pleasure in doing it well. Yet at moments, and particularly, perhaps,

"R. J. Jr.," on the porch of the Fifth Street house, 1906.

during those weeks in August 1906 spent at a lakeside inn in the mountains, Katharine may have had time to think about where she wanted her life to take her, beyond being a wife and mother. She knew that in Charles McIver's view, being a good mother was an authentic calling for a woman, since it contributed in essential ways to the education of tomorrow's citizens. "When you have good mothers," he had said, "you have a good nation."[19] Would that be enough for her? Might she not do more? Perhaps she and Dick had already talked about a dream of hers, to own a place in the country, a farm close to town. What is certain is that less than three weeks after their return from Lake Toxaway, Dick purchased a farmstead of 104 acres in Katharine's name, the first of many ac- quisitions of contiguous rural property to follow, all of it her own. Its significance as the first step of what she hoped would be a truly significant undertaking was underscored, just eleven days after the date of sale, by news that Charles Duncan McIver had died suddenly, at forty-six, "in the prime of his useful life," as the *Raleigh Times* reported.

Once again, the early death of someone she loved must have shocked Katharine profoundly. McIver had been traveling on a special train taking William Jennings Bryan on a tour of the state, two years before Bryan's third campaign for the presidency on the Democratic ticket. McIver had years earlier been the first person to bring the celebrated statesman and orator to North Carolina, and the men had remained close. In a eulogy delivered in Greensboro on the night of McIver's death, in which he praised his friend's extraordinary accomplishments on behalf of women's education, Bryan made a point that would have resonated forcefully for Katharine:

> Dr. McIver had behind his intellectual enthusiasm a moral enthusiasm, and you could not come into contact with his life, consecrated to great work, without feeling that somehow there had been kindled in your own heart an enthusiasm like his. . . . We marvel that one can stand by the side of a telegraphic instrument, and by means of an electric current talk to people ten thousand miles away, but the achievements of the heart are still greater. The heart that is full of love for its fellows, the heart that yearns to do some great good, the heart that puts into motion something for the benefit of the human race, will speak to hearts that will beat ten thousand years after all our hearts are stilled.[20]

Katharine was a wife and mother, bound by obligations to family and to place that were the most important things in her life. She could not have conceived of taking on a role in the world like the one that her older contemporary Jane Addams (1860–1935), the pioneering social worker and founder of Hull House in Chicago's impoverished tenement district, had achieved as a single woman, winning international respect for her labors. But

Katharine knew that there was real potential, nevertheless, both in her determination to make some difference, at least in her own small world, and in the means that were at hand to her—not just because of her husband's wealth, but because she had confidence in Dick's basic goodness and decency.

Still, she could hardly fail to recognize the inherent moral dilemma that shadowed her husband's meteoric rise to wealth and the political influence that came with it. He was, after all, the largest employer in North Carolina, in an era when the American public first became painfully aware of the social and economic consequences of unregulated and brazenly lawless monopolies and corporations. The country's industrial czars had routinely driven competitors out of business, used intimidation and violence to control workers, and bribed legislators to prevent the passage of reform measures. R. J. Reynolds, by contrast, prided himself on his fair treatment of his employees and worked hard to make local government more responsive to the needs of all classes of people.[21] Yet he had done his best to prevent his fellow townsmen from discovering, in 1900, that he had sold a controlling interest in his corporation to Continental Tobacco, a holding company created by and for the American Tobacco Company, a trust headed by archrival James B. "Buck" Duke. In the 1890s, Reynolds had actively supported the editorial campaigns of newspapers in the state calling for action to prevent Duke's empire from relentlessly swallowing up smaller tobacco wholesalers and manufacturers. But Reynolds Tobacco was itself desperate for capital it needed to reduce debt and continue expansion, and the $3 million Duke paid for his shares had put Dick's company in a financially secure position. Moreover, the gamble ultimately paid off, since by 1911 the federal government would force the dismantling of Duke's trust, returning the controlling stake in his strengthened company to Reynolds.

The Smith and Reynolds families, like most southerners, had emerged from the Reconstruction era absolutely committed to the Democratic Party, although southern Democrats expected the party to respect the historic difference between North and South on issues of racial equality. In William Jennings Bryan's first campaign in 1896, the Democrats had found a candidate who espoused many of the same values as the Progressive Party, which had organized farmers and skilled craftsmen in efforts to challenge the economic tyranny of the northeastern business establishment. Alton Parker, Democratic presidential candidate in 1904, embraced the Progressives' attacks on big business with campaign slogans such as "Our country for the masses, not the classes" and "High tariffs breed trusts—Do they help you?" Even his Republican opponent, Theodore Roosevelt, though himself a member of their class, would later inveigh against the "malefactors of wealth," after Jacob Riis and Samuel Gompers had taken him to see at firsthand the brutal conditions endured by American miners and factory workers. Believing that government had an obligation to impose restraints on a capitalism so indifferent to the welfare of laborers—many of them women and children—Roosevelt would try unsuccessfully to get Congress to strengthen federal regulation of corporate strategies that made a mockery of "free" enterprise.[22]

Charles McIver had aligned himself with the Progressive movement, winning support from the influential Farmers' Alliance for establishment of the Normal School and other educational reforms. Such reforms had in fact constituted a central thrust of southern progressivism, since McIver and others believed them to be the most essential avenue to economic recovery for the region. But on every front, progressive coalitions in the South, uniting farmers, educators, and "New South" businessmen in a common cause, were largely composed of moderates, men and women determined that modernity and social reform should not be purchased at the expense of traditional southern values. In a similar way—and predictably, given the role that religion played in southern life—organized humanitarian efforts from the turn of the century onward were usually spearheaded by Protestant churches, which more and more availed themselves of the time and energy of devout middle-class women. The Young Women's Christian Association, to whose work in Winston and elsewhere in the South Katharine Reynolds remained committed throughout her life, was—along with the YMCA—among the most influential advocates of civic improvement and social reform in the region.[23]

Still another distinctive aspect of southern progressivism that helps us to understand the social conscience of Katharine and R. J. Reynolds has been described by one historian as "a yearning for a more orderly and cohesive community." Such an ideal community should manifest, across the barriers of race and class, a serenity and stability based on a shared code of morality and a common assent to a rule of law that would ensure the integrity of elections, honesty in government, ethical business practices, and a decent standard of living for every citizen.[24] Southern reformers most often drew upon the example of traditional rural communities as symbols of an endangered way of life, under siege in a changing twentieth-century South, just as Wordsworth had celebrated the example of Grasmere and its surroundings a century earlier.

Katharine's early exposure to these ideas through her education were only confirmed by Dick's support of many of the reforms being promoted within the progressive wing of his own party. Still, she could hardly have been unaware of the risks attendant on her new life, of the danger that her husband's financial success might tempt her away from the principle of selfless service to the community to which she had been inspired by her mentor, now gone. Seek "one thing in life and but one," his favorite recitation had warned, if you hope "to achieve it before life is done." Since she had already been called to marriage and motherhood, her mission must somehow represent an expansion of this primary vocation. She was beginning to discern the outlines of the path that she must follow into the future.

Katharine longed, first of all, for her husband to experience the kind of religious conversion that had seized her before she was twenty. Dick was a good man, but not a deeply religious, churchgoing one. He had been raised in a strict Methodist household and was put off by the severe piety of his father and other members of his family, particularly their zealous commitment to the temperance crusade. Katharine probably hoped to become her husband's good angel, as McIver had been hers, leading him gently toward deeper faith and drawing out his innate compassion, his instinct for justice, and his natural charity.

Then her new home, the place in which her children's values would be instilled, must be more than just a house like the one, however splendid, in which they now lived. Katharine imagined the country place that they would develop as the beautiful, generously welcoming center of a small rural community. She and Dick between them had so many relatives with whom their daily lives were deeply enmeshed that her notion of "family" easily expanded outward to include her circle of friends, her servants, the townspeople of Winston, and the men and women who would help manage the farm that her husband had begun to develop for her. That place where they would live, token of so many blessings for which Katharine was grateful, must bring blessings to the lives of others, creating new possibilities for good work and the happiness and prosperity that would come from it. She resolved to make it all happen, somehow.

A Darker Shadow Still

Charles McIver had always appeared to be a man of robust good health and physical stamina. His death at forty-six from a sudden attack of "apoplexy" forced Katharine to confront the mortality of her fifty-six-year-old husband, and very likely made her intensely aware of the fragility of her own life. Her heart had been damaged by the rheumatic fever she had probably contracted during adolescence. Doctors of the time, knowing that most survivors of the disease were subject in later life to recurring episodes of debilitating weakness, aching joints, and throat infections, counseled a cautious avoidance of fatigue, stress, and exposure to contagious illness. Katharine's condition certainly added to the ordinary risks of pregnancy and childbirth, as she may have come to appreciate more fully during her first pregnancy. Yet their son was born a fine, healthy baby, making their hope of having more children seem natural and appropriate. Dick's mother had given birth to sixteen children, five of whom grew to maturity; Katharine's mother had seven, losing one (the younger brother who died when Katharine was seven). Moreover, both Katharine and Dick had strong nurturing instincts, which manifested themselves in their relations with younger siblings and other kin. Maxie came for long visits, which allowed Katharine to oversee her sister's courtship with James Dunn of Winston; in the same period, her younger sister Irene lived in the Reynolds home so that she could attend school in Winston. Two of Dick's three brothers, his brother-in-law, and

Dick and Katharine Reynolds, Maxie Dunn, unidentified woman, and James Dunn on porch of Fifth Street house.

a nephew whom he treated as a son all had managerial positions in his company, and after 1906 participated in a profit-sharing program for employees that he had initiated, allowing them to increase their own wealth through stock purchases.[25] No doubt he longed for sons of his own, to guide the R. J. Reynolds Tobacco Company through decades of the twentieth century he would not live to see. And of course Katharine, a loving wife and mother, longed for more children, confident that she had been called to bring them into the world.

The babies came, three more in the five years following her son Dick's birth: Mary Katharine, to be called Mary, arrived in August 1908; Nancy Susan in May 1910; and Zachary Smith, called Smith, in November 1911. While it is impossible to know just how much Dick and other family members understood the actual danger to Katharine's health posed by this frequent childbearing, comments in Katharine's correspondence and a new pattern of family travel reveal that she had indeed suffered physically. The household had no lack of servants, including a nurse. Nevertheless, it is hard to see how Katharine, who breast-fed all four infants,[26] managed not just to maintain her usual level of social activities as her family grew, but to take on more serious obligations of the sort she favored, involving church and community projects of one kind or another.

Just three weeks after McIver's death, for example, Katharine hosted a meeting to discuss erecting a suitable monument in his honor, and made the first donation toward its commissioning. In November of the same year she was fund-raising for the YWCA—starting with a $5,000 contribution from Dick—and, in addition to a flurry of holiday entertaining, held a party in her home honoring Dr. Anna Gove, the professor and resident physician from the State Normal and Industrial College in Greensboro whom Katharine had known during her student years.[27] (Katharine stayed in touch with activities at that beloved institution and with former classmates, becoming a member of the alumnae association even though she had not actually graduated from the

Katharine with Mary,
Nancy, and Dick Jr.
c. 1911.

Dick with Dick Jr.,
Smith, and Mary,
1912.

school.) Early in 1909, the year in which she was elected first vice president of the local YWCA, she hosted a luncheon for the board of directors at a Winston hotel, served as toastmistress, and, according to a newspaper report, "gave a very interesting talk."[28]

In 1910, when Booker T. Washington, the internationally famous educator and spokesman for American blacks, made a seven-day lecture tour of North Carolina, "the richest woman in Winston-Salem loaned her dishes and silver to the Negro family that entertained his party."[29] This gesture of Katharine's may seem to us today a patronizing, "Lady Bountiful" indulgence on the part of a wealthy woman living without protest in a racially segregated society. But to presume that Katharine's intended kindness represented nothing more than that reflects a failure to understand not only the racial politics of that time—Washington, though considered a moderate by most Americans, remained a highly controversial figure in the South—but also the adamantine social protocols that governed relations between the races in any southern city. Katharine's fellow townspeople knew that her contribution to the reception amounted to a political statement, something that those within the white community would judge favorably or not. It showed that she was not afraid to align herself publicly with liberal voices committed to dialogue and progress in racial matters.

The first suggestions of heightened concern for Katharine's health emerge early in 1907, when baby Dick was eight months old. On February 5 the society editor of the *Winston-Salem Journal* noted that Mrs. Reynolds had "entertained very charmingly at a violet dinner . . . in honor of Mrs. Abbie Henshaw of Danville, Illinois. . . . Covers were laid for fifteen and seven perfectly appointed courses were served. A beautiful white basket, filled with Parma violets . . . formed the artistic centerpiece." A few days later Katharine, her husband, the baby, and his nurse departed Winston on what was originally planned to be "an extended southern trip," starting with Mardi Gras festivities in New Orleans and including Texas and Mexico. One of Katharine's cousins, writing to her in the same month, expressed regret that Katharine had been "having the rheumatism."[30] The Reynoldses apparently decided to end their trip at a spa in Hot Springs, Arkansas, likely to have been an important destination for Katharine in the middle of winter in Winston. Dampness and cold were known to aggravate chronic rheumatic disease, and sufferers were urged, if they had the means, to visit mineral spas and to winter in warm, dry climates.

In the summer of that year, the family undertook a more physically challenging vacation journey, a motor trip through New England in Dick's spanking new Royal Tourist automobile. With an entourage that now included a liveried chauffeur, they traveled by train to Philadelphia at the end of July, picked up their car, and began a month-long trip that took them as far north as Maine. Katharine tried to give her mother a sense of the novelty of their mode of travel in a card sent from the falls of the Ammonoosuc River in the White Mountains of New Hampshire: "We are having the finest trip we ever had. . . . We travel entirely by auto and have seen the country over which we travel as we never saw it before."[31] Their itinerary suggests that they were in pursuit of cool

Katharine, Dick Jr., and Dick with chauffeur, nurse, and the Royal Tourist, 1907.

*Mount Washington
from Pinkham Notch,
White Mountains,
N.H., postcard.*

*North Woodstock and
Franconia Mountains
from Parker Ledge,
N.H., postcard,
1905.*

*Hood Farm, Derry,
N.H., postcard.*

mountain air and spectacular scenery; they visited Tip-Top House on the crest of Mount Washington, the highest peak east of the Mississippi River, and Franconia Notch. They had covered a route that took them as far west as Northampton, Massachusetts, before heading north through the Connecticut River valley to the White Mountains. This region had, since the late nineteenth century, become a mecca for wealthy residents of the eastern seaboard—artists, musicians, and writers, as well as business and professional people—many of whom established country retreats on rural farmland. The distinguished American sculptor Augustus Saint-Gaudens, for example, had an estate and studio in Cornish, New Hampshire, a summer colony described by the architectural historian Mark Alan Hewitt as "a kind of arcadian experiment in house and garden design."[32] Charles Platt, whose career as a designer of houses and gardens was to make him America's foremost residential architect in the years before the First World War, had a home there, as did the architectural critic and editor Herbert Croly (co-author of *Stately Homes in America*),[33] artists such as Stephen and Maxfield Parrish, and garden designer Ellen Biddle Shipman, whose husband, Louis, was a playwright.

Two aspects of the landscape associated with the charming resort towns that Katharine and Dick would have seen on their drive through rural New Hampshire—besides Cornish, there were similar, well-established colonies in Dublin, Peterborough, and New Castle—must surely have contributed to the couple's ongoing conversation about the kind of country place they wanted to build for themselves. Katharine would have been familiar with many of these fashionable estates through illustrated articles that appeared regularly in the pages of *Country Life in America* and *House Beautiful*. Some of these properties were maintained as working farms, just as the Reynoldses' acreage would be. More often, New Hampshire's struggling agricultural economy had made the purchase of rural land inviting to those who wanted merely to enjoy expansive pastoral surroundings as a setting for their summer homes. In both cases, however, the favored architectural styles, while conservative in their reliance on building conventions derived from European and American classical traditions, conspicuously abjured the ostentatious design and palatial scale that were the pride of Newport's "cottagers" and had made the fortunes of prestigious architects such as Richard Morris Hunt and the firm of McKim, Mead, and White.

Charles Adams Platt (1861–1933), whose career had begun in Cornish with work on his own house and garden and those of several famous neighbors, was in the vanguard of what astute observers of the time (Herbert Croly among them) recognized as a movement away from architectural grandeur on the aristocratic model and toward a more down-to-earth and practical American elegance, responsive to the natural and cultural character of both the site and local tradition. Platt had progressed in his young manhood from painting to garden design to designing houses that suited their landscape. His work managed to recover for wealthy and middle-class American clients the inspiriting strengths of the Renaissance villas he had studied closely during the sojourn in Italy that culminated in publication of his influential *Italian Gardens* of 1893.[34] Those strengths came not simply from a close integration of house and landscape, but from a richly expressive aesthetic affirmation of the villa's roots in nature and agriculture as much as in human industry and art. Platt's grounds and gardens do not just embellish the house; the landscape fixes the whole in time and place, determines its forms, infuses its atmosphere. Yet his are modest and comfortable houses, admired for a "deliberate plainness and lack of drama" that belie the architect's innovative adaptations of historic forms to the requirements of modern life.[35]

Katharine Reynolds's New England trip introduced her to a picturesque landscape steeped in the nation's history, celebrated beyond any other in American literature and art, and calling to mind the quaint villages and rural countryside of England, though lacking their European aura of worn-smooth, centuries-old habitation. The fine, fresh-looking houses she glimpsed through a stand of trees or across rolling green pastures were not simply *in* the country but *of* it, suggestive of some past time and an earlier way of life, yet belonging just as much to the present, and to a future that seemed to her then full of promise. Her little party drove eastward next, to Portland, Maine, paying a visit to the poet Longfellow's boyhood home before heading south along the coast to Atlantic City, New Jersey, where they stayed at the luxurious Marlborough Blenheim Hotel before starting for home.

Their gay adventure on the road appears to have been a huge success, but Katharine now returned to the round of parties and other social activities that were so much a part of life in town. By November she was pregnant with her second child, and facing the prospect of a return of weakness and rheumatic pain as winter progressed. Was it fear or confidence that inspired Dick to apply at the end of January for passports for travel to China and Japan for Katharine and himself, his toddler son, and the child's nurse? Whatever the case, not long afterward they were off on a less ambitious trip to Florida by train, stopping at hotels in Miami and Palm Beach, among other places, then sailing to Nassau in the Bahamas for a brief stay. About the middle of March, Katharine sent her mother a postcard of Ocean Avenue in Palm Beach, "one of the avenues through which we walk or ride in a rolling chair every day." Tellingly, another postcard sent later the same month, as the end of their trip neared, reassured her mother that "all are perfectly well now."[36]

"To doubt and fear give thou no heed"

Katharine gave birth to a daughter, Mary, in August. After the trip to Florida, the last five months of her pregnancy had undoubtedly demanded some relaxation of her busy schedule in order to ensure safe delivery of this second child. An enforced rest through the warm months of early summer would have given her a welcome opportunity for the intensive reading and planning that she needed more than ever to do, since not one but two domestic projects now occupied her mind. She had resolved to redecorate and improve the grounds of their Fifth Street home, making the house more truly her own, and she would urge Dick to intensify his search for the additional acreage needed to develop the farm that was to become their country estate. If the untimely death of Charles McIver had given rise to fear that her own life or that of her husband might be cut short in the same way, Katharine had her staunch faith to help her move forward nevertheless, hoping to accomplish that one great work to which she had pledged herself.

Until this time, some three and one-half years since her marriage, Katharine had been busy learning to fulfill the expectations of society in her public roles as Mrs. R. J. Reynolds—wife and mother, churchwoman, dazzling hostess, civic leader. Nothing about her life would have seemed unconventional by community standards. Yet neither her religious piety nor her natural decorum prevented her from inwardly refusing to accommodate herself to the traditional expectation that a southern lady must be docile and dependent, concentrating her efforts in the home because she was constitutionally incapable of functioning in the world of business or the professions as men did. Katharine's health was frail, but her mind was strong and her spirit ambitious. She and Dick shared a relationship of remarkable equality for their time and place—owing in no small part, no doubt, to the formative example that the marriage of Charles and Lula McIver had provided, the self-confident feminism instilled in Katharine by her teachers at the Normal School, and her husband's genuine delight in her appreciation of his drive to excel and her interest in his affairs. He trusted Katharine's head for business, and increasingly encouraged her involvement in financial decisions. He may, too, given the difference in their ages, have entertained some unspoken anxiety lest he leave his wife a widow with small children to raise.

Katharine's health was probably as much at risk as his, since she had the perfectionist's habit of adding responsibilities to those already taken on without any compromise of high standards of performance. The new baby was barely two months old when Katharine took her along on an October trip to New York City. Her own mother had come to visit and care for Irene (attending school in Winston) in Katharine's absence. The hastily scribbled notes Katharine sent home at this time suggest that she was already feeling additional stress. She tells Irene to "take good care of Mamma and make her enjoy herself. Will be home on the earliest date can possibly get home. Have been so busy. Mary is well and growing." Then eleven days later, in a card sent to her brother Matt: "We have been expecting a letter from you for a long time. What is the matter? . . . We are trying to get off tomorrow. Am so anxious to get home and see Mamma."[37] In May of that year Dick, who had been looking at rural property around Baltimore and New York City, apparently for investment purposes, had written Katharine from New York about missing the sale of a dairy farm he had planned to attend. He went on to say: "I found from my investigations [of] the dairy farm business that it was [an] unprofitable and troublesome business. You and Dick [Jr.] can get more pleasure and profit out of other investments. I saw several beautiful grass farms for sale, but will not buy unless you should see and like one. . . . I [visited] all the beautiful farms for sale around Baltimore."[38] Katharine the New Woman may have been looking at property in October, while Katharine the homemaker was consulting with decorators and choosing furniture in anticipation of the planned refurbishment of her house. She settled on the Philadelphia firm of Hunt, Wilkinson and Company to take charge of the latter project. New furniture and an array of other furnishings began arriving in December, and the work of painting, papering, and installing new draperies continued over the course of the next two years.

The same period saw a marked acceleration of Katharine's involvement in the purchase of real estate, both for investment and for the planned farm. In January, Dick purchased a lot in her name in downtown Winston, for construction of "the most up to date apartment houses possible, . . . furnished with every convenience, including janitor service and heat . . . [and] similar to those of the larger cities," and also signed a contract for construction of a department store that promised to be "the most modern in the city," having "elevators and other innovations."[39] Not long after, he announced plans to construct in Winston a "mammoth" new factory for the R. J. Reynolds Tobacco Company.[40] The family fled winter weather once again in February, this time visiting New York City and Virginia, then returning to New York again for several weeks in spring. Katharine continued her whirl of entertaining whenever she was at home, having by this time also assumed a leadership role in the local YWCA and with a committee responsible for renovation of the First Presbyterian Church of Winston, of which she was a member. She and the children vacationed again that summer in the mountains of North Carolina, this time at a hotel in Roaring Gap. One-year-old Mary fell ill, and her concerned father corresponded with Katharine faithfully, sending fresh vegetables and fruits whenever he could arrange for delivery. There are tender letters, particularly one sent from New York's Plaza Hotel, where Dick was staying for the first time; hereafter they must stay there, he told Katharine, whenever they visited the city. His letter ends with an apology:

I feel real bad I have not provided more comfort than you are getting on the mountain. You have been such a sweet love of a wife to me and give me greater and more pleasure during 4 years of married life than I have ever received from anybody during my entire life. Whenever you see I have made a mistake you know how to correct me in such a sweet loveable way that I always appreciate what you say and words will not tell how I am grieved over my utter failure to do likewise or as good for you. I regret very much that I had to leave you with tears in your eyes drawn by telling you as I want you to tell me when you think I have made a mistake. My first prayers will be in asking the lord to teach me how to express myself to please instead of displeasing you. From your devoted husband, R. J. Reynolds[41]

In the days before leaving Winston for New York, he had also written Katharine letters that document the renewal of his efforts to add acreage to the original parcel purchased for her farm: "The Conrad land lays on the south side of the road . . . opposite your land and will have to be sold soon. I will buy this land for you whenever they offer it for sale at its value."[42] A second note written the same day let her know that a landscape engineer from the internationally famous Berckmans family nursery in Augusta, Georgia, had arrived for the purpose of assessing the suitability of Katharine's original parcel for development as a golf course.[43] "I have allowed him to begin work. I hope this will be satisfactory with you for them to proceed," he wrote. Three days later their prospects had changed dramatically, as Dick had obtained options to buy three farms, including an "old gin mill pond" tract, on the opposite side of the road from Katharine's property. His excitement is communicated by his haphazard spelling and punctuation:

> The above three farms give you all of the headwaters of the Creek you pass over below the Hooser farm the springs break out high on Hodgins and Grays farm and make beautiful branches through the timber land as the water can be kept clear and looks pretty pouring over the rocks. You can make a pond and rase trout in the water. Mr. Dunn[44] and the Augusta Ga golf man and myself went over the land before taking the options and he says it is an ideal form for golf course so much better than yours. I stopped him from work on your farm and he is now running his line over the farms mentioned above which can be made much more beautiful and enjoyable than your farm. He said it would take your entire farm for 9 whole Golf course and you would not have any farming land. So I don't want to put such a good farmer out of business. We will buy the Golf

and other play grounds. I feel so sure you will be pleased with the land we will go right along with the work.

These three farms, he explained, together formed three sides of a fourth tract, not for sale, that fronted the road. "If you never get [this] place," Dick assured her, "your farm will be complete without it or any other lands."[45] Within less than a year Katharine owned all four of these properties plus two more, then added another two the following year, for a total of almost seven hundred acres—nearly twice what her husband thought would make a large enough estate.

Pregnant with her third child through the fall and winter following the family's return from the mountains, Katharine used the time before and after Nancy's birth in May to begin planning further development of her farm. Three values were uppermost in her mind as she pored over articles and books on farming and house and estate design. First, perhaps the primary impulse driving her resolve was the belief, widely held since the middle of the nineteenth century and still persuasive in the early decades of the twentieth, that country living provided a more healthful environment in almost every respect for adults as well as for children. Epidemic disease was strongly associated with conditions intrinsic to urban life, and Katharine had every reason to be haunted by fears of polluted air and water, swift and deadly contagion. She was by nature a fastidious person, as meticulous in every aspect of her household management as in the accounts kept of her investments. And she trusted authority, particularly when its voice seemed to reflect a modern scientific perspective. "Domestic science" was now being taught in university departments headed by women, often ardent feminists, committed to the belief that women must take an active role in reshaping household design, incorporating new technologies in the interest of greater efficiency, comfort, and health.[46] In 1911 the *Ladies' Home Journal* published a series of articles by Christine Frederick, one of the best known of these household engineering experts, exhorting women to apply the principles of "scientific management" to the functioning of their households.[47] Katharine Reynolds had since the beginning of her marriage made good use of her copy of *Mrs. Rorer's New Cook Book: A Manual of Housekeeping*, with its chapters on "The Chemistry of Food" and "The Kitchen Calendar: Proper Seasons for Different Foods."[48] And she would obtain copies of Lucy Maynard Salmon's *Domestic Service* of 1911 and two books published in 1912, *The Chemistry of Cooking and Cleaning: A Manual for Housekeepers* and H. W. Conn's *The Story of Germ Life*.[49] If up-to-date knowledge and determination could ensure the good health of her family, she would exercise both. Getting out of the city to their farm promised clean air and plenty of physical exercise, pure water and wholesome food, relief from the everyday stresses of living in town, and—just as important to Katharine—a spiritually rewarding closeness to the natural world.

The second value informing her thinking was related to these concerns for improving her own and her family's health: she would transform the land itself, healing and restoring it to fruitfulness, again by means of enlightened scientific management. The patchwork of rural properties that now constituted the site of what was to become her estate included rocky land that had never been suitable for farming—there was even an old stone quarry in one location—as well as acreage that had been "farmed out" and eroded by traditional agricultural methods that failed to maintain the fertility of the soil. Katharine was a faithful reader of *Progressive Farmer*, the most reform-minded and popular of the two dozen or so farm journals then published in the South. It had been founded in 1886 by Leonidas L. Polk, charismatic leader of the Farmers Alliance in North Carolina. At Polk's death the editorship had passed to the equally energetic Clarence Poe, close friend of Charles McIver and a man whom Katharine knew personally.[50] Poe continued to champion a more diversified and self-sufficient agricultural economy for the South, with more cattle and dairy production. He added a "Home Department" feature to the magazine focusing on home economics and the virtues of rural life for families and communities, subjects that helped to increase the number of women in his reading audience.[51] Katharine subscribed as well to Walter Hines Page's journal *World's Work*, which similarly called for a rehabilitation of southern agriculture to be achieved by teaching the new generation of farmers how to apply scientific knowledge in their farming practice.

In August 1903, just a few months after Katharine had first moved to Winston to assume a secretarial position in the Reynolds tobacco factory, *House Beautiful* had published an article describing the "ideal village in the hills of North Carolina designed as a whole and built to order," adjacent to George W. Vanderbilt's vast Biltmore estate in Asheville. Southern readers would have been particularly interested in this account not just of the village—which included a church and parish house, a hospital, a school for children of employees, shops, apartments, and the general office for estate operations—but of the superb dairy farm and a department of forestry, managed by the internationally renowned forester Gifford Pinchot. Although the author of the article includes neither the name of the estate and its owner (described simply as a "New York millionaire"), nor its precise location, few North Carolinians had not heard or read about the astonishing scale and extravagance of this project, begun fifteen years earlier. According to the author of the article, Vanderbilt had insisted on the best that money could buy in every detail of Biltmore's architectural and landscape design and construction, its various industries, and its technological innovations. Once it was completed, nothing short of perfection remained the standard in its farming, dairying, and forest research and production. The Biltmore herd of dairy cows, for example, had been "conspicuous in every great dairy exhibit in the land," winning "prizes without number." The families of the dairymen who tended them lived nearby in "rows of pretty cottages nestling at the foot of a long, green hill, all their surroundings a model of neatness. Prizes are offered for punctuality, neatness, and thoroughness in milking." Even the chickens lived in modern luxury: "Each little house, for

*Biltmore Estate
(1887–1895),
Biltmore Village,
church from Railway
Station, lantern slide.*

*Biltmore Estate,
farmhouse, stable, and
adjacent buildings,
lantern slide.*

*Biltmore Estate,
cottages on Lodge
Street, lantern slide.*

*Biltmore Estate, back
of cottages, lantern
slide.*

each breed, has its own dwellings, has its wire-inclosed grass plot. . . . The incubators are generally full of eggs, which are carefully registered and sold for breeding purposes."[52]

Katharine Reynolds would have devoured such particulars as these, storing them in her memory until she could finally begin to create her own farming operation, significantly smaller in scale but no less sophisticated in its technological and managerial aspirations, inspired by the most progressive ideas of the agricultural reformers. Her farm, moreover, had the potential to offer farmers of the North Carolina Piedmont and elsewhere in the South a model with more relevance to their own circumstances than grandiose Biltmore. It must be both a working farm and a profitable enterprise, yet one that was in all respects solidly rooted in a historic place and within an existing community. This last aspiration—that the country estate that she and Dick were building should somehow manage to dispense its advantages of health, happiness, security, and beauty beyond their immediate family to others—was the third good to which Katharine committed herself as her mission began in earnest.

She was not unaware that both twentieth-century architectural modernism and the domestic science movement were proposing alternatives to conventional house design that aimed to be more practical, more responsive to changes in the way families and individuals now lived and worked. Growing numbers of single working women, for example, needed housing options better than rented rooms in the homes of strangers or dreary group dormitories provided by employers. The YWCA had actually been created in response to this need, but the facilities it could provide stopped far short of the innovations being proposed by housing reformers, many of whom were women. Some of these, Jane Addams among them, criticized the increasing isolation of America's middle class from the working and poorer classes, a process accelerated by suburbanization. Yet at the same time, as we have seen, many middle-class southern women were, like Katharine Reynolds, becoming actively involved in a variety of social reform agendas, including campaigns for decent housing and improved working conditions, through organizations associated with religious denominations or church ministries. Playing an active role in support of such causes frequently had the effect, according to one historian, of instilling "a sort of unself-conscious radicalism which would have turned the conservative southern male speechless if he had taken the trouble to listen to what the ladies were saying."[53]

Katharine's social conscience had, of course, been formed earlier by her exposure at the State Normal College to liberal humanitarian ideals cautiously framed within the gospel message of orthodox Protestant Christianity. Now she had come to understand that the burdens she bore—her cycles of recurring illness, the responsibilities of child rearing, the manifold social obligations that wealth and status imposed—must not prevent her from accomplishing her unique personal mission. The work she was assuming as part of her estate-building project—an occupation unusual for any woman, but especially so for a lady of the South—would amount to much more in the long run than writing checks for the design services and construction costs entailed in developing a handsome country house or a "gentleman's farm"; it had the potential, Katharine believed, to improve in substantial ways the lives of many less fortunate than she. The pious and industrious Moravians, who in the eighteenth century had founded Winston's neighboring town of Salem, wanted their little settlement to be a godly place, a just and loving community modeled on the ideal of a caring human family, the "Unitas Fratrum." In many respects, the hopes of Katharine Reynolds for the community she was about to bring together seem to have been inspired by the same ideal.

The Work Begins

An important change in Dick and Katharine's fortunes was also occurring in these years, one that would soon affect many of the decisions to be made as her projects moved forward. In 1907, aware that the federal government had initiated an investigation of the American Tobacco Company, her husband had boldly defied a stipulation in his agreement with Buck Duke requiring Reynolds Tobacco to confine any future expansion of its products to the manufacture and sale of plug tobacco, in order not to threaten Duke's domination of the market for smoking tobacco. Dick now patented and began production of a brand of smoking tobacco he named Prince Albert, which before long proved to be a phenomenal success nationwide, with sales climbing at the rate of 4 million pounds a year.[54] By the time government action in 1911 forced the American Tobacco Company to relinquish its stake in Reynolds Tobacco, Dick and those of his employees who had elected to participate in his profit-sharing plan were substantially wealthier men, just as his company was now poised for still further business expansion. Never content to savor a victory without beginning at once to plan another, he next began looking into a promising machine technology for rolling smoking tobacco into cigarettes. For her part, Katharine understood that she was now freer than ever to indulge her fondest dreams for the kind of country place she wanted to create.

In the meantime, she spared no expense in transforming their house in town into a mansion much more sumptuous in its decor than it had been when she came there as a bride. The massive turreted Queen Ann–style house had by this time a distinctly old-fashioned look, and Katharine was eager to replace its equally outmoded systems with such modern improvements as a McCray Sanitary Refrigerator (ads for which advised, "For the health of your family . . . keep your foods sweet and pure, free from odors, impurities, and contamination"), electric vacuum cleaners, and new bathrooms.[55] Its interior decoration, however, apparently still seemed to her best served by an eclectic blend of traditional styles of furnishing, including a Louis XVI bedroom suite and an Adamesque sitting room. For the grounds—larger now, after purchase of an adjacent property—the Reynoldses commissioned a landscape plan from the firm of Buckenham and Miller of New York City and Somerville, New Jersey (the Somerville office was occupied in design and ongoing supervision of projects on the local estate of James B. Duke, who had probably recommended the firm to Dick and Katharine). Their plan for the Reynolds property called for the addition of tennis courts, more trees and ornamental shrubs, and a formal garden centered on a large pergola with trellises and beds of flowers.

The extent of these improvements to the Fifth Street house suggests that Katharine had anticipated from the outset that the construction of their new house was still a long way off. She had decided, in fact, that the farm and its supporting facilities—the entire landscape within which their home would one day be embraced—should be developed prior to building the house. She and Dick each had some farming operations already under way on land he owned in his own name and on portions of the acreage he had acquired for Katharine. Now Katharine initiated measures aimed at achieving her goal of more diversified production on her farm, ordering fruit-bearing plants and a hundred white Leghorn chickens by mail during the last months of her pregnancy in the spring of 1910.[56] At about the same time she arranged for a civil and hydraulic engineer to draw up topographical surveys of those parts of the site she intended to develop and to assess the potential of her springs and Silas Creek for supplying water for a variety of uses, including the lake that Katharine still pictured in her mind's eye as a central feature of the landscape to be seen from the house. These maps and plans were ready by summer, at which point they were forwarded to Buckenham and Miller, who had been commissioned to produce a master plan for the entire estate.

Katharine would certainly have drawn up a detailed program for this work, explaining to the architects exactly what facilities and features she wished the plan to accommodate: house site, lake, lawns, greenhouse and gardens, housing for staff and servants, power plant, farm buildings, post office, stables and garage, perhaps a chapel. It was characteristic of her to begin in this very deliberate way, following the advice of the many books and articles now addressing the subject of what author E. P. Powell had dubbed the country house "revolution." In his introduction to *The Country Home* of 1904, Powell had managed to link the retreat of growing numbers of middle-class Americans from cities to a "real" place in the country with several of Katharine's most heartfelt convictions—her faith in science, in nature as a manifestation of God, in landscape design as a form of high art, and in rural life as a foundation of ideal community. Powell wrote:

> Our first care must be the creation of real country homes. Here we shall have the primal art of nature to assist us, with its latest interpretations by science. It is a new thought of high art that is growing among the people, that instead of buying pictures to hang on our walls, we may better create them on the sod, with living plants and running brooks. Literature also is turning its face countryward. Nature books rival novels in popular use. They express the new stage of social evolution, and confirm the desire to escape from city conditions. In other words, we are going back, and to what God wrought—intending to cowork with him. . . .
>
> What we want in the country is men and women who intend to live as common-sense folk; will lift the social level with simple brotherhood, high aspirations, and a humanity filled with Godliness—unaffected, pure in heart, and democratic.[57]

Katharine did not give herself much time to recover from the birth of her third child in May. Acutely aware, however, of the fear that any illness in the family aroused in her husband and herself, she had earlier decided to hire a live-in trained nurse. Perhaps the addition to their household in the months before Nancy's birth of the highly qualified Henrietta van den Berg of Baltimore (whom the children nicknamed "Bum") helped

Bum with Mary on her pony at Fifth Street, c. 1911–12.

Katharine to regain sufficient strength for a six-week summer trip with the whole family, including Bum and two-month-old Nancy, to visit the Thousand Islands region of New York State. It had seemed best to remove the family entirely from the Fifth Street house while so much construction and redecorating was going on. Katharine even managed, once they had arrived in Philadelphia by train in mid-July, to keep an appointment at Hunt, Wilkinson and Company to review the latest designs and materials prepared for her redecorating project. The Reynoldses then set out on their tour, having once again arranged to have the chauffeur meet them with the car. They drove first to Atlantic City for a brief stay at their favorite seaside resort, then headed north, having given family and friends in Winston mailing addresses at the Thousand Island House at Alexandria Bay and at another hotel on Lake Frontenac.

It seems likely, however, that they would not have missed a chance to make a stop along the way in Somerville, in order to review progress on the master plan that Buckenham and Miller were preparing; clearing and grading for the first phase of construction was to commence before Katharine and the children returned to Winston at the end of September. The press of business obliged Dick to return two weeks earlier, after seeing his family safely installed at the Plaza in New York City. He wrote Katharine there, advising her to finish the work that remained for her to do in Philadelphia, then to go back to Atlantic City and "remain there until I write that your house is in condition for you and the children to live in."[58] Two days later another letter from him reassured her that "all of your horses, mules, cows, and stock of every kind look well," and then, auspiciously, promised that by the time she got back home, she should be able to see the results of clearing the sites of both her lake and the first hole of her "golf ground," close to where the house—"your bungalo"—was to be located.[59] This exciting news probably influenced her decision to leave for home as soon as possible, whether or not the house was ready. Just a few days later she and the children moved to the Stafford Hotel in Baltimore, where four-year-old Dick received a note from his father filled with mechanical information of the sort a little boy might delight in receiving, since it sounded grown-up and manly: "Your mother now has 40,000 gallons of running water per day at Gray springs. The water shoots out of a two-inch pipe ten feet above the level of the bank of the branch and can be piped to the lake and pumped two hundred feet high without any cost of operating the pump."[60] As if Katharine were not already eager enough to start for home, the next letter from Dick reported that her personal automobile had been delivered. Now she would have a fast and comfortable way to travel back and forth between their house in town and her farm.

Her elation probably did not last very long. As with most construction projects, the promised completion of renovating and redecorating stretched into fall, even as the usual round of social gatherings and meetings of the various clubs and boards on which Katharine served picked up intensity. Sometime after the holiday season, in late winter or early spring 1911—around the time when she and Dick celebrated their sixth wedding anniversary—Katharine knew that she was expecting another child. In just a few months she would have to endure the combined effects on her stamina of advancing pregnancy and the heat and humidity of summer. Of course both her doctor and husband would insist that she plan on spending the summer in the mountains, this time leaving as early as June, just as construction of the spillway and dam for her lake would be getting under way. She made reservations for the family at Eseola Inn in Linville, North Carolina, which at least offered the advantage of a golf course for her to study.

It would not be for Katharine to play on, however; there is a hint of wistfulness in her observations of her companions and children at play in a note she sent to her brother Gene in August: "The people here spend most of their time on the links. Senah and Ruth Critz [daughters of Dick's sister Lucy] are up with me and they play most all the time. The children are getting on fine and enjoy the river so much, they do not want to go home. Dick [Jr.] in bathing this morning and Mary wading. . . . Come to see us when we get home."[61] There is evidence, too, that her husband's

Linville golf course, postcard, 1911.

concern for what he refers to as "her condition" moved him to insist on a passivity so contrary to Katharine's nature that it was a form of suffering for her. In the same letter in which he tells her not to let her new automobile be driven faster than fifteen miles an hour while she was in it, he pleads with her to "take the best care of yourself. My life would not be worth living without you."[62] Knowing her restiveness, he was as attentive as ever in writing frequently to keep her informed about small things that mattered to her—"the flowers around our home are now in full bloom and our house looks beautiful"; "your peas are not suffering much for rain"—and about progress made in her farming and building operations. He hired a Mr. Fowler, a "common sense man" who came well recommended, to manage the farm, instructing him, as Katharine had requested, to send soil samples taken from her "golf land" to the New York offices of Peter Henderson and Company, a nursery from which Katharine regularly purchased books on landscape design and horticulture as well as seeds and plants.[63]

Even after the family's return to Winston in the fall, life seemed to slow as the days grew shorter and Katharine waited for the birth in November of the boy who would be named for her own father, Zachary Smith. She had two sons now and two daughters. They were handsome, healthy children, perfect in every way. Her beloved husband was sixty-one years old and supremely contented, as was Katharine, with their home life. The two of them, fond lovers still, must have enjoyed a peaceful, happy sense of accomplishment and of gratitude when Christmas came that year, although they may also have shared a sense of standing at the threshold of something new, as if one chapter of their lives was ending and another just beginning.

THREE

Creating Reynolda

KATHARINE REYNOLDS SEEMS TO HAVE HAD A FAIRLY realistic sense of the scale and complexity of the work she was about to undertake in turning her dream of a unique kind of country house estate into a real place—a landscape restored to health, beauty, and productivity; a family home at the center of a community of learning, work, and play. Although farming operations were already under way on her acreage, a significant expansion of these agricultural enterprises awaited completion of supporting facilities—dairy barns and poultry houses, for example—that were

Detail of 1911 Buckenham and Miller master plan.

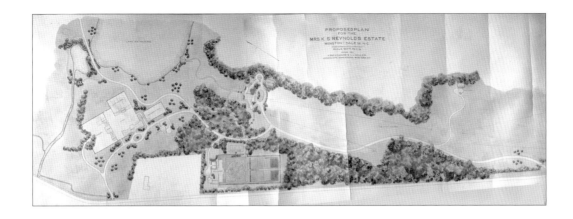

Reynolda, land cleared for the lake, c. 1912.

still in the early stages of siting and construction. Having begun her project by commissioning a master plan for the entire estate, Katharine expected to have the working parts of that scheme functioning smoothly by the time the family's new house, their "bungalow," would be finished and ready for their move to the country. Apparently anticipating that this process might require years rather than months to accomplish, she continued to initiate major projects at the Fifth Street house, purchasing an adjacent lot in January 1912 to use as a play area for her children, since so much of the existing site was slated for additional embellishments of the formal gardens.

The priority she attached to the transformation of her severely eroded, "farmed-out" rural land into a fertile, self-sustaining, and beautiful agricultural landscape, delighting as well as nurturing those fortunate enough to dwell within it, suggests the continuity of Katharine's vision, in certain respects, with the ancient Roman tradition of the *villa rustica*. This ideal type of the rural estate had been rediscovered and celebrated by the patrons, artists, and architects of the European Renaissance and the Baroque age, and later inspired an American translation in Thomas Jefferson's design of his home and farm, Monticello. Jef-

Monticello, aerial view, 1985. Photo by William Rieley.

ferson shared the view of the classical poets and writers he admired that industry and trade were morally inferior to "the culture of the earth," farming and husbandry. He chiefly prided himself on being a dedicated agriculturist, relishing as well certain precious advantages of a rural domestic life. To Jefferson's mind, life in the country offered, at least to men and women of his class, opportunities for invigorating fresh air and exercise, closer family relationships, and heightened enjoyment of those arts of civilized living that meant more to him even than his distinguished public life: friendship, hospitality, conversation, correspondence, reading, reflection, and the study of nature. Katharine and many of her contemporaries in the new Country Life movement in America were in a real sense the inheritors of this Jeffersonian idealization of rural life, in spite of the fact that their wealth derived from business and commerce.[1]

Just as important, both Katharine's passionate commitment to restoring the patchwork of small farms she had assembled to healthy productive life and Jefferson's deep love of his Virginia plantation had their roots in the shared ground of the South's distinctive history and culture. In 1930, less than twenty years after Katharine Reynolds began to introduce innovative design and scientific management to every component of her farming complex in the hope that such a wholesome environment might serve as a catalyst for a revitalized familial and community life, a group of southern academicians, historians, and men of letters came together to voice their alarm over the accelerating erosion of the South's agrarian culture and folkways. In the view of these "Vanderbilt Agrarians"—who included such nationally prominent figures as Allen Tate, John Crowe Ransom, and Robert Penn Warren—their region's capitulation to "New South" industrialization and urbanism increasingly threatened to sacrifice the traditional spiritual and humane values of southern society to the Yankee god Mammon, a totem of material prosperity disguising itself as genuine civilization. An anthology of essays by members of this coterie of aggrieved southern intellectuals, *I'll Take My Stand: The South and the Agrarian Tradition*, insisted that "an agrarian society is hardly one that has no use at all for industries, for professional vocations, for scholars and artists, and for the life of cities," but is primarily committed to agriculture as "the leading vocation." Such a society, they argued, had proved more likely to cultivate both a religious and an artistic sensibility in its members, as well as a "sensibility in human affairs" fostering gracious rituals of social exchange. These essential relationships—with God, with the natural world, with one's neighbors and friends—had been shaped in distinctive ways by a place and a people, so that the South's "native" humanism was not, as elsewhere, an abstract ethical system but "a culture, the whole way in which we live, act, think, and feel. It is a kind of imaginatively balanced life lived out in a definite social tradition . . . rooted in the agrarian life of the older South."[2]

Echoes of Jefferson's pleas for an American republic of yeoman farmers rather than urban factory workers sound again in this new "declaration of independence" across the century and a half that separates him from the Vanderbilt Agrarians. What is perhaps more remarkable, however, is the degree to which, earlier in the twentieth century, the vision of Katharine Reynolds for her thousand acres of farmland incorporated the values and view of south-

ern history set forth in the "Statement of Principles" that introduced *I'll Take My Stand.* Katharine was not an intellectual; hers
was a practical intelligence, although one highly receptive to new
ideas. But the girl to whom classmates gave the title "Ruler of
Hearts" had grown into a woman ruled by her own. If Katharine
Reynolds, now in her thirties, was open-minded, there is no want
of evidence that she was even more open-hearted—to a surprising
extent, a woman even more driven by feeling than by thinking.
Moreover, her vision was simultaneously conceived in religious
terms as a mission. It owed less to ideas and images culled from
books and magazines than to her deeply felt love of the South's

Katharine and Dick Jr.
at Fifth Street,
c. 1914.

traditional rural culture, and her zealous belief in its potential to ensure an "imaginatively balanced life," not just for her own family and friends but for a wide circle of farmers and working people. There was not another American country house estate, north or south, quite like the place Katharine had in mind, and intended to bring into being.

From the outset, too, she knew herself to be resolutely committed to a time-consuming standard of perfection in every detail. Her copious correspondence from these years, with engineers and designers she employed as well as innumerable other suppliers of goods and services to her building projects, clearly demonstrates her determination never to cut corners in the interest of getting something done more quickly or efficiently. However much Mrs. Reynolds might be admired within her community as an exemplary southern lady—unfailingly modest, gracious, and accommodating in her dealings with people of every station—she was now assuming a role and an authority that had few precedents within the society to which she belonged.

From her training in business skills at the Normal School to her experience as the wife of R. J. Reynolds, Katharine had developed her natural propensity for management. She would now prove to be an exceptionally formidable client, never surrendering for a moment her ownership of every decision. One is struck, in reading through her correspondence, by the sheer number of business letters she typed personally, even after she hired a personal secretary, Evie Crim, in 1912; many of these address relatively insignificant matters of design, cost, or procedural details. She once responded to an invoice for overdue payment sent to her husband's office rather than directly to her with a curt formal clarification of exactly who was in charge of this project.[3] And from the start of their business relationship, all plans and drawings submitted by the landscape engineering firm of Buckenham and Miller carried the title "Mrs. K. S. Reynolds Estate"—not even the more common usage for a married woman, "Mrs. R. J. Reynolds." It took a little time for townspeople and tradesmen to discover that the great work commencing just outside of town was "Mrs. Reynolds's Farm," and no one else's.

"I am doing the very best I can . . ."

After spending the winter afternoon of January 19, 1912, inspecting the progress made thus far in implementing the site plan for the estate—the grading of lake, lawns, and drives; the staking out of several village and farm structures; and continuing construction of roads, bridges, dams, and spillway—Katharine wired an excited note to Dick, who was away from home on business. She announced happily that if the weather remained favorable, construction was finally about to "begin in earnest."[4] Less than three weeks later, however, she developed a respiratory infection following a trip with her family to Asheville to participate in a friend's wedding, and was "a long time getting over it."[5] Indeed, this illness, like so many before it, appears to have triggered another attack of the symptoms to which she always referred as "rheumatism." Each flare-up of this kind carried the risk of further devastating damage to her heart, and Katharine occasionally acknowledged more openly in her correspondence the disabling pain and fatigue that sapped her strength in the months that followed. She entertained a small gathering of family and friends when her infant son Smith was christened at the end of February, but traveled to Baltimore just a few days later to consult with a doctor on the staff of the Johns Hopkins Hospital. The decision was ultimately made to try a tonsillectomy—a procedure believed to reduce the incidence of serious infections originating in the throat—and surgery was scheduled for early May.

The year had started with so much promise of steady progress, especially since Katharine had decided on the architect she would commission to design the bungalow, Charles Barton Keen of Philadelphia. Keen had even submitted preliminary plans for the house sometime during these early months of 1912, then wrote a rather peevish note to his new client on the third of May asking why he had heard nothing back from her. He reminded her that there was at least another month of "hard work" involved in producing any necessary revisions, then specifications and estimates, and she had told him that she was anxious to begin.[6] Anxious indeed, but Katharine was confined to bed during the week or so before leaving for Baltimore. She had also been reviewing plans prepared by Buckenham and Miller for a large pergola that was to be the central feature of the gardens being installed at her Fifth Street home, and preparing to solicit proposals for design and construction of the greenhouses associated with her estate's formal gardens. So she found herself uncharacteristically behind in her correspondence, and forced by her illness to withdraw from serving as a delegate to the tenth annual convention of the North Carolina Federation of Women's Clubs, whose meeting that year in Winston would coincide with her hospital stay in Baltimore. She carried out her duties as chair of the hospitality committee, nonetheless, by hosting the delegation at the Hotel Zinzendorf and arranging for a fleet of automobiles to take officers and volunteers on an outing to a neighboring country town, still a novel adventure for these ladies in 1912.

Dick accompanied Katharine to Baltimore for her surgery but returned to Winston during the period of her convalescence. She penciled a note telling him how much she missed him and the children, then typically reassured him with what seems under the circumstances an excess of fervor: "I am to get up in a rolling chair for one hour today. I know I shall enjoy it. In fact, I am enjoying everything—coming in, as I did, hardly hoping to go out alive—and feeling so good now—just makes me enjoy everything."[7] The same vein of determined optimism, as if she might overcome her chronic condition by sheer force of will, reappears in a note to a cousin written a month later, in which she announced that the operation had "relieved me entirely of rheumatism."[8]

At her doctor's suggestion, Katharine had postponed her trip home in order to spend an additional week recuperating at the family's favorite hotel in Atlantic City. Before leaving Baltimore, however, she invited Charles Barton Keen to meet with her there, a decision that probably says less about a miraculous return to health than about her eagerness to get back to work, to keep the farm and construction projects moving forward on several fronts. Earlier that month, Keen and Katharine appear to have agreed on a new siting of the bungalow, different from the one proposed in Buckenham and Miller's master plan. A letter and a print of the revised plan sent by Louis Miller, the partner who had taken principal responsibility for both her estate project and the ongoing renovation of the house in town, reached her shortly after she arrived in Baltimore. He reported that he had also sent copies to R. E. Snowden (the engineer Katharine had placed in charge of all the work being done, construction as well as farming), with instructions that he should stake out the new footprint of the bun-

Bungalow, front and rear elevations by Charles Barton Keen, 1912.

galow in anticipation of her return home, so that she could see for herself that the changes would demand additional quantities of fill along the north foundation wall. Then, perhaps with some pique because his own work in siting the house had been discarded, he added, "Of course this high foundation wall would, in a measure, destroy the squatty appearance you are after[,] looking from the lake side."[9] A telling remark, since it suggests just how much of her own preference for a particular massing of the building, affecting its relationship with the surrounding landscape, Katharine had brought to her discussions with both Miller and Keen.

There are many such indications of her close personal involvement in the design process. Katharine had been back home barely a week before writing to Miller: "Kindly let me know . . . if you think we could make a small island in the lake where it would look well, and at the same time, be in deep enough water to make a good fishing station. This could be very easily made while we are cleaning out the lake bottom."[10] The inspiration for this gesture of scenery-making was, of course, the travel account published in the Sullins College yearbook when Katharine was editor. The writer had singled out Loch Katrine in the picturesque Scottish Highlands as "the prettiest" of several small lakes dotting the valley near Aberfoyle; it was also the inspiration for Sir Walter Scott's long poem of 1810, "The Lady of the Lake," whose heroine lives on an island in Loch Katrine. Since the sixteen-acre lake still under construction on Katharine's estate was to be named Lake Katharine, it must have a little island as well. But not just to make a charming picture from the porch and windows of the house that would overlook it. The romantic imagination that made Katharine Reynolds such a bold dreamer was tempered by a solid Presbyterian frugality that considered everyday usefulness an added grace to ornament. The island would therefore serve as a "fishing station" in a lake stocked with trout and bass. Miller replied that he thought the idea for "placing an island in Lake Katherine [sic] . . . a very pretty one," and supplied a sketch showing survey lines and sections for staking it out.[11]

Strenuous action on behalf of good health was apparently high on Katharine's list of priorities for this summer of 1912. She had recently organized a group of six local women into a walking club, whose activities she described in a letter to a friend: "We walk out [from town] to the end of my farm every morning and have an automobile to come out for us at ten o'clock. We wade in the branch, climb cherry trees, sit on the grass, play mumble-peg and have a good time in general."[12] Believing after her return from the hospital that her health *ought* to be much improved, she had plunged into a "catch up" round of activities, in spite of the fact that she had now assumed full responsibility for the children's care. Miss van den Berg had been forced to leave in haste for Baltimore just days after Katharine's homecoming, and would spend the next six weeks recovering from emergency gall bladder surgery. Concerned that her mistress would not be sensible about her own limitations, Bum had written a note of warning shortly after arriving at the hospital: "I believe I am keeping my promise better than you are yours. How about being in bed at 10:15 every night and sleeping late if you had a restless night with the little chap[?] . . . You know you cannot stand that sort of thing, and you will have to find some way to slip away for it will break my heart to have you get sick now when I could not be there to take care of you. Now don't shake your head and say 'I am doing the very best I can.'"[13] In a subsequent letter, Bum tried to reassure her about a still-painful throat: "It sometimes takes a small place a long time to heal."[14]

There was too much happening for Katharine even to consider slowing down. She wrote her sister-in-law: "I am very busy these days working on my new lawn and building a pretty pergola and garden there [on Fifth Street], in early fall will put out some trees, shrubbery, etc., am also doing a great deal of farming."[15] Several letters to Louis Miller written that month include detailed descriptions of changes she had found it necessary to make "in the field," as it were, to his original design of the landscape being installed at her home in the city. Then, having settled on Lord and Burnham, premier designers of glasshouses nationwide (with an

Pergola, Fifth Street, c. 1911.

office in Philadelphia as well as other major cities), to take responsibility for her own greenhouse complex, she initiated a flurry of correspondence with that firm, arranging for preliminary visits to the site and so on. There are similar letters to Keen, asking for specific changes to his design of the bungalow. A single paragraph from one of these may convey the tone of Katharine's voice in such correspondence: "A toilet room for the children to use when playing on the lawn, which is to contain a bathtub, so that it will make a good room for the care-taker during the winter. However, I agree with you that it will be better to have simply an enameled brick wainscoting, with the painted plaster finish above and think the floor of this room had better be of tile, similar to that used on the porches. It would also be desirable to have a WINE CLOSET adjoining the STOREROOM in the basement."[16] There was no detail of design or construction, no choice of materials, whether in barn or bedroom, too small or insignificant for her to think about and decide.

Toward the end of June, eight-month-old Smith came down with whooping cough, a frightening disease in an infant. As Bum's absence stretched into the middle of July, Katharine was feeling the strain; now it was her turn to strike a note of vexation in writing to Charles Barton Keen:

> I have had a right sick baby the past week and my trained nurse also being . . . in the hospital, I have been delayed in taking up the study of the bungalow foundation. There is only one change that I feel I would be justified in making and that is, that there should be an *outside door*, opening on a level with the outside ground somewhere in the rear end, and I do not see why it could not be under the stairway, and the wood basin be moved further down. It would be too bad that the ashes from the pits, down-sweepings, cleanings, etc. should have to be carried out through the door of the children's plaything room.
>
> We are not hurrying about the bungalow, as we had originally planned to do, as the greenhouse plans from Lord & Burnham came a week or more ago and the stone mason we have can begin work on this, instead of having to go on [to] the bungalow foundation as we had thought he would have to do.
>
> I had counted on you, Mr. Keene [sic], making the plans for a stables, dairy, garage, etc., and I wanted them to be equipped with the very newest and best conveniences; and these are what we are needing so much at present. It had been our plan to take these right along with the bungalow and rush them to a finish much earlier.[17]

The letter concludes with a list of spatial and other requirements for the stables, dairy, and garage. Another letter typed the same day enclosed a check to help a woman, suffering from opium addiction, who was unknown to Katharine but vouched for by her minister and close friend, Neal Anderson.[18]

Thus at a time of year when she usually preferred to have her family safely away from the city, she found herself coping with difficulties that threatened to undo whatever benefits to her own health the recent surgery might have provided. A friend writing her in mid-July expressed concern over "all the anxiety and worry that you have had lately."[19] At the very least, weariness and apprehension must have tempered the delight Katharine would otherwise have felt in seeing her dream finally taking on tangible, three-dimensional form in the foundations and walls of the little cluster of buildings rising along the edge of the road that connected her farm with town.

Laying the Groundwork

Most women of her generation confined any responsibility they may have been given for influencing the design and development of a residential property to the house itself, and perhaps to garden areas associated with it. Yet much as Katharine relished thinking through the layout and visual character of the bungalow that was to be the heart of the larger complex—what came to be described as the "home place"—her vision had always embraced the entire estate, of which this symbolic center was only a part. One of her roommates at the Normal recalled years later a conversation in which Katharine, thinking about her future, expressed her intention one day to own a great estate, where she would have "a thousand cattle [grazing] on a hill . . . and flowers all around."[20] The travel account published in the Sullins College yearbook may have added further details to her ideal image of a an English countryside of hills and valleys, orchards and fields, and villages of charming cottages, as did the books and poems she loved, the magazines she subscribed to, and her own experience of travel.

She was familiar too with a variety of American adaptations of English landscape gardening tradition in both park and residential design, traditions that came together at a property Katharine knew especially well, George W. Vanderbilt's much publicized Biltmore estate. The Reynoldses and Vanderbilts "visited back and forth,"[21] and the Biltmore nursery became an important source of plants purchased for Katharine's estate. At the inception of what would become a project of enormous scale, the largest residential property in the United States, Frederick Law Olmsted had persuaded Vanderbilt to abandon the notion of transforming the original two-thousand-acre tract into a landscaped park on the English model. Instead he advised his client to "make a small park into which to look from your house; make a small pleasure grounds and gardens; farm your river bottoms chiefly to keep and fatten livestock with a view to manure; and make the rest a forest."[22] Vanderbilt responded so enthusiastically to the economic as well as aesthetic wisdom of this recommendation that he purchased an additional four thousand acres for an experimental forest management program, a project that eventually comprised more than a hundred thousand acres, most of it now part of Pisgah National Forest.

Olmsted had initially been somewhat dismayed, however, by Vanderbilt's decision to build a 250-room mansion in the style of a French Renaissance chateau, since he confessed himself "not quite at home when required to merge stately architectural work with natural or naturalistic landscape."[23] Nevertheless, his design solution achieved a remarkably successful integration of stately formal features—a tree-lined allée, broad terraces, walled gardens—within a dense lushly planted woodland in the master's signature style. Katharine Reynolds would not have missed an opportunity to stroll along the path winding down the slope that leads from the upper terrace of the house to the formal gardens below, which front an elegant greenhouse forming a wall on one side, much as the greenhouse adjacent to her own gardens would later do. Although the greenhouse and garden complex at the

edge of Katharine's estate was the only strictly formal design ele-
ment in the entire landscape, the shorter stroll from her bungalow
down the path to the gardens would recapitulate, on a much
smaller scale, the walk through Olmsted's "Ramble" at Biltmore
to the walled gardens below.

Another estate that undoubtedly influenced Katharine's
thinking about her project, since she hired its designers, Buckenham and Miller, to produce her master plan, was that of Duke
Farms, the 2,700-acre New Jersey property of James Buchanan
Duke, with whom the Reynoldses maintained a fairly close friendship over many years in spite of strains created by the men's ongoing rivalry in the tobacco wars. Their shared ties as successful
sons of the South were no doubt responsible for at least some of
this fellow feeling, as was the grudging respect they apparently felt
for each another. Buck Duke, who had begun buying land for his
New Jersey estate in 1893, later shared the fruits of his experience
in estate building with Dick and Katharine. Duke, however, had
chosen to live mostly in the North; he maintained a mansion near
Central Park in New York City as well as the property being de-

Duke Farms, rendering of proposed residence by Horace Trumbauer.

veloped along the Raritan River, close to the Somerville office of Buckenham and Miller, whose client he remained for many years. Like Vanderbilt at Biltmore, Duke had intended to build a French chateau-style mansion as the crown jewel within an extensive park landscape, but at the outbreak of World War I impetuously donated to the war effort all the steel he had acquired for construction. Although he continued to spend millions on the estate, with its thirty miles of manicured drives, nine constructed lakes, waterfalls, stone bridges, terraces, fountains, and statuary, he lost interest in finishing the house, of which only the foundation had been completed. A director of the recently restored property speculated that Buck "lived [there] as a country farmer. Other wealthy families were going to Newport and Long Island, but he wanted to play with his farm and his hydroelectric plant on the Raritan River," which supplied power to outlying areas as well as to Duke Farms.[24]

Katharine Reynolds would have admired in Buck Duke this fondness for country ways and commitment to real work—a kind of inherited rural sensibility that remained strong among many southerners well into the twentieth century.[25] It distinguished Duke from the larger class of very wealthy northerners, including

Vanderbilt, who fancied themselves "gentlemen farmers," and it would similarly characterize Katharine's approach to the management of her farm. If there is a sense in which it is fair to say that they both "played" at farming and other rural occupations, since their livelihoods did not depend on such activities, in their case the "play," however pleasurable, was also intensely serious and absorbing, and was directed toward outcomes that they hoped would reap benefits for many other people. For the same reason, Katharine must also have been impressed by the unconventional approach that Duke took toward his property during the years when she and Dick visited, in freely sharing its splendors with the general public, for he welcomed any and all visitors to Duke Farms as if it were a public park. When some took advantage of his hospitality, he simply hired a constable to encourage civility. Finally, though, after an incident in 1915, when a touring party of 180 cars left the lawns littered with picnic trash and stripped flower beds of their blooms, he was forced to discontinue his open-door policy—but not before setting an exceptional example of Christian charity to which Katharine Reynolds would be highly receptive.[26]

Each of these high-profile estates contributed in different ways to Katharine's creative musing, not just on the physical layout, architecture, and landscape of her own property, but on the management philosophy that would govern its operations. Olmsted had awakened a sense of environmental stewardship in George Vanderbilt that found expression both in the forestry operation at Biltmore and in the sensitive restoration of native woodland species within its park. There, Katharine would have seen with her own eyes that good design can produce places that are simultaneously beautiful and ecologically sustainable (a contemporary concept that she would have understood simply as maintaining the continuing health of the land's natural systems). Earlier in her life, the politically potent alliance of educational and agricultural reformers in North Carolina had planted the seeds of her eventual ambition to make her estate a regional model of agricultural reform based on modern science, as well as an educational resource on a variety of subjects for her community and for the Piedmont South. And even if Buck Duke had embraced the fashion for manorial European Baroque in the styles he chose for his New Jersey house and its park, his personal manner and values were still those of a man born and raised in the rural South. With that same strong sense of southern identity, Katharine Reynolds decided to seek out architectural and landscape types more appropriate to a farm on the edge of a rapidly expanding southern city, and to the simpler, traditional family-centered way of life she intended to foster there.

At the same time, Katharine was young, and enough of a "New Woman" to embrace wholeheartedly the national trends in home design that were responding to two closely related developments, the application of new technologies within the household and the expansion of leisure activities among the middle class. With her customary pursuit of perfection, she intended to have "the very newest and best conveniences," not just for her farm operations but throughout the estate. She was equally determined to build into its very fabric an array of opportunities for recreation, since she shared the growing conviction among women of her day that physical exercise was essential to the health of mind and body. Hence the effort to find an appropriate location for a nine-hole golf course almost before the ink was dry on the deeds of sale, and hence too the prominent siting of the links bordering the entrance drive to the house in Buckenham and Miller's plan (a far cry from the experience of winding past the "quarters" that commonly greeted visitors to many otherwise elegant antebellum southern plantations). Places for swimming, boating, riding, tennis, and later polo fields were all to be part of this landscape of play. As women's hemlines steadily rose to permit easier mobility and to avoid the transfer of soil from the street to skirts and petticoats, Katharine had herself fitted out with jodhpurs for morning rides around the farm astride her saddle horse, Kentucky Belle.

What was less conspicuous but perhaps even more essential to her obsessive pursuit of a healthier way of life was the network of underground utilities that made Mrs. Reynolds's farm more sophisticated in its engineering than many estates in more cosmopolitan places. Katharine was hardly alone among her country house contemporaries in placing the highest priority on ensuring an abundant supply of clean water, and then preserving it from contamination; E. P. Powell devoted a whole chapter of *The Country Home* to this subject, explaining that "wells are contaminated not only by surface water, by slops, and by barnyard drainage, but by subterranean streams that encounter cesspools or other contaminating substances."[27] Katharine Reynolds, haunted by the memory of the typhoid outbreak at

Lake Katharine boathouse, view toward barns. Photo by Thomas Sears.

the Normal during her years there, took as much pride in the system being established on her estate as Louis XIV took in the elaborate fountains of Versailles, pumping "at full throat." Her water supply, regularly monitored for purity, would move thirty thousand gallons a day through pipes connecting three artesian wells to every corner of the property where water was needed. Aboveground, this bountiful presence of water served equally important aesthetic ends, whether moving or contained; the boulder-surfaced dam connecting the placid surface of Lake Katharine with a lower pond created a sparkling, rushing rustic waterfall at the spillway.

Numbers of New South cities had embraced electrification with great enthusiasm and pride before the turn of the century;

The waterfall. Photo by Thomas Sears.

R. J. Reynolds had been instrumental, with other members of the local business elite, in organizing the Winston Electric Light and Motive Power Company in 1887. Nevertheless, even when Katharine began installing state-of-the-art electrical machinery and service systems (and later a steam power plant) on the estate she was building, electric lights and telephones were still rare and unattainable marvels throughout most of the rural South. To her mind, of course, these were not so much amenities as an arsenal of defense against the threats with which modern medicine, domestic and agricultural science, and social reform movements had to do battle: ignorance, dirt, and disease; the kind of grueling labor that wasted time and exhausted a worker's strength; inefficiencies that reduced productivity; and isolation that threatened family and community. "Light" was as important a metaphor in these decades for many Americans as it had been during the age that came to be called the Enlightenment, synonymous in both periods with rationality and the discipline of a refined and harmonious order in the individual and in society. These were precious values that no doubt helped Katharine to hold at bay the unspoken fears that haunted her. For her, the roar of generators, the hum of refrigerators, the pulsing of pumps, the lively ringing and buzzing that would soon fill the air were as reassuring and as beautiful as the sound of water cascading over the stone-faced spillway from her lake.

During these early years of engineering the site, the gully-riddled fields of the old farms were scoured even more deeply by teams of mule-drawn "drag pans" and squads of laborers with shovels digging underground tunnels to carry the vital arteries of pipe and wire. Tons of native diabase rock excavated during grading and construction were reserved, at Katharine's instigation, to be used for walls, piers, foundations, and chimneys. Cleared fields intended for cultivation were enriched with manure and cover crops. Elsewhere, huge expanses of ground were cut into or filled; the earth itself was recontoured, sculpted into new forms to produce a "recreation and pleasure ground"—a landscape transformed by art into something more like a park than a North Carolina Piedmont farm. Except for the rectangular area of formal gardens sited below the west wing of the house and parallel to the road leading from town, Buckenham and Miller's design was more "naturalistic" than "natural," to use Olmsted's terms. Rather than a state of untouched nature, the landscape was meant to convey a visual impression of serene and pastoral rural scenery: an expanse of lawn resembling open meadows picturesquely framed by groves of trees; meandering streams and a natural-looking manufactured lake and pond; narrow roads and paths winding through acres of woodland, past orchards and cultivated fields; and finally, a large "farmhouse"—Katharine's bungalow—close to a cluster of farm buildings in a village of quaint cottages.

No wonder Olmsted had misgivings at Biltmore about using the design formula derived from English landscape gardening tradition as a setting for an enormous French chateau—a difficulty he overcame by extending the formal architecture of the mansion out into the landscape through a sequence of grandly scaled classical garden elements. At Duke Farms, as at countless other princely private estates across the country, a sprawling "naturalistic" landscape in the English style was lavishly embellished with classical garden structures and statuary. Katharine Reynolds chose not to imitate either of these approaches. From the very start of her planning, long before she hired Charles Barton Keen, Katharine and her husband had always referred to the house they would build as their "bungalow," a popular type of middle-class American house that represented the antithesis of a mansion or "stately home" (the term Herbert Croly used in the title of his 1903 study of high-style residential design).

Moreover, her wish, to which Louis Miller referred, that the house should have a "squatty appearance" suggests that she wanted a long and low massing of the bungalow, not very different from the midwestern Prairie Houses of Frank Lloyd Wright, which in the years since the first publication of the designs in two 1901 issues of *Ladies' Home Journal* had become almost as well

House of the Democrat, Rose Valley. Photo by Robert Linzer Edwards.

known among Americans interested in domestic architecture as they were among Europeans attracted to modernism.[28] Wright's less well known contemporary and fellow member in the Chicago Architectural Club, Robert Spencer, published seven designs for farmhouses in the same magazine that year, including one for a "Southern Farmhouse," a long, low building with deep eaves, open porches, and a two-story living room; in 1904, Spencer's "Attractive Farmhouses for Real Farmers" appeared in *Country Life in America.*[29] A loyal subscriber to both magazines, Katharine Reynolds was exposed over the years to many such examples of the new style, which, in spite of owing a debt to the more modestly scaled and boxier bungalows associated with the American Arts and Crafts movement, aimed for a tighter integration between the house and its grounds. Wright suggested that a house should seem to have grown up out of the earth organically, as a tree grows, an effect achieved by "extension and emphasis of the planes parallel to the ground."[30] While it is unlikely that Katharine found classic Chicago School architectural modernism to her taste, she did want her home to appear comfortably nestled within the land on which it stood, which on her site plan was a narrow ridge defined by a broad shallow bowl of green lawn to the south and a more steeply descending grassy slope on the north side, with the lake at its base.

What is intriguing about Robert Spencer's adaptation of the modern movement's simplified, strongly horizontal architectural forms to farmhouses is that he managed throughout his career to combine this aesthetic with historic traditions of English building, finding no inconsistency in using such nostalgic features as half-timbering and casement windows in otherwise chastely modern stuccoed structures. This hybrid style, unembarrassed by a deliberate evocation of English villages and farms in the vernacular style, appealed as well to the conservative Philadelphian Charles Barton Keen, who found a uniquely sympathetic client in the wealthy young southern matron who intended to live within a

Aerial view of the bungalow with Lake Katharine and barns.

landscape as picturesque and quaint in its visual effect as it was "modern" in function.

Katharine's sure judgment in selecting Keen to design a project significantly larger and more complex than any he had yet tackled (and ultimately the most important of his career) had much to do with her confidence that he thoroughly understood the appearance and atmosphere of the English landscapes she so admired. Another country house architect of the period, Aymar Embury II, though himself an advocate of regional revival styles in American domestic architecture, singled Keen out in a discussion of the dangers posed by the enormous popularity of English house and garden design: "The best of architects cannot mix the oil and water of English cottage and Colonial styles; and when, as for example, Charles Barton Keen sometimes has, the architect gallantly makes the attempt, the old motives undergo a strange sea-change, and though the result may be beautiful, interesting, and even coherent (if the architect is skillful and able), it is not a compound of the old motives but a new and hybrid species."[31] If Katharine Reynolds came upon this passage in Embury's book *The Livable House*, published in the spring of 1917, the year the Reynoldses finally moved into their new home, she would have felt even more convinced that she had made the right choice, since she never intended to choose between modernity and the romantic aura of historic places that had sheltered a small community over generations of time.

The Village and Five Row

Katharine would not have seen her wish to borrow something of English landscape tradition for the design of her estate as mere stagecraft, any more than Frederick Law Olmsted thought that adapting forms derived from the practice of the English school in his designs for American parks and suburbs represented a shallow eclecticism. Just as Olmsted believed that certain landscape forms were capable of generating specific physical and psychological responses in those who experienced them, Katharine shared the conviction of the Progressive Era that environments characterized by beauty, cleanliness, and order contributed to the health and well-being of those who lived and worked in them. She knew and loved numbers of small southern towns, like the Mount Airy of her childhood, and believed that they possessed a pleasing visual simplicity and restorative, quiet charm.

The mix of styles that Katharine—with the guidance of her interior designers at Hunt, Wilkinson and Company—had selected for refurbishing the family's quarter-century-old house in Winston was conventionally sumptuous in the manner of countless fashionable homes that she and Dick had visited when they traveled. Their new home, however, represented an opportunity for her to start from scratch, producing something more in keeping with her own evolving taste, although the very meaning of the word "home" had shifted in Katharine's mind from a house to a thousand-acre landscape. She had no intention of pretending to cultural associations that did not seem natural to her and to a farming estate in the still largely rural South. At the same time, she had never had reason to question the steadfast conviction of white middle-class southerners that the region's political, religious, and social mores were a legacy from the peoples of the British Isles—the legions of English, Scots, Welsh, and Irish settlers of the South in the eighteenth and nineteenth centuries who were their forebears.

For this reason, and in spite of his being a northerner, Charles Barton Keen's work seemed to Katharine to have the potential to capture precisely the expressive landscape qualities she was after, without sacrificing any of the benefits that modern technology and sanitary systems could provide. She was familiar with the country estates being built in Chestnut Hill and the developing Main Line suburbs of Philadelphia by architects associated with the T-Square Club, a group of designers unabashedly conservative and Anglophile in their admiration of twentieth-century English Arts and Crafts masters such as Edwin Lutyens, C. F. A. Voysey, Baillie Scott, and W. R. Lethaby. Like his colleagues, Keen sensitively drew upon rural vernacular building traditions to produce an architectural ensemble that appeared inseparable from the historic agricultural landscape that surrounded it, that was "coherent," in the way that Aymar Embury recognized, as well as "beautiful" and "interesting."[32] A magazine writer of the time summed up the signature style of Philadelphia's gentlemen architects as "picturesque, practical, and straightforward, and rendered with an agreeable dash of personality, and with that peculiar *friendliness* towards materials used that characterizes the works of the modern English architects."[33]

The photographs of Keen's architecture included among the illustrations in Katharine's 1909 edition of Charles Edward Hooper's book on country houses[34] looked for all the world like the photographs in one of several popular books on English villages and cottages by the British author Peter Ditchfield, published shortly after the turn of the century.[35] In a prefatory note to Ditchfield's 1905 *Picturesque English Cottages and Their Doorway Gardens*, published in this country as part of a *House and Garden* series, the American architect and author Ralph Adams Cram urged American readers to discover, through careful study of Ditchfield's documentation, the difference between an architecture that merely imitated superficial details of rural English building traditions—what he called "architectural scene-painting"—and work that reflected an architect's deeper understanding of those "sound principles of proportion and composition" that in times past had informed a "living art" of building, passed down from one generation of craftsmen to the next.[36] Katharine Reynolds clearly appreciated the agricultural and historic sources of this conservative approach to American architecture; only those familiar with the evolution of southern architecture in the twentieth century can appreciate the remarkable boldness of her decision to claim its appropriateness for the New South

Inner court of a house near Bryn Mawr, Pa., and children's playhouse at Cedarhurst, L.I., by Charles Barton Keen, illustrated in Hooper, The Country House *(1904).*

by commissioning Charles Barton Keen to design her "home place."[37]

The remodeling of the Fifth Street house had allowed Katharine to reserve an upstairs room there as her office, where she now managed her various affairs with the help of her secretary. The steady flow of plans and elevations sent from Keen's office during July 1912 culminated in the arrival of a full set of prints and specifications for the bungalow by the end of the month. When Keen subsequently wrote to arrange a site visit and review of the work thus far, Dick replied for his wife, explaining that she was "now sick in bed" and unable to meet with him.[38] So much was going on at both properties, however, that the irrepressible Katharine was up and about by week's end, writing Keen to suggest that he plan to come in mid-August, and busying herself with countless details related to ongoing construction in the gardens at the Fifth Street house and at the farm.

In spite of coping with illness in the family, this may have been the most exciting summer of Katharine's life, as she saw what she had only imagined gradually becoming a real place. Her voice in correspondence is confident and proud, as if she felt more than equal to every task required for the project's realization. Her farm was flourishing, expanding and advertising its summer production, and grading and clearing of the lake bottom was almost completed. Two days before her superintendent's weekly progress report informed her that twenty-four acres of golf links were ready to be sown, she had written *American Golfer* magazine to inquire about "the best book available on golf grounds."[39] Then, unwilling to wait until her dairying operation could move into its new facilities, Katharine sent the superintendent a list of detailed directions spelling out the precise sequence of steps that she wished him to enforce in the milking and storage process, warning that each particular in this sanitary regime must be "carried out to the letter."[40]

After signing the final contract with Lord and Burnham for the greenhouse complex early in August, she pressured them immediately to provide working drawings for various parts of the plan, sending a telegram requesting "at least, the excavating plans . . . at once."[41] She had already plunged into negotiations with construction contractors, and hired a local architect, Willard C. Northup, to help with parts of both Lord and Burnham's and Charles Barton Keen's plans; he supplied specifications for a florist's workroom and gardener's cottage in the same month. She had also initiated a search for a qualified horticultural professional to oversee the greenhouse, gardens, and all other ornamental plantings, even as building and installation of these components got under way. Later that month she sought Louis Miller's advice in this matter, asking if he was familiar with the work of a candidate for the position who was currently employed as superintendent of a New Brunswick estate not far from Buckenham and Miller's New Jersey office. She wanted to know if this person might even be suited to the job of superintendent of her own estate, to replace Snowden, and added exultantly: "We are starting at the farm this week . . . the gardener's cottage and the superintendent's house and office. The plans complete for our barns, dairy, garage, bungalow and servants quarters are well under way and we hope to begin active operations about October 1st." (By "active operations" Katharine referred to beginning construction of the several buildings for which final plans and specifications were still pending.) She assured Miller that by the time of his forthcoming visit to stake out additional beds and walks at the Fifth Street house, she would also be ready to take up with him the matter of design of the formal gardens adjacent to the greenhouse and the planting beds on either side of the front lawn.[42] Miller must have spoken favorably about the candidate in question, W. P. Mahan, since Katharine hired him almost at once to be her superintendent, anticipating that he would begin work as early as September.

Katharine and Keen had decided on a palette of building materials and an architectural style that reinforced the primary visual effect they were after, which was that of a cohesive, gracefully articulated landscape composition. To Keen's credit, this would be achieved without sacrifice of a subtle visual play between the imagery of past and present, between suggestions of long-settled, industrious human habitation and a striking modernity, manifest in the immaculate perfection of every detail, as if a historic place had been so lovingly cared for over the course of time that its usefulness and beauty had been preserved intact for a contemporary generation. The round, tawny-colored boulders harvested from the site to be used for landscape features, chimneys, and the foundations of the bungalow, dairy, and other buildings as grading required did more than just affirm the connection between these

Stone pillars at the south entrance to Reynolda.

Entrance to the village with rocks defining landscape features.

Foundation of the dairy and retaining wall.

structures and the very ground of the original site. The stonework—particularly, as it turned out, in situations requiring the high retaining walls about which Miller had fretted—proved to be more boldly handsome than even Keen could have anticipated when he agreed to Katharine's wish to use the native fieldstone, and inevitably evoked primitive building traditions.[43] Taken together, these stacked rounded stones of variable size provided a pleasing contrast to the civilized classicism of Keen's robust Tuscan columns on the bungalow and several houses in the village, and the uniformly white stuccoed or painted facades of residential and farm buildings. The same aesthetic of restraint, emphasizing formal simplicity, the repetition of elements, and traditional building types (not necessarily drawn from Piedmont ex-

Tuscan columns on the bungalow front facade, 2001. Photo by Carol Betsch.

amples), integrated the small community of homes with buildings serving a score of other functions—barns, stables, sheds, shops, cribs, offices, power plant, and a dairy which, in spite of being one of the most technologically sophisticated in the entire country, appeared reassuringly familiar from the outside. At the skyline, the sheer expanse of so many green clay tile roofs—a flat mid-green, close to the color of copper patina—would prove no less impressive as a unifying device, in this case tying the entire complex to the woods that encircled and framed the village, orchards, and fields of Katharine's farm on either side of the road connecting it with the city.

In a similar way, houses of varying scale and refinement, from the most modest of the worker's cottages up to and including the Reynolds family's home, were to be deliberately unpretentious, inviting and comely rather than intimidating and grand. The final plan for the bungalow seems to give physical expression to this ideal of the hospitable home, since wings on either side of the central block extended forward at an angle from the entrance facade like a pair of welcoming arms ready to embrace visitors approaching on the drive leading to the porte-cochère. It is possible, of course, to read the tidy, conventional prettiness of Keen's village houses as nothing more than a signature style of the conservative Philadelphia School—what Augusta Owens Patterson, art editor of *Town and Country*, would describe in her 1924 survey *American Homes of Today* as a variety of the "Modern Picturesque" which, in imitating English cottages, "must be intimate or it fails."[44] In fact, Katharine Reynolds had discovered in Keen's deft blending of rural English and American vernacular prototypes an architectural style uniquely suited, with its suggestion of a timeless, unassuming, and yet fine simplicity, to her missionary purposes—those educational and social goals that elevated to virtue what might otherwise have seemed a dangerously consuming personal ambition in a Christian wife and mother. Katharine's intention to inculcate among resident employees of her estate a strong sense of belonging to a mutually supportive and caring commu-

OPPOSITE:
Post office at the entrance to the village and greenhouses. Photo by Thomas Sears.

The stables. Photo by Thomas Sears.

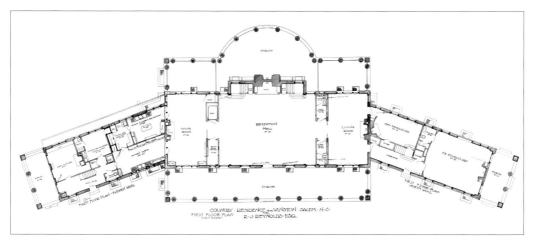

First-floor plan showing the angled wings, 1919. Traced from Charles Barton Keen's drawings by J. E. Ellerbe.

Watercolor drawing of a gardener's cottage by W. C. Northup.

nity meant that every building must contribute in some measure to the general impression of a well-kept, thriving neighborhood, just as each person would have a part to play in maintaining a vital, healthy, and beautiful environment for work, domestic life, and health-giving leisure.

Perhaps it is only a coincidence that in the late summer of 1912, a time of such excitement and high hopes for Katharine, the Reynolds Tobacco Company initiated a profit-sharing opportunity that was, according to historian Nannie Tilley, "unique in the tobacco industry" in creating a loyal "community of interest" in the company's future among employees at every level, who were subsequently enabled to purchase shares of Class A stock.[45] Katharine had always admired her husband's entrepreneurial genius, and he equally valued her good judgment and her interest in his affairs; we know that the two loved to talk business together. Although Dick's failure to share her deep religious faith was a continuing source of anxiety for Katharine, they were alike in being unstintingly public-spirited, working together diligently on behalf of civic improvements and an elevated standard of living for people of every class in Winston. Tilley credits Katharine with influencing her husband to initiate a number of major improvements to working conditions in his factories— such as providing chilled drinking water, sanitary restrooms, wholesome lunches furnished at cost in a pleasant cafeteria— and subsidized housing.[46] For her part, the model farm she was establishing was in a real sense Katharine's *business*, and she was determined to make at least a modest financial success of it, since if it were not economically viable, her effort to provide North Carolina farmers with persuasive examples of how they might improve their own operations was doomed to failure. Her determination to make the farm profitable, however, was a relatively minor consideration in comparison with more essential, complementary goals for her project—first to bring into being a unique kind of southern place, a life-enhancing physical environment, and then to make sure that through wise management it created manifold opportunities for the people of its exceptionally favored small community.

In the South of 1912, it was still possible, even natural, for Katharine to think of all of her farm's residents as a single community. As a matter of fact, she began quite early in its operations to invoke the metaphor of a family, enlarging a common practice among southerners, reaching back even to the time of slavery, of referring to household servants, black or white, as members of one's "family." (On his most benevolent day, neither R. J. Reynolds nor any of his peers is likely to have thought of his employees as one big family; it remained for the human resources departments of late-twentieth-century corporations to discover the psychological potential of such a notion.) For Katharine Reynolds, however, using the word "family" to describe her community of employees was meant to define a relationship of mutual obligations, but also one of mutual respect and even, it was hoped, of genuine affection. Her use of the metaphor was certainly not meant to convey, as it might today, any blurring of social distinctions in the direction of equality. Katharine's conception of her estate's "family" was determined, inevitably, by her place and time. But also, her Christianity exhorted her to recognize that the "neighbors" she must love were not just the people next door but the least powerful and neediest members of her society. Her education had exposed her, probably for the first time, to the radical idea that descendants of African slaves, given the same advantages as members of the white race, had the potential to achieve just as much. Indeed, no one did more to improve the lot of black people living in the "Twin Cities" of Winston and Salem than Katharine and Dick Reynolds.[47]

To presume, however, that these two dedicated philanthropists ought to have perceived and rejected the morally atrophied assumptions undergirding the paternalistic system that governed relations between the classes as well as the races in the South (and, to a lesser extent, other regions of the country) is to hold the Reynoldses accountable for an inherited, solidly entrenched way of looking at the world that, to their minds, represented not simply the way things were but the way they probably ought to be for the foreseeable future. Patriarchal society took its authority from religious tradition, in which the hierarchy of authority within the family, moving downward from father to mother to child, established a model for other social relationships, including those that governed the world of work. Allen Tullos has vividly described the implications of southern paternalism for black families seeking employment opportunities in and around the tobacco and textile factories of the Carolina Piedmont during the Jim Crow era:

For a subsistence pay of dimes and starch, table scraps and castoff clothes, black women took in the laundries and cleaned the houses not only of middle-class but also of many mill-hill families. Black men worked as construction laborers and were consigned to the most strenuous and hazardous of jobs, such as the firing of steam boilers. Black men and women undertook the dirtiest, dustiest, hottest, and heaviest tasks in the tobacco factories of the Reynolds family in Winston-Salem and of the Dukes in Durham. All but a relative handful of blacks were excluded from the Piedmont's textile mills and from the operation of to-bacco-processing machinery until after World War II.[48]

This is the background against which to judge, to the extent that surviving information allows, Katharine Reynolds's treat-ment of the "colored" farm workers, gardeners, household ser-vants, and their families who worked, and in many cases made their home, on her estate.

Both tradition and documentary evidence help us to under-stand how Katharine treated these people, what she expected of them in return, and how they might have thought and felt about her. On the one hand, of course, are all the obvious reminders of inequality; on the farm as in the factory, the physically hardest and lowest-paying jobs were most often assigned to black work-ers. Schools, churches, hospitals, and housing were segregated in town, so it is hardly surprising that when Katharine built the first five houses at the farm to accommodate black families, the site chosen was outside the village area on her master plan. This be-came the "Five Row" neighborhood, expanding over the years with the addition of a building used as both church and school and more houses, including a twelve-room log structure accom-modating three families, in addition to the original group of white frame cottages. Unlike houses in the village, these homes did not have indoor plumbing; residents obtained water for cook-ing and bathing from a line of spigots spaced along the dirt road,

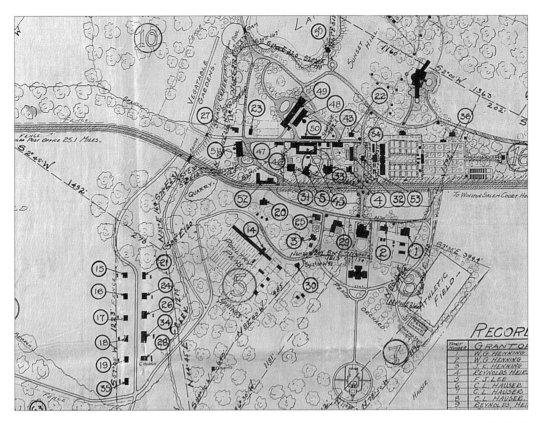

Detail of the "General Plan of Reynolda" by J. E. Ellerbe, 1925, showing location of Five Row (at lower left; bungalow at upper right).

The Five Row schoolhouse and church.

Flora Pledger and Lilly Hamlin, Five Row residents. Photo by Mrs. Sarah F. Hamlin.

and an outhouse maintained by the estate was located at the rear of each property. Kerosene lamps were used for lighting, and small coal-burning stoves for winter heating. Residents were strongly urged to plant and tend vegetable and flower gardens; Katharine supplied whatever was needed, then encouraged high standards by periodically giving prizes—most likely cash—to those with the prettiest yard or a superior show of produce. On a road behind the house lots, families could keep chickens in separate fenced yards with coops. Men and women who grew up in the Five Row settlement recall that Katharine Reynolds kept a close eye on what went on there; she frequently arrived on horseback, unannounced, and saw to it that the least thing in need of repair or refurbishment was attended to promptly, at no cost to the occupants. While she lived, no rents were charged. She managed the place, obviously, with a man's authority, in a style that reflects classic southern paternalism, however tempered by matriarchal benevolence.[49]

There is no question, however, that for those on the receiving end of Katharine's benevolence, the offer of a job on her farm, especially if it came with accommodations in Five Row, meant something close to dramatic rescue, a passage out of routine poverty in bleak surroundings to a place and a life that offered security, hope, and self-respect. Our own twenty-first-century sensibilities are instinctively suspicious, and rightly so, of any "yes, but" defenses of historic patterns of racial discrimination, and none is intended here. Yet we ought to be able to appreciate the difference between Katharine's determination to educate and improve the lives of black people working on her estate and more ordinary—even, in Katharine's society, more socially acceptable—gestures of charity toward members of a black community whose civil and human rights, almost half a century after emancipation, remained tightly restricted, even by law. Katharine never shirked the obligations of charity. Her friend and pastor Neal Anderson privately praised her for all the help she consistently rendered "in such a quiet and unassuming way to the sick and poor. Its influence is far wider than I believe even you realize."[50] Nevertheless, while there is ample testimony to frequent small kindnesses that Katharine extended to individuals and families living in Five Row, it is equally clear that she did not think of her black employees as properly the recipients of charity. Her relationship to them was based instead on a conviction that, in spite of social disparities literally enforced by her society, simple justice established the right of each of these workers, men and women equally, to consistently fair treatment, a living wage, and opportunities to learn and to improve their lot. In return, Katharine expected each one of her employees to demonstrate not just a commitment to hard work but a sense of responsibility for seeing that every task was performed to her own high standards, and she praised and rewarded those who pleased her in this way. Infringements of any of the codified rules governing workers' behavior were grounds for dismissal.

The records of conversations with black people who worked for Katharine provide a sense of how unwelcome such a fall from grace might be, since those interviewed described both their work and the experience of living in the Five Row community in largely idyllic terms. Harvey Miller, for example, whose father worked on the estate and who began earning wages himself as soon as he was old enough to take on appropriate jobs, expressed pride in the quality of the education that he had received in the Five Row school, since public schools in the city—all of them segregated, of course—offered fewer advantages. He pointed out that Katharine had hired two well-trained teachers, and provided the students, several of whom came from outside the Five Row community, with the same textbooks, equipment, and supplies as those used in the white children's school. Miller described a curriculum that included history, geography, spelling and grammar, arithmetic, penmanship, hygiene and health, painting and drawing, and "a little music, too," since one of the teachers had musical training. He recalled fondly the large hedge-bordered yard used for exercise and games, and stressed that children from both schools regularly played together on the grounds of both schools.[51]

Former residents of Five Row also praised the abundance of fresh fruits and vegetables, milk, eggs, and farm-raised chicken and pork that they could produce for themselves or obtain from the estate at little or no cost. James Holmes considered the availability of piped water just outside one's home a great improvement over the situation of most rural southern blacks, and added that Katharine also arranged with a local company to deliver ice to the Five Row houses. Similarly, Ed Lash contrasted the wooden floors in the houses with the dirt floors that were still common, noting that although the houses in the village proper were of a superior quality, the houses in Five Row "for their time and place were real good houses," and the people who lived in them "loved Mrs. Reynolds" because she had seen to it that their homes were comfortable and well maintained.[52]

Although Katharine obviously acquiesced to the expectations of her society in providing segregated living accommodations for farm workers, at least two black employees on her household

Major-domo John Carter and his wife, Marjorie, maid and later cook.

staff—Cleve Williams, her chauffeur, and John Carter, who ultimately functioned as her household manager—were assigned homes in the village rather than in Five Row. Katharine had personally trained Carter, as she did many other of her employees, making it possible for him to move from a job in her husband's tobacco factory to service as valet and then butler at the Fifth Street house, and finally major-domo of the estate for the remainder of his working life. In deciding that these two retainers deserved housing commensurate with their positions on her staff, without consideration of race, Katharine seized an opportunity to confirm a social status they had earned by their diligence, superior skills, and dedicated service—exactly the model of virtuous industry in which she so firmly believed, and which she held up, without compromise on her part, to anyone who came to work for her.

Pressing Ahead on Many Fronts

Katharine came out of that heady summer of 1912 in high spirits, charged with excitement over the progress being made at her estate, and ready, typically, to tackle several new initiatives. The fall social season in town was, of course, as busy as ever; she and Dick hosted a party for the visiting governor of Virginia early in November. Far from allowing such affairs to be the chief preoccupation of her life, however, as they were for so many of her peers, Katharine tried to manage their details in a businesslike way, refusing to neglect the various missionary causes, secular as well as religious, to which she had pledged her energy and her resources. She had for some time been taking advantage of programs and publications offered by the extension service of the U.S. Department of Agriculture in planning her farm operations, and was now preparing to introduce formal instruction in improved farming, dairying, and food processing techniques to her own farmworkers and their wives, and to as many people from Forsyth County as she could attract to classes and workshops, using staff from the local county extension office. Hoping to involve the young people from these families as well, she ordered a set of instructional pamphlets on the formation of agricultural "corn clubs" for boys and "canning clubs" for girls, a national movement with which the clubs she eventually sponsored would become affiliated.[53]

In the meantime, Katharine arranged to bring to her Winston home from the Asheville area an academically trained professional "domestic scientist," Annie Jean Gash, to teach a month-long course in sewing and in what today might be described as "gourmet" cooking for a small group of women friends and relatives. That this was meant to be a serious educational effort rather than merely a pleasant diversion is suggested by the fact that the ladies in the sewing class earned credit toward an "Efficiency Certificate," although Katharine's subsequent correspondence with Miss Gash suggests that the participants had a very good time in the bargain. A letter written early in December, in fact, gives us a rare glimpse of Katharine in a relaxed and playful exchange with a woman whom she now considered a friend:

My dear Miss Gash:

It was a great pleasure to have your recent letter and I enjoyed it more than I can tell you. . . .

Knowing Methodist preachers as I do, I imagine they must have thought they had died and gone to heaven when they got some of your cooking; however, I never thought that Methodist preachers made very good husbands. I would advise you to wait and come back to Winston. . . .

The farm is flourishing now. I am acting Superintendent and good (?) management is beginning to tell. You would have been quite pleased, had you heard a couple of answers I had over the telephone this morning, when I invited two of your recent cooking class to go with me to the farm: one could not go *because she was making suet pudding for dinner.* The other was showing a neighbor how to stuff her turkey with tomato dressing. So you see the good work is going on.

. . . Max [Katharine's sister] wore her dress, about a week ago, to a party and she was paraded up and down the floor, right and left and most hugely admired (the dress, I should have said).[54]

The parenthetical question mark following her announcement that she was acting as superintendent of the farm is revealing, since it is obviously meant to soften the ring of what might otherwise sound like boasting about one's management skills, something a proper southern lady would never do. It hints at the possibility that Katharine Reynolds was occasionally sensitive to what others thought about the exceptional responsibilities and authority to act in her own behalf that she had been "allowed" by a wealthy and indulgent husband. Similarly revealing is Katharine's comment that "the good work is going on," because it reminds us that she had from earliest young womanhood appreciated and valued traditionally feminine domestic and artistic occupation as an important part of a vocation that increasingly challenged her not to limit her activities to the domestic sphere, but to take responsibility for improving her community in ways that women of her generation were only beginning to do.

Just a short time before writing to Miss Gash, Katharine had written to Anna D. Casler, executive secretary of the South Atlantic Territorial Committee of the YWCA, headquartered in Charlotte, to ask for help in drafting a constitution for a civic improvement league she was helping to organize for the Winston-Salem association. Miss Casler was impressed by the request, since neither the Civic Club nor the Civic Department of the Women's Club in her own community had a constitution. She promised Katharine that she would obtain suitable models for her from a young man, "an expert on the subject . . . associated with the firm of John Nolen, First Vice-president of the American Civic Association." Then, in a second letter written the same day, she urged Katharine to accept nomination for a position on the field committee, serving as liaison between the Twin Cities and both the territorial committee and national board of the YWCA: "This I know you would enjoy because of the [opportunity to keep in] touch with those women whom we are all so glad to know and to work with. I need not tell you how much we need you." While reassuring Katharine that very little travel away from home would be required of her, she did press her—using language that underscores the still problematic nature of such activities for married middle-class southern women—to attend a meeting of the National Board that would convene the following spring in Richmond: "You remember that Mr. Reynolds practically promised that you might [attend the convention in Indianapolis], so now that we are to have it nearer home (probably the only time in twenty years in *this* field) I hope you will ask him to see that you come. Membership in the South Atlantic Committee, of course, will mean that you will have the privilege of meeting with the National Board for its special councils during the Convention; and we need you there."[55]

This invitation to serve on a regional board of the YWCA (which also encouraged Katharine to participate in meetings of the national board if she happened to be in New York City at a time when it was convenient to do so) represented an opportunity for her to move beyond involvement with local programs and issues to join forces with those seeking progressive change on a number of fronts throughout the Southeast, an experience that was likely to lead ultimately to being considered for a national position. It must have been very hard for Katharine to turn her back on such an opportunity, and we can only assume that circumstances forced her to do just that. If her husband was wary of her traveling to conventions, it was probably out of concern for her health, since so often her rheumatic flare-ups followed stressful or exhausting departures from routine. Then, at the very time in early December when she would have been trying to decide whether or not to accept the nomination, she found herself once again faced with a worrying confluence of physical and mental pressure. She wrote to Miss Casler that she felt obliged to decline, saying that her time was 'too taken up" to allow her to do justice to the position, but that she would do her best to attend the April convention in Richmond.[56]

A lot of Katharine's busyness had to do with her insistence on giving personal attention to a staggering list of tasks in preparation for Christmas—even as winter planting of trees and shrubs continued in the Fifth Street gardens—and for once she was not able to achieve perfect success in spite of the difficulties. Her order for Christmas cards sent to Tiffany's in New York arrived too late for engraving; on the tenth of December she wrote in clear desperation to a New York furrier wanting to know "what kind of FUR COATS and what price you could furnish me immediately for a gentleman who is 6 feet-2 inches and weighs about 215 pounds?" On the eighteenth she placed a large order with a North Carolina nursery for delivery of fresh greens and cut flowers for herself and as gifts for friends; her own house, she wrote, would need "your best pair of pyramidal box trees six feet tall," in addition to smaller matched pairs of boxwood and cedar "in nice tubs." A second letter that day, sent to a woman from whom she ordered "stocking stuffers" for the children, provides the first hint that the pace of holiday preparations might be dangerously taxing: "Winston was quite gay last evening—a good theatrical performance at the Auditorium, William Jennings Bryan at the Liberty with a reception after at the YMCA and Mrs. John Hanes' reception." (Bryan's address on this occasion would have been even more than usually exciting to hear, since he was credited with having recently secured for Woodrow Wilson the hard-won Democratic nomination for the presidency.) "I attended pretty much all of them," Katharine confessed, "and am feeling pretty well 'washed out' today."[57]

Perhaps fearing that her surgery the previous spring would not, after all, prevent the recurrence of yet another bout of debility, she wrote at about this time to Susanna Cocroft, described on her letterhead as "Originator of the Physical Culture Extension Society" and author of no fewer than a dozen books on such topics as *The Vital Organs*, *The Nervous System*, *Self Sufficiency*, *Ideals and Privileges of Woman*, and a title Katharine ordered for her own library, *What to Eat and When*. Cocroft replied to Katharine's original query with absolute confidence that "you are suffering with difficulties which I can relieve, Mrs. Reynolds." The pitch that followed—"I cannot make people realize just what my pupils are doing by Nature's methods of exercise, breathing, bathing, and a slight regulation of diet instead of by drugs"—would have appealed strongly to Katharine, who placed so much faith in the power of fresh air, exercise, healthy foods, and sheer determination to restore physical strength and well-being.[58] By the time the letter arrived, however, the Reynolds household had been placed under quarantine after an outbreak of measles among the children that began just a few days before Christmas.

It meant another of those rounds of infection, fevers, and the risk of even more serious complications that must always have reawakened terrible memories. As late as the second week in January, Katharine wrote Miss Gash that the quarantine was still in effect, that Nancy had "just the right temperature and pulse to break out at any time," and "the baby had pneumonia and measles and was quite sick . . . but is able to be up today."[59] Even with these preoccupations, she had taken time on the day after New Year's to respond to a series of urgent letters and wires from Louis Miller asking for a decision on his request to purchase evergreens from Buck Duke's New Jersey estate to be used for the entrance plantings at her farm. Miller had informed her a month earlier that he was severing his partnership with Buckenham and setting up a landscape engineering firm of his own. "I can do this work much cheaper for you than under the old regime," he told her, and while her reply at that time assured him that she would remain his client, it ended with a challenge to a bill he had sent charging her for a pergola design that she had rejected in favor of one proposed by a local firm. "I look upon your landscape architectural plans in the same way that I would architectural plans for buildings," she wrote, "where we pay only for what we accept."[60] Now her tone was even more cool, in a letter that offers further evidence of Katharine's continual absorption in the landscape design process:

My dear Mr. Miller:

We are ready to put in the planting along the fence and around the gate at the farm, or will be by the time we could get the plants here.

We had several bids on this planting, . . . the one from

Biltmore Nurseries being the cheapest one of them. This I believe you wrote me at the time was due to the fact of the plants being smaller. As we have no water near where these plants will go, I am inclined to believe that the smaller plants will prove the more satisfactory [as compared with those available from the Duke estate], and am, therefore, prepared to accept the bid of the Biltmore Nurseries. . . .

Your plan shows no planting on the outside of the gate, but I feel sure that you intended to put some in there, as it would look a little bare; there is no hurry about this, as we have piled rock there at present. . . .

I note what you say in your favor of the 19th of last month, in regard to being able to work much cheaper in future.

Whenever you come down be sure to call to see me, as I would like to advise with you with regard to the best place for locating our small farm houses, namely: cottage for poultryman, dairyman, gardner [sic], etc. I had an idea that they might be well placed if along the side of the hill on the other side of the highway, opposite greenhouses, gardner's cottage and present farm buildings. The property on this side, as you, perhaps, remember, slopes down from this road to a little brook, with the hill rising beyond. My idea was to run a road along the side of this hill beyond this brook, some three or four hundred feet from the present macadamized road, communicating with this road at both ends[,] building the houses a little back from this road on the far side [and] leaving a space in between for a small natural park.

The houses then would be easily accessible to our water plan and sewerage system.

With best wishes for the New Year. . . .[61]

At the very least, the language of this letter is more technical and the understanding of the relationship between topography and scenic effect that it demonstrates more sophisticated than one might expect of a woman of Katharine's background and circumstances. It confirms the impression, in fact, that she spent a lot of time visualizing and evaluating exactly what she wanted in given situations before soliciting ideas from her professional consultants. Although it is impossible to know for certain whether this was also true in matters of interior design, at least in architectural and landscape decisions she brought an educated eye and a designer's absorption with alternative options to her dealings with the firms she commissioned.

For a brief period in mid-January, Katharine found herself still well and increasingly hopeful as each of the children steadily improved and she could start planning, at her doctor's suggestion, to take them to a warmer climate for the balance of the winter. A thank-you note to Miss Gash written on young Dick's behalf for a gift sent during his illness reported that "the farm is coming along nicely. The [gardener's] cottage is almost finished, the greenhouses are also nearing completion and the lake lacks just about one and a half feet of being full. It certainly is beautiful. I have been going out daily to see it."[62] But toward the end of the month she did succumb, not to measles but to an unspecified illness (almost certainly her familiar "rheumatism") that persisted for weeks, leaving her very weak and unable to travel. In a letter written in late February to her Asheville friend Mollie Bernard, Katharine played down the seriousness of her symptoms—"I am just going to Atlantic City for a little strengthening up"[63]—but two other letters of the same date, one to Katharine's favorite Baltimore dressmaker and one to another clothier she favored in that city, warned that although she had hoped to visit them during her family's upcoming stay in Atlantic City, the fact that she had been "quite ill for three weeks" made it unlikely that she would be strong enough to travel to Baltimore and so "might have to make selections from cuts, samples, descriptions, etc." sent to her hotel.[64] A postcard sent to her mother from the Marlborough Blenheim barely ten days later reported cheerily that the children

The children playing at the beach in Atlantic City, Marlboro Blenheim Hotel in the background, c. 1912.

were all well and that she herself was "feeling fine now."[65] In fact, Katharine had not fully recovered even by the time the children returned to Winston with Bum at the end of their brief holiday, and she moved into the Belvedere in Baltimore with her sister Irene as companion. She wrote more candidly to her husband once they were settled in, a letter that begins with a tender recollection of her first trip to Baltimore with her bachelor cousin years earlier:

> Well, my dear, it is just about ten years ago, lacking one week, that I was here for the first time, when you brought Nancy O'Hanlon and myself. How different Baltimore

looks now! I couldn't see its dirt then; it was all wonder and beauty. Now it seems that Winston is far more wonderful and decidedly prettier. How I would love to be home with you and the children; but just as you have your business, so I have my work, and this is part of it, getting the children's spring clothes and mine. I suppose Miss van den Berg told you I would have to go very slow for the next day or so; that will prevent my getting home as soon as I had hoped, as I cannot stand until Monday to be fitted. . . .

I have several invitations next week for card parties and teas, but, of course, cannot go.

The letter closes—after sending "my best love and many, many kisses"—with an amusing conspiratorial postscript: "They are not showing 'Prince Albert' in the tobacco stores on the 'board walk.' I didn't dare enquire on inside."[66]

Since Katharine regularly took advantage of the opportunity to see doctors connected with the Johns Hopkins Hospital whenever she was in Baltimore, this most recent serious recurrence of symptoms just a year after her hospitalization there may have forced her finally to admit, to herself if not to others, not only that her health would probably not improve significantly but also that it might very well become worse if she failed to rein in her habit of "overdoing." This meant more than simply avoiding another pregnancy, as her doctors insisted, although it was probably as difficult for them as for her to determine precisely what restrictions to her usual routines might be prudent.[67] If she sincerely regretted having to miss card parties, teas, and dances—and Katharine seems to have thoroughly enjoyed this kind of socializing—how much more did she dread any limitations on the multiple responsibilities she considered to be "her work," which embraced everything from planning wardrobes and vacations to overseeing the construction, development, and management of a large farming estate. Her symptoms, when they occurred, were bound to have been as frightening to her as to her loved ones, but the idea that she should start thinking of herself as an invalid and behave accordingly was totally repugnant to Katharine's nature. She was thirty-two years old and her eldest child just seven. She probably reasoned that if her damaged heart was always going to require periodic regimes of physical rest, her mind and imagination might still be occupied and productive. And work of this kind so richly satisfied her creative drive; it was play for her, refreshing her spirits, and she relished all of it, even the most mundane details. Moreover, the religious faith that informed her understanding of herself and her mission in life affirmed that hard work in service to others was the path to salvation. Thus when dark apprehensions gnawed at Katharine's hopes for the future, threatening to undermine her trust that God would give her the strength she needed to do his work in the world, she must certainly have prayed about her condition, accepting it as a cross that she, so richly blessed in other ways, must bear in patience.

Then, as if to confirm her expectations that her farm, however much it might superficially resemble agricultural estates elsewhere in the country, was providentially intended to be an instrument of good, the year 1913 produced a cornucopia of good fortune for the Reynolds family. Even the inauguration in March of President Woodrow Wilson would have seemed propitious. Wilson, the son of a Presbyterian minister, had spent much of his youth in Georgia and South Carolina, understood the implications of what the South had suffered during and after Reconstruction, and represented the progressive wing of the national Democratic Party. Also that spring, after several years of secret research on the technology of cigarette manufacture, the R. J. Reynolds Tobacco Company, which even after the success of Prince Albert was chiefly a producer of plug tobacco, informed the Winston Board of Trade that it was preparing to launch a brand of cigarettes. The story of how Dick Reynolds and his brothers subsequently acquired the necessary machinery, developed a better-tasting blend of Turkish and domestic tobacco, then named, packaged, and advertised Camels, "the first truly American cigarette," is a now classic tale of revolutionary merchandising, full of such colorful incidents as a last-minute decision to take advantage of the timely arrival of a circus in Winston to get a picture of "Old Joe" the dromedary, whose photograph served as the model for what became a famous label almost from the start of production in October. Another part of the story credits Katharine Reynolds with having shrewdly improved the copy on the back of the Camel package to read: "Don't look for Inserts or Coupons, as the cost of the Tobaccos blended in CAMEL cigarettes prohibits the use of them." For the second time in five years, according to historian Nannie Tilley, "R. J. Reynolds had hit the bull's eye in public taste."[68] Auspicious, too, that in the same year that guaranteed the rapidly expanding profit potential of Winston's largest employer, the Twin Cities of Winston and Salem consolidated as Winston-Salem. It is hard to imagine what the plain-living Moravian brethren who founded the historic Salem settlement would have thought of a merger that married their fortunes to an increasingly rich and powerful "tobacco town."

Once again, however, a new year began with chilling reminders of Katharine's physical frailty. At some point early in 1914, while still riding a tide of good fortune and happiness, she and Dick had conceived another child. When worrying symptoms developed, Katharine turned, as she always did, to specialists at Johns Hopkins. The only record of her hospitalization there in late April is a letter written to Bum by a nurse, obviously a friend, who attended the doctors and cared for Katharine during her stay. This woman's hastily penciled note ("Hope you can make out this awful scratch . . .") describes in poignant detail a four-day ordeal that started when Katharine suffered a heart attack during an obstetrical procedure, followed later the same day by a second, more severe attack before finally responding to drugs administered by her physicians. "At first," the nurse reported, "she begged Dr. Thayer [and] Dr. Williams to let her go on a while longer but after the heart attack she was perfectly resigned and realized [termination of the pregnancy] was the only thing to do." Although she was far enough along for the sex of the fetus to be noted, Katharine—exceptionally "brave and wonderful," in the nurse's view, throughout a grueling experience—"did not wish to know anything about the baby and we have told her nothing."[69] Since records show that she stayed for a time in May at the Marlborough Blenheim in Atlantic City, Katharine apparently went there directly for a period of convalescence after her release from the hospital.[70]

The year was almost half over by the time she was back home and strong enough to resume her normal round of activities. Since by then it had become even more certain that the Camel brand was destined to increase the family's personal wealth no less dramatically than Prince Albert had done, Katharine was free to do more than simply see their current building program through to completion. During her enforced leisure in recent months she had had time to ask herself if any part of the existing plans for the estate might be improved or expanded. As the framing of the bungalow and other construction in the village moved steadily forward, she had managed to maintain, as we have seen, extremely close oversight of Charles Barton Keen's drawings of interior details and design revisions, but none of these had involved a major rethinking of the house they were building. The remodeling and redecorating of the Reynolds home in town was finished now, as was its surrounding landscape of lawns and gardens. Louis Miller remained actively involved with development of the estate landscape, of course, and had submitted to Katharine in the fall of the preceding year his final design for the formal gardens fronting the greenhouse adjacent to the village, a plan that included detailed lists of the botanical names, quantities, and location of all the fruits, vegetables, and woody or herbaceous ornamental varieties he was recommending.[71]

At some point after receiving this design from Miller, Katharine must have had second thoughts about the quality of the work he had produced. The landscape surrounding her residence on Fifth Street was old-fashioned looking, but that may have seemed appropriate enough for the Queen Anne–style house. The design of its garden and gazebo (both Miller and Katharine always referred to this roomlike structure as a "pergola") were conventional at best, and Katharine had accepted Miller's recommendation of a sentimental commercial figure ordered from a catalogue for the fountain. For the master plan of her estate property, his firm of Buckenham and Miller had drawn upon the English landscape gardening tradition that Katharine admired, and the conceptual plan they produced in 1911 had satisfactorily provided at least the preliminary outlines of a suitable setting for Charles Barton Keen's architectural translations of nineteenth-century English estate villages and parks. But Miller's design of the formal gardens, intended to complement and bring to perfection the entire greenhouse complex, now seemed to Katharine as uninspired as those in Winston that she had recently paid for—and getting good value for money spent was extremely important to her. Some of the fault may have been her own, since she continually urged Miller to frugality; he lost the contract for the pergola at the house in town because the contractors who supplied services to R. J. Reynolds Tobacco offered to build essentially the same structure for much less, and she then balked at paying his design fee.[72] Now she realized that in this critically important component of her estate, its formal gardens, his design skills were no match for the quality of a steadily evolving site plan and architectural program that reflected Katharine's increasingly sophisticated landscape design aspirations.

If she went to Keen with her concerns, as seems likely, he would not have hesitated to recommend to her the landscape architect Thomas Sears, also of Philadelphia. (Louis Miller's professional title was "landscape engineer.") Perhaps Katharine had already seen residential landscapes designed by Sears among the many homes of friends she had visited in the environs of that city, or she may have encountered photographs of his garden designs in books and magazines. However their first meeting came about, Katharine was sufficiently impressed with his credentials that she decided not to proceed any further with installation of Miller's plan but to hire Sears, not just to redesign the formal gardens but for all additional landscape architectural services she would need as work at the farm continued. Resetting her course toward a more contemporary and a more exceptional landscape provided Katharine with an exciting new challenge, one that suited the optimism about their future that the brilliant national success of her husband's latest product had generated.

As if to acknowledge and seal, in a formal way, their recovered happiness—the pride and pleasure that both Katharine and R. J. Reynolds took in the remarkable place that she was creating—the name of "Mrs. Katherine Reynolds Farms . . . formerly known as 'Reynolds Farms' was legally changed on the first of October 1914 to 'Reynolda.'"[73]

FOUR

The Landscape of Home

IN COMMISSIONING THOMAS SEARS TO REPLACE LOUIS Miller as her landscape design consultant for Reynolda, Katharine was making a choice that favored youth over age, fresh and stylish approaches to garden design over distinctly stodgier ones. The 1911 master plan Miller had produced while still a partner in the venerable firm of Buckenham and Miller had by this time been substantially modified and expanded by programmatic and siting decisions that reflected Katharine's own thinking and ongoing discussions not just with Miller but with Charles Barton Keen and others from whom she sought advice. A list of "Liabilities and Assets" published as part of the October 1914 legal notice of her farming estate's change of name conveys a good sense of the progress that had been made. This record itemizes expenditures made to date by "Mrs. K. S. Reynolds" for acquiring and improving her land and farming operations; construction costs for each component of the infrastructure, the lake, the golf course, and individual buildings; and all purchases of equipment and furnishings. Only $1,500 had been spent on the bungalow, an amount even less than the $1,837.51 cost of preparing its site. The other figures, too, suggest that Katharine had spent most of her money and energies on getting the farm up and running, installing utilities and roads, shaping the contours of a picturesque landscape of village and surrounding park, finishing the first of the homes and offices needed by workers and members of her staff, and building the greenhouse complex.

Louis Miller's task in redesigning the expanded grounds around the Reynolds family's Victorian mansion in the city had chiefly involved the composition of lawn and trees, a formal garden, and numerous beds of shrubs and flowers. At Reynolda, by contrast, he had been occupied with engineering the site, creating the "big picture" in a sense, and had only recently turned his attention to selecting trees and shrubs for planting along the drives and at entrances, and completing his design of the three-acre formal gardens. The unusual decision to site the greenhouse complex along an edge of the property adjacent to the village and parallel to what came to be called Reynolda Road had been made very early in the planning process, well before Keen was commissioned as architect; its location and configuration in the 1911 master plan of Buckenham and Miller were, in fact, among the few features of that plan that survived intact. An oral tradition holds that Katharine Reynolds herself, not Miller, was responsible for choosing this location for the gardens because she wanted them to be part of the village, seen and enjoyed by the whole community of Winston-Salem, rather than a more private adjunct to the family's residence—a gesture of southern hospitality for which Buck Duke's liberality at his New Jersey estate may have provided the immediate inspiration.

There were other considerations, however, related to her expectations of how this garden complex should function that may have been even more important in determining its location. Late in the spring of 1912, Katharine had written Lord and Bumham that she wished to expand the design program on which their preliminary plan of the preceding year had been based. In addition to a "palm room" and specific "compartments" dedicated to American Beauty roses, other roses, and carnations, she asked them to

provide plans for the following features (typing the letter herself, then inking in bullets before the separate items):

The Palm House, c. 1921.

- a good-sized grapery.
- a tomato section, a large vegetable section and an assorted plant section.
- a propagating room and a section for fruits.
- a nice work room, a pit and about 200 feet of cold frames.

Explaining that she "might not want to build at once, but would want the plans complete before starting," she reminded them that "as I told you before, I want neat, well-built houses that would be in keeping with our bungalow. . . . The foundations for these houses, I wish to build of native stone . . . [and] to build myself, but want you to furnish plans."[1] As it turned out, she would contract locally or use her own crews for a good deal of additional

Greenhouses (Reynolda Presbyterian Church and manse in left background), c. 1921.

The New York Botanical Garden Conservatory and Lily Pond, c. 1925.

construction preliminary to installation of the framework and furnishings of the greenhouses.

Katharine knew very well that she was in conversation with the firm whose name had long since become synonymous with design and construction of the finest glasshouses in America. Their projects for public gardens included the 1878 conservatory at San Francisco's Golden Gate Park and the magnificent acre-sized domed greenhouse of the New York Botanical Garden, built in 1902 and modeled on the Palm House of London's Royal Botanic Gardens at Kew. Their private clients included such wealthy and socially prominent Americans as millionaire Jay Gould, for whose Lyndhurst estate in Tarrytown, New York, Lord and Bumham had produced in 1881 a structure almost four hundred feet long, housing one of the finest horticultural collections in the country. It is most unlikely that the firm's staff had had much experience in dealing with female clients, and still less likely that they were used to dealing with a steady stream of hand-typed letters or telegrams of the sort they received from Mrs. Reynolds of Winston-Salem:

> My Dear Sirs:
>
> I am enclosing check, covering second payment on greenhouses.
>
> The iron and frame work was not completed as soon as you seem to think it was.
>
> I am wiring you the enclosed message, regarding basin for shower bath. You forgot to send this with the other fixtures. Of course a shower bath is in no way complete without something to hold the water and keep it from running all over the floors, and I feel sure that it is only a matter of calling your attention to this fact to insure its being made good, as the price certainly includes this.
>
> Your lack of completing plans of my architect in the workroom has caused your men some trouble as well as myself; but I believe we are about to get this matter straightened out now.
>
> The houses seem to be progressing nicely, and I think we shall be much pleased with them.[2]

What this most unusual southern lady had in mind for her estate's greenhouse complex, starting with those "neat, well-built houses," would also have seemed rather unconventional to these gentlemen, since they were accustomed to more dramatic descriptions of their glass buildings, whose aesthetic effect was that of a dazzling crystalline splendor. In insisting on an architecture that connected the greenhouses to the bungalow, particularly through repetition of rustic stone foundation walls hand-built by her two masons, Katharine was deliberately avoiding the introduction of an incompatible formal grandeur into buildings and a garden landscape that should express instead the aesthetic of a working farm and village settlement possessing a simpler, less pretentious beauty of their own. Moreover, she expected much more than the visual beauty of ornamental gardening from the greenhouses and gardens; their primary function, as her list of necessary facilities bears out, was closely linked to her farm's agricultural enterprises. The rows of cold frames, the grapery, and the "large vegetable section" in the greenhouses would produce food crops as well as plants and flowers, all marketable to the public. Reynolda's greenhouse complex, in other words, was to be at once a pleasure garden, grocery, florist shop, and—like the rest of the farming operations—an accessible model demonstrating the benefits of the latest scientific, technological, and horticultural ideas and practices.

Such a combination of ornamental pleasure gardens and productive vegetable gardens and orchards on residential properties represented a well-established American tradition. Its roots lay in the eighteenth-century English landscape gardening school's concept of the *ferme ornée*, or ornamental farm. In the nineteenth century, the great popularizer Andrew Jackson Downing, using the example of his English mentor John Claudius Loudon, had translated the aristocratic villa and country house tradition represented by Jefferson's Monticello to the scale of middle-class rural estates and suburban properties. More often than not, however, Downing and his followers included utilitarian gardens in their plans without managing to integrate them successfully with either formal pleasure gardens or the preferred picturesque style of the grounds. The 1911 Buckenham and Miller master plan of Kathar-

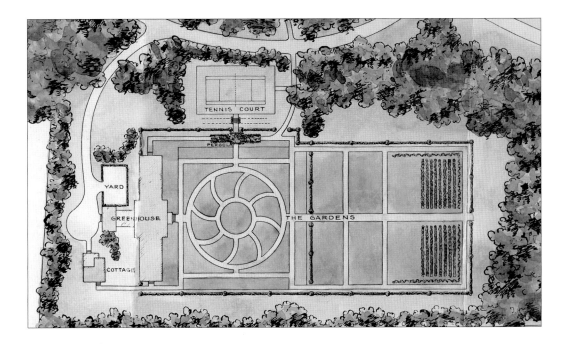

ine Reynolds's estate shows a long rectangular garden area divided at its center between a garden of flowers and shrubs immediately fronting the greenhouses, and beyond it on the same axis a slightly narrower vegetable garden. A pergola is indicated on the eastern edge of the ornamental garden's cross-axis, between that garden and a proposed tennis court.

The "Garden Planting Plan" that Louis Miller submitted two years later essentially refined this design and supplied names and quantities of recommended plant and tree species for the entire area. Miller proposed long narrow beds of roses along the facade of the greenhouses, bordered on either side by walks from which a short, central flight of stairs descended to the sunken ornamental garden. Here, within four rectangular sections formed by the intersection of walks on the central and cross-axes, identical geometric patterns of narrow grass paths would define a traditional arrangement of oval parterres, each centered on an urn in a large bed of roses and lilies, with compartments of massed perennials forming an outer ring. Separating the oval paths containing the parterres from the major walks on the axes and on the perimeter

Detail of 1911 Buckenham and Miller master plan showing the greenhouse gardens.

Detail of Miller's 1913 "Garden Planting Plan."

HERBACEOUS GARDEN

are large beds that Miller had simply crosshatched in the plan, with a note indicating that they were to be filled with "summer annuals." Trellises for climbing roses and clematis were spaced at regular intervals to arch over the main walks, which at their junction defined a diamond-shaped space with what appears to be a small pool or similar feature at its center. The entire ornamental garden was to be enclosed on four sides by a peony hedge—275 of the herbaceous variety interspersed with 60 tree peonies—and a perimeter walk; beyond the walk, a U-shaped outer hedge of "PeeGee" hydrangea shrubs (*H. paniculata grandiflora*) tied in on either side to the block of greenhouses forming the northern edge of the gardens.

The longer and narrower vegetable garden was divided into twelve large beds, six to a side, formed by paths—two beds each for currants, gooseberries, and mixed blackberries and raspberries, two for asparagus, and four for strawberries. Artichokes, rhubarb, horseradish, and a variety of herbs were to be accommodated at the edges of three of the strawberry beds. Parallel rows of fruit trees—apple, apricot, peach, pear, and plum—were specified for either side of the central walk just inside the beds, as well as along the outer edge of the perimeter walk on the east and west sides of the garden. Except for the repetition (but without a pool) of a diamond-shaped space at the intersection of the walks and the addition of a small semicircular form shown in the plan at the terminus of the central walk, the design of the vegetable garden is straightforward, a workaday solution to the problem of dividing a large outdoor space between a display garden of flowers and another for food production.

It is easy to understand why Katharine Reynolds would have been disappointed with Miller's design. She was a perfectionist, after all, with little tolerance for work that failed to reflect fastidious standards of craftsmanship and attention to detail. Furthermore, she knew enough about gardening, horticulture, and floriculture to review the plan intelligently and see in her mind's eye exactly how the gardens Miller was proposing would look. She was prepared to compare them not just to gardens she had studied in books and magazines, but to a number of other professionally designed residential gardens she had visited. By this time, Katharine's appreciation of fine garden design was easily more sophisticated than Miller's plan. We can imagine the questions that would have occurred to her. Fully half of the space in the parterre garden is given over to unspecified "summer annuals," presumably those massed "bedding out" varieties so popular in the late nineteenth century. Wasn't that too old-fashioned-looking, like the tired choice of urns at the center of the parterres? So many peonies, too—a whole hedge of them around the entire garden. What would it look like in winter? For that matter, what about the even more important hedge of PeeGee hydrangeas, the enclosing wall on three sides that would be constantly on view from outside the garden? These shrubs are lovely in bloom, of course, but tall, coarse, and straggly after they lose their leaves in the fall. Then the path through that double row of hedging: wouldn't the vegetable garden seem a little tacked-on and homely? And so on. Perhaps such questions were never put to Miller directly, only the decision that his services were no longer required. In the end, however, it was not a problem of failed aspects of the gardens' design so much as a pervasive failure of imagination, the sheer banality of the whole scheme, that sealed his fate.

An architect with as strong a landscape sensibility as Charles Barton Keen would certainly have been sympathetic with Katharine's reservations about Miller's recent work, and with so many landscape projects still to be undertaken on the estate, Keen may have encouraged her to engage a landscape architect with greater competence in garden and planting design. The name of Thomas Warren Sears would have immediately come to mind, since Sears, too, had his office in Philadelphia and moved in the same circle of T-Square Club architects and wealthy suburban and country house clients as Keen himself. For her part, Katharine would no doubt have responded favorably to whatever Keen was able to tell her about Sears's education and experience, and then been delighted to discover, if she had not already met him, how charming and intelligent a man he was. Since the recent dramatic increase in the Reynolds family's fortunes, she could afford to be less concerned now than in the past about the prospect that Sears might charge more for his professional services than Miller had. She probably even liked the fact that he was young—exactly her own age, in fact; in the spring of 1915, when he began to work for Katharine Reynolds, they were both just thirty-four. Sears had practiced during the early years of his career in business partnerships, first in Providence, Rhode Island, then, after moving to Philadelphia, with a man named Wendell; an opportunity to work on a project for the Philadelphia Museum of Art may have provided the incentive for that move.[3] He was soon expanding his client base in the Philadelphia area, making a name for himself locally as an urbane and talented young man who particularly enjoyed residential garden and planting design. His fortunes took quite a dramatic turn, however, when Mrs. Reynolds of North Carolina approached him about designing the farming estate she was developing. He had to have sensed from the beginning that the Reynolda project, much larger in scope than any of his previous commissions, had the potential to become, if all went well, the most significant of his career.

Sears was a Bostonian by birth, having grown up in suburban Brookline, where the firm of Frederick Law Olmsted had its office. For Katharine, who considered a good education second in importance only to righteousness, the fact that Sears had earned a bachelor of arts degree from Harvard in 1903 and then a bachelor of science degree in landscape architecture from Harvard's Lawrence Scientific School—making him one of a still small number of academically trained landscape architects in the country—was an impressive credential. The American Society of Landscape Architects had been in existence for just seven years when Sears was elected to membership in 1906. Equally persuasive from Katharine's point of view, however, were his artistic interests, which were not confined to landscape design but were equally strong in photography. His camera served as a useful tool in his practice (critically important in working on properties located far from his office), but Sears also had pursued photography professionally since his undergraduate days at Harvard. As a member of the Harvard Camera Club he had regularly exhibited his work, winning a second-place prize in 1904 and first prize the following year, awards that helped to finance the first of at least two periods of extended travel, photographic work, and landscape study in Europe. At the time he began his conversations with Katharine, Sears would have been in the final stages of preparing a collection of his photographs published in 1915 as *Parish Churches of England*.[4] In the same year, pictures he had taken on visits to the vast English-style park of Prince Pückler von Muskau's nineteenth-century estate on the border between Germany and Poland were published in Samuel Parsons Jr.'s *Art* of *Landscape Architecture*.[5] Katharine, whose own library contained an earlier book by Parsons, could appreciate the significance for Sears of having his photographic work represented in the latest publication of this eminent New York City landscape architect and prolific author.

Perhaps, though, nothing would have endeared Sears to Katharine so much as his familiarity with the same English landscapes that had inspired her own earliest imaginings of the kind

Thomas Sears's photograph of Pückler-Muskau estate from Parsons, Art of Landscape Architecture *(1915).*

Badgeworth church, from Thomas Sears's Parish Churches of England *(1915).*

of rural home and community she longed to live in and had re-solved to create at Reynolda. She could feel confident that the study trips Sears had taken in 1906 and 1908 during which he had photographed so many lovely old parish churches in rural villages had given him an opportunity to absorb, as Olmsted had in an earlier time, the visual lessons of that serenely ordered pastoral landscape. On his first visit to Reynolda, Katharine would have taken him to the site, directly across the road from the entrance to Reynolda village, at which her own church, designed by Charles Barton Keen, was under construction, its cornerstone having been laid in November 1914; the Reverend Neal Ander-son, her pastor and dear friend, would help to arrange affiliation of the Reynolda parish with the Presbyterian Church. The archi-tectural design that Katharine and Keen had settled on for the church—with its gables, columned side porch, and half-timber-

Reynolda church under construction, c. 1915.

Reynolda church, rear elevation, 1918.

ing—represented a fusion of traditional pre-Reformation English parish church architecture with a design vocabulary borrowed from the residential work of Arts and Crafts movement architects on both sides of the Atlantic, thus allowing Keen to extend the domestic iconography he had established elsewhere at Reynolda to this religious structure. It is probably significant that the rear elevation, in particular, looks a little like a two-story manor house with a navelike central hall—grander, in other words, than a bungalow or a cottage, yet hardly majestic. Katharine's hand is evident here, since it was her program for the building that had thus elevated the Presbyterian mission of fellowship, education, and work for church and community to equivalent importance, in its spatial requirements, with worship. Except for a revised topographic plan of the bungalow's site submitted in February 1915, the first extant plans for Reynolda to which Sears (still in partner-

Reynolda Presbyterian Church.

The manse, c. 1920 (after restoration of original structure damaged by fire).

ship with Wendell) set his hand were planting designs for the area around the chapel and the three finished cottages on that side of the road.[6]

An Eye for the Architecture of Landscape

Katharine's move to replace Miller with Sears had more far-reaching consequences for the subsequent evolution of Reynolda's landscape than even she may at first have appreciated. There is no lack of evidence that in her discussions with Sears, as was the case with everyone who supplied her with design services (or, for that matter, any kind of service at all), she would have begun with at least a few cherished ideas of her own and then enthusiastically participated in the often arduous process of expanding or discarding possibilities, weighing costs against advantages, seeing every detail through to what she hoped would be a perfect resolution. Once Miller's work no longer met her expectations, she must certainly have tried to explain to Thomas Sears, at least in a general way, her vision of how the various parts of Reynolda's landscape should look and function, and then—perhaps in a conversation about the greenhouse gardens—suggested some specific landscape features she wanted him to consider. For his part, Sears brought to these discussions not just the substantial advantages of his professional training and his understanding of contemporary currents in garden design, but a personal style and commitment to a well-defined set of aesthetic values that together made him singularly qualified to satisfy Katharine's expectations over the course of the succeeding years.

Anglophilia was not least among the several shared sympathies that made good working partners of Charles Barton Keen, Thomas Sears, and Katharine Reynolds. The school of architects practicing in Philadelphia during the five decades stretching from 1880 until the Great Depression was more heavily indebted to English practice, historic and contemporary, than any similar regional group in the country. The T-Square Club "followed the practice of such English institutions as the Royal Academy and Art Workers' Guild," and its members were "full of the romantic views of architecture that were held by modern Ruskinians in England."[7] Sears would later be remembered by those who knew him as "a real gentleman of the old school," "rather shy and proper," who wore highly polished high-top shoes, spoke with a Boston accent, and gave the impression of being "somewhat aloof" and "proper."[8] Katharine would read such demeanor as courteous, refined, and serious, qualities she would value highly in the man responsible for the future development of the gardens and grounds of her estate.

In his approach to design, Sears—even more than Keen—preferred to work within a conservative tradition grounded in historic prototypes without pressing the limits of its conventions, much less proposing more radical innovations in landscape form. It is interesting to compare his work in this respect with that of Fletcher Steele, a contemporary who had spent two years in the new graduate program in landscape architecture at Harvard before embarking on a six-year apprenticeship in the Boston office of Warren Manning, another of the founding members of the American Society of Landscape Architects and a man with a widely known and respected national practice.[9] Steele opened an office of his own in Boston in 1914, about the time that Sears decided to move his practice to Philadelphia. Both men, clearly talented and hardworking, subsequently prospered primarily by finding clients among the expanding class of wealthy Americans who were building country houses and suburban estates. In contrast to Sears, however, Steele was an extrovert whose reputation as a designer was enhanced by an equally active career as lecturer and author of numerous magazine articles on garden subjects, many of them articulating his own questions about prevailing directions in American and European garden design. He would later become the first American landscape architect to describe for a general audience the influence of European modernism on landscape design practice, and one of just a few who began to experiment with the new aesthetic in his own projects.[10]

If the thought even occurred to her, the likelihood that Thomas Sears was more an astute craftsman than a creative artist would hardly have made a difference to Katharine Reynolds, since stylistic departures from the landscape imagery she had already identified and wholeheartedly embraced would please her even less than Louis Miller's recent lackluster efforts. She was after quality, not originality; Reynolda's scenic landscape compositions and gardens must measure up to those she admired in *Country Life in America*, complementing Keen's architecture in the way that Gertrude Jekyll's breathtaking borders and romantic woodland walks animated the virile geometries of Edwin Lutyen's architecture and garden layouts. Americans of Katharine's class, and especially the many women for whom understanding of the landscape arts had become a desirable distinction, were likely to be more familiar with the key players in the recent history of garden design in Britain than with their American counterparts,

Millmead, designed by Jekyll and Lutyens, from Gardens for Small Country Houses *(1920).*

whose work increasingly reflected the determining influence of British models.

This recent education in landscape taste had been closely observed by the American writer Wilhelm Miller, who, after earning a doctoral degree in horticulture under Liberty Hyde Bailey at Cornell and helping to edit Bailey's landmark 1901–2 *Cyclopedia of American Horticulture,* had accepted his mentor's invitation to serve as horticultural editor of *Country Life in America.* By the time Miller became founding editor of *Garden Magazine* in 1905, his intellectual and professional interests were increasingly centered on the theory and practice of landscape architecture and garden design. Just as Thomas Sears had done, Miller set out in 1908 to study examples of traditional English design at firsthand, later sharing his observations and conclusions with his American readers in a series of magazine articles and then in the 1911 publication *What England Can Teach Us about Gardening.*[11] It is no accident that the title of Miller's book paraphrases Andrew Jackson Downing's *Theory and Practice of Landscape Gardening, Adapted to North America,* a work many times revised and reprinted that was still known and respected sixty years after its original 1841 publication. Like Downing, Miller struck a conversational tone with his readers, acknowledging as indisputable the superiority of English landscape gardening to anything America had yet produced—"after my first ride into the country around Plymouth I threw myself down in despair," he declared—but holding out hope that the application of a few simple principles would remedy the embarrassing aesthetic deficiencies of typical American practice. Miller argued that Americans had imitated the English styles they admired in too literal a fashion, foolishly striving to achieve the same visual effects in prospects and gardens by using the same materials, ignoring inherent differences in climate and soils as well as the potentially greater beauty that native trees and shrubs and suitable species imported from the Far East could provide. "Our serious task," he proposed, "is to study our own national life and to contribute what we can toward an American style of architecture and gardening."[12]

The authority most frequently invoked by Miller was William Robinson, whose estate, Gravetye, he had visited on his English tour, as had Thomas Sears.[13] A number of photographic views of the landscape at Gravetye are used to illustrate *What England Can Teach Us about Gardening.* By the time Americans such as Sears and Miller came under his influence, the Irish-born Robinson had already established his reputation as the dean of British gardeners and garden writers; indeed, his writing had been the instrument through which he launched a crusade against what he considered to be the vulgar excesses of late-nineteenth-century formal gardens. A series of popular books, including *The Wild Garden* of 1870 and *The English Flower Garden* of 1883, as well as two successful journals he founded, *The Garden* and *Gardening Illustrated*, set forth and eloquently defended a new set of aesthetic standards in garden and landscape design. These are the precepts Wilhelm Miller would later effectively summarize for his American readers. In describing, for example, how the design of a genuinely beautiful formal garden must express the actual "home life" and interests of its owner rather than imitating a style that had nothing to do

William Robinson's Gravetye. Photo by Thomas Sears.

A view of Gravetye from What England Can Teach Us.

with lived experience, Miller posed a list of questions about various conventions associated with such gardens—"Shall architecture be dominant?" "Shall an historical idea be dominant?" "Shall water be a dominant feature?"—for which he then provided appropriate "common-sense" answers. These responses, not surprisingly, described the landscape effects characteristic of the English style first inspired by Robinson's writing, put into practice at Gravetye, and perhaps even more succinctly illustrated in the work of his friend and disciple Gertrude Jekyll, whom he had introduced to the gardening world by publishing her work in his magazines.

Although they have specifically to do with designing formal gardens, Miller's answers also sum up certain of the informing values and physical attributes that Katharine could have expected to find in any of the landscape designs that Thomas Sears produced for her. Chief among the desirable values to be enforced was the avoidance of ostentation. Miller warned, for example, that if lavish displays of water in the garden involved "great expense," they should be avoided. Similarly, statuary may be an important feature "if confined to your one exquisite piece which perfectly expresses your ideal of character or achievement." When overdone, however, "collections of statuary . . . only serve to remind visitors of Fourth Avenue shops and the fat commissions of architects who let us buy all we want." In answer to the question whether flowers should be the dominant feature of a formal garden, he replied: "Yes, if they are chiefly hardy and perennial. No, if they are chiefly annuals and bedding plants, for the latter speak of ceaseless vigilance and expense where the only suggestion should be gaiety and repose." He admitted, then, to having had to learn to prefer the "careless grace" of Penshurst and "dozens of other English gardens" to that "perfection of detail" that "makes many American gardens restless" because "it inevitably suggests straining after effect." While acknowledging that formal gardens were inherently more "architectural" in character than an encompassing landscape laid out in the English manner, Miller maintained that once designers and their clients abandoned the pursuit of wasteful and exhibitionist displays of wealth, three additional values essential to a new American style—simplicity, naturalness, and practicality—would finally find expression in this country's residential gardens and grounds.[14]

Miller's analysis of English practice continued in chapters examining a number of specific landscape types and features—hardy borders, water gardens, rock gardens, rose gardens—that Americans might usefully adapt to their own situations. Here, too, he was at pains to describe precisely those standards and methods of design, copiously illustrated by references to the work of Robinson and Jekyll and photographs previously published in *Country Life in America*, that distinguished English practice from what was commonly done on this side of the Atlantic. In lamenting the "woful [sic] shortcomings of most American examples" of the hardy border, for example, Miller held up the model of that type represented by the work of Gertrude Jekyll, and then explained, using her 1908 *Colour Schemes for the Flower Garden* as an authority, exactly how the ideal of "a perfect succession of flowers and a perfect colour scheme" might be achieved. He cautioned his readers, however, that "the great objection to the system" Jekyll employed was that "it makes of garden design a fine art, and therefore calls for life-long devotion on the part of conscientious and well-trained workers. Not one flower lover in a thousand can realize such an ideal."[15] Katharine Reynolds already had a well-established reputation among friends, family, and readers of the local newspapers' society columns for her great love of flowers and, equally, the art of arranging them well. She exchanged flowers and cuttings with friends, frequently contributed arrangements needed to grace local civic events, lavished attention on those prepared for her own entertaining, and saw to it that her house was filled with bouquets in every season.[16] She would certainly have made Thomas Sears aware of her intention that Reynolda's garden and greenhouse complex should become the principal source of flowers and plants for the house, for Reynolda's church and schools, and for sale to local people. Even more important, Sears would quickly come to appreciate the extent to which his new client was one of Miller's "one in a thousand" Americans, determined to establish in her new gardens the demanding design and management regime responsible for Jekyll's extraordinary perennial borders.

The revitalized English movement made its influence felt well beyond the garden's walls; Robinson had something challenging to say about virtually every aspect of an estate's landscape. His assumption of authority on such a wide range of issues had, in fact, fomented a lively literary debate in England after the publication of two books in 1891–92, J. D. Sedding's *Garden-Craft Old and New* and Reginald Blomfield's *The Formal Garden in England*,[17] both of which took aim at the growing popularity of Robinson's view that even in formal gardens, designers needed to imitate the natural world more closely—in their choice of plants, in the way they composed planting groups in beds and borders, and by rejecting such costly and, to his mind, sterile conventions as topiary, bedding out, pleached allées, and the like. Finding such strictures presumptuous, his critics questioned Robinson's credentials, insisting that no amount of horticultural knowledge and gardening experience could substitute for an educated understanding of the essential role that strong spatial structure and architectural ornament had historically played in well-designed gardens.

On the basis of only his own design work, Robinson might have been vulnerable to the charge that he lacked a sophisticated architectural sensibility. Blomfield had ridiculed, for example, his plan for a "non-geometrical garden" encircled by "a path which as nearly represents a tortured horse-shoe as Nature would permit; and his trees he puts in a happy-go-lucky way, and allows them to nearly obliterate his path at their own sweet will! No wonder he does not fear Nature's revenge, where is so little Art to destroy!" When the gifted and articulate Gertrude Jekyll rose to Robinson's defense, however, rejecting as false the notion of an inherent opposition between the demands of nature and art, she could point to her own collaborative practice with Lutyens for evidence. Their landscape designs absolutely depended on a fine reciprocity between formal elements—the plan and its various architectural features—and the deceptively "careless grace" of her well-orchestrated horticultural displays. Lutyens used handsomely crafted walls, walks, basins, and pergolas to establish a sense of serene classical order extending outward from the house. Over this firm foundation, Jekyll's intricate painterly compositions of layered colors, textures, and shapes added lushness, sensuosity, and a subtle tension arising from the illusion of naturalness, as if human control had indeed yielded, just as Sedding and Blomfield feared, to nature's own processes, risking even the possibility of a collapse into disorder. By the time Wilhelm Miller published his recommendations for how Americans might best adapt the underlying principles of the English Arts and Crafts movement to their own way of life and the natural circumstances of the places in which they lived, such arguments had lost their urgency, since a rapidly enlarging American audience for illustrated articles and books on these subjects was eager to embrace the new aesthetic.

In domestic architecture, this meant that the long-standing preference for historic styles broadened to include vernacular and folk traditions, a shift manifesting itself in the move away from complex structures and toward natural and hand-crafted materials, and the evocation of a time, now perceived as threatened by accelerating social change, in which rootedness, integrity, and modesty achieved a beauty presumably indifferent to the requirements of any "style." Analogous values found expression in landscape design, the English having been encouraged by Robinson and Jekyll to open their eyes to the "artless" beauty of their country's cottage gardens and hedgerows, even as Americans were reclaiming their colonial heritage of dooryard gardens and flower-filled parterres. Taken together, the architecture of house and landscape was expected to convey the impression of a seamless whole through which the most essential properties of the site's natural and cultural identity had been given not just visible and palpable form in the present time but meaning and relevance as well. What distinguishes this architectural ideal from earlier varieties of eclecticism—a difference dramatically illustrated by a comparison of Vanderbilt's Biltmore to Reynolda—is that Americans such as Keen, Sears, and their client Katharine Reynolds laid claim to English building and landscape design traditions as a legitimate extension into the present of their own and Reynolda's historic legacy.

Their task was to evoke the spirit and substance, what Miller called the "effects" of that tradition, not through futile efforts to replicate English models but by creating a place that in every detail captured its ethos, as Keen's messuage of house, village, church, and farm buildings seemed to do. Thomas Sears had embraced the same aesthetic vision well before he came to work at Reynolda. Both passionate garden-maker and well-trained *archi-*

Thomas Sears's garden, Ardmore, Pa., 1931. Photo by Thomas Sears.

tect of landscape, he understood three-dimensional spatial form as a vital language, a way of communicating that was no less essential to the expressive and experiential quality of a garden or landscape design than the materials and structures selected for its implementation. Having already committed himself to the design principles of the English Arts and Crafts movement made popular among Americans by Wilhelm Miller, Sears was prepared to offer Katharine Reynolds design proposals that reaffirmed, expanded, and translated into landscape form many of the same values—and not simply artistic or architectural values—that had from the first inspired her vision of Reynolda.

Reimagining Southern Landscape Traditions

As the pace of construction work on the bungalow picked up during the same months in which Thomas Sears began his employment at Reynolda, Katharine no doubt felt alternately elated and overwhelmed by the steady stream of plans, drawings, and revisions arriving every few days from Charles Barton Keen's office that required her attention and a timely response. Sears, too (still in formal partnership with Wendell during the late winter and spring of 1915), began submitting design proposals for areas of the grounds in the vicinity of the house and village for which a grading plan had recently been drawn up by a civil engineer, who had probably been hired for this task during the interim between Miller's departure and the hiring of Sears.[18] The plan shows the road layout, a boathouse by the lake, the central block and one finished wing of the bungalow, the greenhouse complex (illustrated with Louis Miller's rejected proposal for the gardens), a "boarding house" for workers, "farm building," "machinery shed," and two cottages near the entrance gates to the village. Perhaps its most notable feature, however, is the strong axis running perpendicular to Reynolda Road that now connected Buckenham and Miller's formal entrance, with its central "office" on an oval island in the drive, to the new chapel on the opposite side of the road, framed on either side by the site of the future manse and two existing cottages, a configuration giving forceful symbolic expression to Katharine's faith in the essential bonds joining the work of the church to that of her farm and community.

How fitting, then, that one of the first tasks entrusted to her new landscape architect was to design plantings of trees and shrubs to border both sides of the short drive leading from the road across a narrow stream to the chapel entrance. If Katharine was hoping for dramatic proof that Sears would do work of an order altogether different from what Louis Miller had provided, his plan for this area, however modest in scale, fairly shouted out the difference, particularly in his choice of plants, most of them native, including several species not commonly available as nursery stock. Ever since Robinson and Jekyll had argued so persuasively

Aerial view showing entrance to the village drive on east side of Reynolda Road, opposite entrace drive to chapel area c. 1927.

for the beauty and innate adaptability to designed landscapes of wayside and woodland trees, shrubs, and flowers, the most dedicated of their American converts had been motivated to search out and learn the cultural requirements of promising indigenous species to incorporate in their own designs. Wilhelm Miller had been among the first to point the way, even recommending specific substitutions of this sort to his readers:

> The largest flower show in English woods after the leaves come out is made by the Pontic Rhododendron, but this has a coarse, unpleasant colour. Our own catawbiense, which blooms in June, is no worse in colour, and decidedly hardier, while our maximum is altogether lovely in July. Then, too, there is no evergreen native to Europe which is half so beautiful as our mountain laurel. I am happy to say that we are really beginning to appreciate these three evergreens. It is now quite the fashion to plant them by the car load. England cannot grow *Rhododendron maximum* at all.[19]

Miller was also responsible for bringing to the attention of his American readers what he considered to be the exemplary work of three midwestern landscape architects, Ossian Cole Simonds (1855–1932), the Danish-born Jens Jensen (1860–1951), and Walter Burley Griffin (1876–1937), an architect in Frank Lloyd Wright's Chicago office who practiced both professions. Miller identified these men with a growing landscape movement committed to the idea that instead of continually reworking the inherited corpus of western European styles, Americans should be designing parks and gardens that managed to convey, through their forms and materials, the unique geographic character and atmosphere of the various regions of this country. He even named the midwestern movement for its adherents: "I called this manner of doing things the 'prairie style' of landscape gardening, defining it as an American mode of design based upon the practical needs of the middlewestern people and characterized by preservation of typical western scenery, by restoration of local color, and by repetition of the horizontal line of land or sky, which is the strongest feature of prairie scenery."[20]

Although Miller's articles on this subject had appeared in *Country Life in America* and elsewhere, Thomas Sears would have encountered closely related ideas even earlier, as part of his New England upbringing and education. He may even have been drawn to the profession of landscape architecture through the towering influence of such Boston-area figures as Frederick Law Olmsted (1822–1903), Charles Sprague Sargent (1841–1927), Charles Eliot (1859–1897), and Warren Manning (1860–1938), all of whom were early and vociferous spokesmen for the cause of preserving native plant species and distinctive natural landscapes in every region of the country. Olmsted insisted that the natural characteristics of any site should find exalted expression in its design, and he deplored the frequent sacrifice of such features to the requirements of conventional formal styles. The work of Sargent—first director of Harvard University's Arnold Arboretum, founder of the influential journal *Garden and Forest*, and author of both *The Silva of North America* (1891–1902) and *Manual of the Trees of North America* (1905)—helped to advance Olmsted's philosophy in countless practical ways, while fostering both scientific and popular understanding of the rich botanical diversity of the North American continent. Before his tragic early death, the landscape architect Charles Eliot, a frequent contributor to *Garden and Forest*, had conceived and led a movement to create an association of citizens representing the various towns of metropolitan Boston with authority from the state to select, purchase, and manage distinctive "small and well-distributed parcels of land free of taxes . . . for the use and enjoyment of the public,"[21] a vision successfully realized with the establishment of the Trustees of Public Reservations in 1891 and the Boston Metropolitan Parks Commission in 1893. Warren Manning was among the first in the profession to have his designs for gardens based on a palette of native plant species published in national magazines, including an

article on his own home's "bog garden" that appeared in *Country Life in America* in 1908.

Thomas Sears had been exposed to the influence of both these groups, the midwesterners credited by Miller with grounding their landscape design in an authentic regional identity and "spirit," as well as the easterners building on Olmsted's Transcendentalist faith in the spiritual and psychological benefits accruing to urban societies that provided their citizens with opportunities to experience the world of nature at close hand, even if what appeared to be "natural" landscapes were the product of human design. For her part, Katharine Reynolds appears to have been enthusiastic about the idea of retaining desirable natural features on her property and integrating native trees, shrubs, and herbaceous plants in suitable compositions; her library included a brochure titled "Uses of Native Plants."[22] She could not have been unaware of the growing national fashion for such "wild gardening," as it was described by Miller, Parsons, and others, and may actually have encouraged Sears to produce a planting scheme that went further than

A view of Charles Sprague Sargent's Holm Lea, from Parsons, Art of Landscape Architecture *(1915).*

Miller's sensible but cautious inclusion of native species along woodland drives and paths. Knowing how intensely she focused her own imaginative energy and strong opinions on any work she commissioned, we may presume that Sears and his client had at least a preliminary conversation—perhaps with reference to specific magazine articles or photos—about the kind of landscape through which visitors would approach the chapel.

Although the axial alignment of the arrival drive might have suggested a more formal design, there was nothing restrained or predictable about the planting scheme that Sears proposed. Instead, he offered Katharine a highly diversified, almost startling composition of forty-six different species of trees and shrubs, well over half of them natives, several, such as fragrant sumac (*Rhus aromatica*), having been originally introduced but long since naturalized, and many that would have been either entirely unfamiliar to gardeners of that time or commonly associated with weedy natural thickets. Native plant enthusiasts of our own day would, in fact, be surprised to discover species on this list that within recent years have been singled out as unusual, neglected, but garden-worthy, such as the cucumber and big-leaved magnolias (*Magnolia acuminata* and M. *macrophylla*), or the southern stewartia (*Stewartia ovata*, formerly *pentagyna*), while the native minnie-bush (*Menziesia pilosa*) is still not commercially propagated. Two rampant native woody vines, American bittersweet (*Celastrus scandens*) and Virginia creeper (*Parthenocissus* [formerly *Ampelopsis*] *quinquefolia*) were sited close to structural supports near the drive. Katharine would have immediately appreciated the potential of many of these wildlings to furnish spectacular fall color and bright berries. The nonnatives mostly included species of popular large woody shrubs such as forsythia, four different varieties of spiraea, mock orange (*Philadelphus lemoinei* "Mont Blanc"), and the white-flowering form of persian lilac (*Syringa Persica* alba).

Sears grouped each separate species into one or two large masses, weaving these together with individual specimens of dogwood, hawthorn, maple, holly, sourwood, or pine to form large, roughly crescent-shaped borders on either side of the drive. The two borders were similar in character but differed in length, width, and composition. Each curved upward toward the drive from the stream banks—for which he had specified such moisture-loving shrubs as the Virginia sweetspire (*Itea virginica*), pussy willow (*Salix caprea*), and wild elder (*Sambucus canadensis*)—then edged both sides of the little bridge before broadening out along the intersection of the entrance drive with an interior drive running parallel to the facade of the chapel. Specimens of the two species of native magnolia—deciduous trees whose very large, coarse-textured leaves possess almost a tropical luxuriance in summer, then carpet the ground with layers of downy gray-backed leaves in fall—were randomly dispersed on the grass lawn framed by the borders, where they would have space to achieve a majestic height and spread.

Katharine Reynolds certainly knew that a planting composition of this sort might well seem outlandish even to those towns-folk who cared enough about landscape design to enjoy something new and unusual. She would also have been aware, however, that

Borders along entry drive to the chapel area.

departures of the sort that her new landscape architect was proposing were the subject of numerous articles in her favorite home and garden magazines. If she had to choose between the way things were traditionally done in Winston-Salem and making sure that the landscape of Reynolda met a national standard of "quality," she was as determined to be open to innovation in this area as she was in her pursuit of couture, measuring success not only by good design and fine materials but also by a tasteful and elegant "stylishness" for which she was well known. Katharine had always to think of herself as simultaneously a progressive modern woman and a loyal daughter of the South. Everything she had accomplished thus far had been made possible by her willingness to walk a fine line between resolute respectability and a quiet determination to stretch the limits of convention in pursuit of a goal she considered important. It would be inconceivable for her, at least at this point in her life, to affront the moral, social, or aesthetic sensibilities of the familiar world into which she had been born. Neither, however, did she intend to let her beloved region languish behind the rest of the country as a new century opened up so many possibilities for becoming a more efficient, more prosperous, more equitable and enlightened society. Had Katharine not recently influenced her husband's decision to provide lunchrooms and meals at cost for workers in his factories? Her eldest son would remember in later years countless discussions between his parents on this subject, until his mother had finally convinced his father that "warm, wholesome food was important for the health of his employees."[23]

This was the same woman who had discovered in the architecture of Charles Barton Keen and the landscape architecture of Thomas Sears an image appropriate to a country estate that was to be quite unlike anything seen before in the American South, and yet, to Katharine's eye and imagination, looked as though it belonged there in ways that styles based on aristocratic European models did not. She knew that in rural and suburban areas outside Philadelphia, New York, and other cities she had visited and read about, American architects, inspired as Keen had been by the English Arts and Crafts movement, were trying to achieve a similar balance between old and new, tradition and modernity, technology and craft traditions. Whether they drew on sources borrowed from England, or from the colonial experience of this country, or from the historic practice of a particular region was not a critical issue for them; neither was the principle espoused by architects of the Prairie School that the geographic character of a region should have a determining influence on design. Thus, when Thomas Sears chose to include an unusual number of species either native to or naturalized in this country among more familiar ornamental trees and shrubs in his design for the chapel area, the surprising visual effect of his novel combinations was likely to have been his principal motivation—and the source of his client's satisfaction. Neither of them adhered to a more stringent ideology of replicating natural communities of indigenous plants. Miller's articles in *Country Life* had celebrated the "wild gardening" of Robinson and Jekyll years before the theoretical extension and expansion of those ideas exemplified in the work of Jensen and others; the work of Sears comes closer to the earlier approach, and to Olmsted's more flexible integration of native and exotic species.

The absence of any imperatives other than consistency with the aesthetic values informing Katharine's original vision and Keen's architectural program undoubtedly had a liberating effect on the exchange of ideas between Sears and his client, while at the same time it explains their apparent lack of interest in making the landscape of Reynolda distinctively southern in character. Sears may have felt both a measure of anxiety in designing for a climatic zone so different from that of the Northeast and a hands-on gardener's excitement in having the opportunity to work with plants whose precise cultural requirements might be unfamiliar to him. There were inevitably occasional failures to anticipate how well a given species would perform in Piedmont North Carolina,[24] although Sears may have been deliberately experimenting with the tolerances of plants successfully grown in adjacent zones, as many garden enthusiasts enjoy doing. His work at Reynolda subsequently created a demand for his services among other wealthy families in and around Winston-Salem, and it would have been natural for him to want to introduce at least a few new or unusual plants to the gardens of his southern clients. In doing so, he would unwittingly have tapped into a well-established tradition of southern garden culture, fostered by the region's climate and agricultural economy, that favored horticultural innovation of this kind even within the conventions imposed by a historically conservative design tradition.

Nineteenth-century southerners had largely resisted efforts made by reforming editors of regional farm journals to persuade them to embrace northerner Andrew Jackson Downing's pronouncements, whether on the subject of "scientific" agriculture or on what constituted good taste in rural and suburban residential landscape design. It was not until the twentieth century, when the South joined the national trend encouraging women to take responsibility for the design of house and garden, that fashions in such matters, circulating through magazines addressed to this audience, began to influence the way southerners laid out their gardens and grounds. This development coincided, as we have seen, with a widespread diffusion of images illustrating the practice of designers associated with the British Arts and Crafts movement and its American counterpart. Although Arts and Crafts architectural styles proved to have relatively little influence on southern taste—Katharine's commissioning of Charles Barton Keen to design Reynolda was hardly a conventional choice at the time—middle- and upper-class southern women did discover in these sources a congenial model for designing their gardens. As elsewhere in the country, Arts and Crafts gardens in the South were used in combination with a variety of popular architectural styles, particularly Colonial Revival.

The work of Lutyens and Jekyll and their followers simultaneously reaffirmed the spatial structure and geometries of the European classical tradition (still the wellspring of practice in the American South) and liberated the art of planting design from the long tyranny of Victorian mechanizing. Here was a much-celebrated "new" style that seemed close both in form and in its visual and sensuous character to traditional southern gardens—old-fashioned flower gardens like the one that Katharine's mother would have tended in Mount Airy, in which trim lines of box or a swept path seemed scarcely able to contain the teeming, fragrant tides of colorful flowers and shrubs brimming above them. Although the formal gardens that Thomas Sears was to help her create must be fine and fashionable in a way that visitors from outside the South would appreciate, it was just as important to Katharine that they seem familiar and welcoming to friends, family, and townsfolk. Like the house itself, the gardens—visible from the public road and combining the functions of "working" and pleasure gardens—must project the warm hospitality that in the end was to be the only distinctively southern thing about them.

A Woman's Home, a Woman's World

For Katharine Reynolds, hospitality was more than a social grace; at a deeper level, it was an expression of charity and love of neighbor, and was therefore essentially tied to her mission in life as she conceived it. In the years since her marriage to the famously convivial Dick Reynolds—a man who enjoyed a good story, a joke, or a party as much as he relished the challenges of managing an industrial empire—she had earned a reputation in her own right for the exceptional energy and generosity with which she had assumed the traditional role of hostess. Well beyond such customary domestic and familial responsibilities, however, involvement in church work had provided opportunities for her, as it did for many southern women of her day, to take on the more active public life of a "New Woman." In Katharine's case, this expansion of her duties involved countless commitments as citizen, club-woman, patron, and volunteer to a host of worthy causes, often in a leadership role. In addition to those noted earlier, in 1915 she accepted the presidency of the North Carolina drive to fund a memorial honoring the recently deceased wife of President Woodrow Wilson, and in the following year served as president of the Winston-Salem YWCA, which she had helped to found and for which she now purchased and helped to furnish a building downtown.[25] Although in some instances, certainly, Katharine had only to lend her name and financial support to a civic or charitable effort, the sum of her other commitments produced enough pressure and hard work, especially given her penchant for thorough research and reporting, to exhaust even someone unburdened by chronic illness. Yet to her resolute mind—continually formed by a life of prayer and participation in worship and Sunday school programs (including those she would establish at Reynolda)[26]—to labor in this way even at the risk of her health was simply her way of living out the injunctions of gospel.

Yet among all these commitments, none compared in importance to the development of Reynolda as a model family home, community, and farming estate, since Katharine believed that this endeavor had greater potential to improve the lives of her "neighbors"—both nearby and throughout the South—than anything else she could possibly achieve. If her conviction suggests a naïve optimism, it at least bears comparison with an observation once made by Frank Lloyd Wright that every house he built was a "missionary." "I don't build a house," he declared boldly, "without predicting the end of the present social order."[27] Katharine Reynolds seems not to have been any less confident that she could personally bring about a new social order, at least at the scale of her own small southern community. Katharine's religious motivation distinguishes Reynolda from comparable projects of the same period, but it also helps us to understand more fully certain aesthetic meanings and intentions embodied in the landscape she shaped. Although it is unlikely that she was sufficiently aware of what amounted to an iconographic program to describe it as such to Keen or Sears, she seems to been guided intuitively toward its realization as the cumulative effect of countless incidental design decisions made from day to day during the period of planning and construction.

Interior decorator Elsie de Wolfe's best-seller *The House in Good Taste* arrived on the scene in 1913. If Katharine found an opportunity to read it—and it is hard to imagine that she did not—she would have approved of de Wolfe's observation that if a designed object simply "fulfills its mission, the chances are that it is beautiful."[28] De Wolfe argued for "modern" translations of only those traditional styles of architecture and furnishings that were designed to function well, achieving whatever beauty they possessed as a consequence of simplicity and usefulness. The house on Fifth Street in which the Reynoldses still lived did not meet that standard, but Keen's designs for the bungalow and other buildings now under construction at Reynolda certainly would. Nevertheless, although Katharine was determined to arrive at modest and practical solutions to the needs of every structure and interior on the estate—in the spirit of those "neat and well-built" glasshouses she had demanded of Lord and Burnham—the mission of Reynolda as a whole, as a physical landscape, was to respond to a greater human need than the desire for useful and beautiful surroundings, important as these were. The estate must present itself to the world in a way that metaphorically opened the door wide to welcome, to reassure, and to enlarge the experience and well-being of those who lived, worked, or visited within its precincts.

In deliberately setting out in this way, in considering the "mission," in de Wolfe's terms, not simply of a building or a piece of furniture but of the total environment of a large estate, Katharine was seeking to achieve on a grander scale many of the same values that helped de Wolfe's book launch a revolution in the way Americans—and more specifically her women readers—approached the design of their homes. Although any number of talented men would soon follow her into the profession inspired by her own career, de Wolfe's witty, ingratiating, and distinctly feminine voice might be considered rather sexist by today's standards:

> We take for granted that everyone is interested in houses—that she either has a house in course of construction, or dreams of having one, or has had a house long enough to wish it right. And we take it for granted that the American home was always the woman's home: a man may build and decorate a beautiful house, but it remains for a woman to make a home of it for him. It was the personality of the mistress that the home expressed. Men are forever guests in our homes, no matter how much happiness they find there.

The delightfully unorthodox history of the evolution of the modern house that followed this pronouncement gave credit for the most significant progress toward genuinely civilized residential environments to two women, Isabella d'Este, marchioness of Mantua, in the fifteenth century, and Catherine de Vivonne, marquise de Rambouillet, in the seventeenth. Madame de Rambouillet, having taken personal responsibility for the renovation and redecoration of her Paris residence—in its quietly beautiful austerity "really the first modern house," according to de Wolfe—made it home to a salon renowned for the unusual social diversity of those invited and the brilliance of the conversation stimulated by its intelligent, vivacious, and good-natured hostess. De Wolfe contrasted the influence on French life and letters of this artistic, intellectual, and humane achievement to the "official success" of Louis XIV's Versailles, a palace universally recognized as "the most comfortless house in Europe." In the eighteenth century, she remarked, visual beauty became the *ne plus ultra* of residential design, while in the nineteenth, architects and engineers turned to science as a source of "magic-making convenience," sanitation, and comfort. To this inheritance the twentieth century had thus far added only a certain "human quality": "There are no dungeons in the good modern house, no disgraceful lairs for housekeepers, no horrors of humidity."[29]

In spite of their appearance of perfection, however, most modern homes addressed only the needs of the body and the restless craving of the mind for "things" while failing to engage the higher faculties of mind and spirit. Here was the challenge, she said, for those women of the new century who were clever enough to recognize that something important was missing from the domestic environments they had created, and serious enough to acquire through reading and study the skills needed to bring about dramatic change. But "be careful and go warily," de Wolfe warned, starting with the selection of an architect who was not "too determined in [his] own way."

> We must stop and ask ourselves questions, and, if necessary, plan for ourselves little retreats until we can find ourselves again.
> What is the goal? A house that is like the life that goes on within it, a house that gives us beauty as we understand it—and beauty of a nobler kind that we may grow to understand, a house that looks refined.

The vagueness of her language suggests that she had lost her own way at this point; maintaining a tone of unexamined spontaneity throughout the book frequently worked against a careful development of her ideas. Having proposed a provocative distinction between a predictable, easily recognized beauty in the design of one's home and a potentially more exalted, more complex and "nobler" beauty requiring for its appreciation a different order of knowledge and imagination, she risked trivializing the notion of that higher beauty by equating it with the appearance of an unspecified "refinement." Nevertheless, de Wolfe was struggling to describe an elusive quality of exceptionally fine interiors in which significant "meaning" as well as beauty has been achieved, perceptible in each carefully considered detail and in the impression of the whole. The rooms of a house "will always have meaning in the end," she assured her readers, if their arrangement and furnishings reflect the hard-won "wisdom" and ideals of the woman overseeing their creation, her "sense of the pleasure and meaning of human intercourse" and her confidence that she has a "right" to make her home as comfortable, suitable, and inviting as it is beautiful. These new American homes should be "individual expressions of ourselves, of the future we plan, of our dreams for our children. The ideal house is the house that has been long planned for, long awaited."[30]

Apart from her husband's unfailing admiration and support for everything she did, Katharine could not have encountered so strong an affirmation of the ideals and goals of her Reynolda project as that provided by de Wolfe's book, which burst upon the national scene just as elements of the larger mission of Reynolda were beginning to take form. Katharine needed to be reassured that a woman should feel no embarrassment in assuming responsibility for a costly, complex, enterprise if it was simply a modern expression of traditional feminine homemaking. Moreover, the aesthetic and humane values to which she hoped to give expression everywhere on her estate were analogous to those that de Wolfe admired in distinctive, unpretentiously lively and gracious private homes. Katharine had long since expanded her own dream of such an ideal modern family home to include a beautiful and productive landscape embracing a farm, a small *community* of ideal homes, and places of work, play, worship, and learning. If Reynolda was to represent her ultimate fulfillment of the commitment to educational and social reform that Charles Duncan McIver had expected of every graduate of the Normal School, then it must possess and communicate meaning to the world beyond its gates and garden walls, a meaning far "nobler" than mere charm, tastefulness, or good design. Moreover, since the physical appearance and disposition of the estate must somehow give expression to the unique character of the "life that goes on within it," in de Wolfe's words, the qualities of that life, its exemplary virtues, must first have been carefully cultivated.

To say that her upbringing and education predisposed Katharine to frame her sense of the ideal life of a community in religious terms raises the specter of a grimly authoritarian management regime, and it is true that her understanding of the teachings of her church is likely to have been influenced in some measure by the stern legacy of John Calvin. Nevertheless, in expecting an honest day's work for wages received and punishing lapses in sobriety or other standards of respectable conduct among her employees, Katharine was acting in sympathy with the convictions of countless numbers of her Protestant brethren active in the Country Life movement and church-sponsored social reform endeavors who believed that educated people had a moral obligation to help those less fortunate accept the Ten Commandments and the two "Great Commandments" of Christ as the foundation of good citizenship.[31] At the same time, this call to uplift the wayward gave reformers the courage to confront a number of injustices previously tolerated by public policy and capitalist business practice. The Southern Presbyterian General Assembly had, for example, strenuously condemned the practice of lynching in 1899, and in 1914 the national General Assembly issued a "Declaration on Christian Faith and Social Service" that affirmed the obligation of the church as an institution and all of its members to improve "social relations in this present world." This document condemned, for example, the exploitation of women and children in the labor force and the failure to pay workers a wage sufficient "to support the man and his family against illness and old age."[32] Her education at the Normal School had first awakened and given direction to Katharine's social conscience, but the ongoing discussions with her husband about improving the working conditions at his factories must literally have brought home to her the realization that these ecclesiastical initiatives profoundly challenged the self-serving assumptions of southern paternalism, for so long the foundation of the only way of life they had known.

For this reason if for no other, Katharine's determination to so order and oversee "life as it was lived" at Reynolda that it might finally achieve the great mission she had conceived for it—to be, every day and in as many ways as humanly possible, a corner of God's kingdom on earth—involved risks that she would not have assumed lightly. Just as her marriage to the czar of an industrial empire gave her a healthy awareness of the social and economic implications of even modest efforts to improve workers' lives, her close attention to agricultural reform movements (as a subscriber to Walter Hines Page's progressive journal *World's Work*) helped her to understand the formidable resistance to new ideas and new ways of doing things among poorly educated southern farm families.[33] All the same, nothing less than a "righteous" society in religious terms was Katharine's ideal, and that meant making sure that everyone associated with her farm and estate had opportunities to enjoy a better life, in the spirit of Christ's promise that his followers should "have life, and have it more abundantly" (John 10:10).

Her conception of the better life to be led by those connected with Reynolda had nothing about it, however, of a coldly engineered utopian or sectarian community. For even though the scope of Katharine's instigation and administration of her project far exceeded anything for which a married woman in her society typically took responsibility, she seems to have succeeded brilliantly in framing all of her activities within the context of a southern lady's traditional homemaking preoccupations—admittedly enlarged, in her case, by the scale of the farming operations that her husband's wealth made possible. If there was a perceptible yet subtle and ineffable difference between the look and feel of Reynolda and comparable country house estates during the years when its unique economic, social, and cultural life was gathering force and expression—if the place did seem, in fact, to convey some larger meaning than contentment, serenity, or physical beauty—that impression had to do with the degree to which Katharine's personality informed the whole. Several decades after her death, the architectural historian and critic Brendan Gill, in justifying his claim that Reynolda House represented "an unprecedented development in American domestic architecture . . . perhaps the first of an entirely new genre," invoked a language surprisingly rich in feminine associations. He observed that in spite of its actual scale, the residence "assumes an exterior demeanor almost as modest as that of a bungalow. We are not in the presence of wealth made formidably manifest . . . but in circumstances charmingly of the family; the intention here is plainly not to show off but to be happy among friends—a pleasing novelty in the first decades of the twentieth century."[34]

Gill was describing expressive qualities in the architecture of the house, an unpretentious simplicity and hospitality that bear a striking similarity to the qualities Elsie de Wolfe most admired in interior design, and which she specifically attributed to the influence of a woman's personality and her sensitivity to the needs of her own household. De Wolfe would have found much to admire in the work that Mrs. Reynolds of Winston-Salem had taken in

The bungalow, c. 1917. Photo by Thomas Sears.

The bungalow, 2001.
Photo by Carol Betsch.

OPPOSITE:
The reception hall,
c. 1918.

The library,
c. 1918.

hand. Katharine had boldly expanded the historic role of women in determining how their homes should be designed, first by taking charge of the site planning and architectural programs of a large farming estate, and now in overseeing the development of its village, gardens, and landscaped grounds—the area that would be called, significantly, the "Home Place." In doing so, Katharine was driven by a wider and more radical vision, one that expanded the conception of "family" beyond the southern understanding of kinship based in blood to the whole community bound by attachment to a special place, respect for shared values, and concern for the needs of others. The aura of genial hospitality that Reynolda projected and to which so many voices have testified—that sweetly refined and gracious, mythically feminine "demeanor" that Gill later observed in the architecture of the house but that

228   *A World of Her Own Making*

The semicircular lake porch, c. 1918.

belonged properly to the entire landscape—was a work of art that Katharine achieved over the course of years, the ultimate expression of all those decisions and revisions into which she had poured her intellect and her heart.

"The world's dark night is hast'ning on / Speed, speed thy work!"

However much religious and aesthetic values, local traditions of hospitality, and her own maturing design sophistication contributed to Katharine's ideal of a Reynolda landscape that would welcome, delight, and enrich every person touched by it, the assurance with which she managed to translate the intangible into reality, a desired atmosphere into requests for specific physical features, is remarkable. The designers she commissioned had to adjust to dealing with a client who was committed to exploring her own preferences, explicit in her directions, and unwilling to delegate any responsibility for seeing that all the parts of the work in progress would eventually come together in the home and landscape she imagined, the experiences she wanted to engender. None of these men could have understood the nature of her vision, its sources and intentions, in the way that she did herself, although Katharine, ever the student, was eager to learn from Keen and Sears, both of whom consistently helped her to consider new possibilities in the design proposals they submitted for her consideration. In the end, no single feature of Reynolda's design would stand as a historic "first use"; it was only as an ensemble—a physical environment inseparable from its context of lived experience—that it achieved a rare distinctiveness.

But how slowly, even painfully that longed-for reality came into being, particularly after the traumatic events of 1914. On the twenty-eighth of June, while Katharine Reynolds was still recuperating from her recent surgery, the assassination of the Austrian archduke Francis Ferdinand by a Serbian nationalist furnished the spark that ignited the conflagration of world war. As military conflict in Europe intensified rapidly, President Wilson found himself increasingly hard-pressed, despite the isolationist sentiments of Congress and most Americans, to maintain the neutrality to which he had pledged the country. Although Wilson steadfastly insisted that a neutral United States had the right to maintain trade with countries engaged in the conflict, German submarines repeatedly attacked American merchant vessels on the grounds that their cargoes often included ammunition and other matériel destined for Allied combatants, which was the case. The still more provocative sinking of a passenger ship, the Cunard liner *Lusitania*, with 128 Americans among more than a thousand civilian fatalities, helped to turn the tide of public opinion against Germany. As the war dragged on without significant improvement in the fortunes of the Allied forces, and in spite of previously unimaginable loss of life and destruction, the smug optimism and indifference of the American electorate gave way to fears that European civilization itself was at stake, and with it the social, cultural, and political life of the New World as well.

The conflict would come home to Reynolda even before the government of the United States declared war in 1917 and sent troops overseas. The increasing scarcity and expense of raw materials, manufactured goods, and transportation considerably slowed progress in finishing construction of the house and other building projects, just as it affected the operations of Reynolds Tobacco, which relied on essential imports of cigarette paper from France and flavorings from southeastern Europe.[35] Moreover, as the possibility of American participation in the fighting increased with every passing month, the Reynoldses had to anticipate the impact that the inevitable military draft would have on the operations of their factories, farms, and home. Threats to his business never failed to stimulate Dick's creative energies, and the challenges presented by the war proved no exception. Cigarette sales and profits would rise dramatically during the war years thanks to government contracts, with growth in the labor force even after the draft was initiated; by 1917, Reynolds Tobacco accounted for 40 percent of all U.S. cigarette production.

However much she might share her husband's zest for challenges, Katharine had learned to fear the debilitating effects of stress and fatigue on her health, and was used to steeling herself against any eventuality that threatened her peace of mind or accomplishment of her goals. A number of strategies helped her to cope—with her own perfectionism and tendency to overdo as much as with circumstances complicating her life. Prayer was undoubtedly one of these, as well as an ingrained optimism and confidence in the goodness of life and human nature. Her devotion to hospitality was as much a source of pleasure as a response to duty; much everyday happiness came from her caring involvement in the lives of family, friends, employees, and countless others, some of whom she would never know personally. During these years before the house was ready for the Reynoldses' move, Reynolda already functioned as a country estate, since the fam-

Bum with Smith, unidentified guests, and Dick at Reynolda, c. 1914.

Camping at Reynolda during house construction (from left: unidentified woman, Nancy, Dick Jr., Smith, Dick, and Mary), c. 1915.

ily, relatives, and guests drove out regularly for camping out, golf, and swimming parties—the exhilarating sorts of recreational and physical exercise that Katharine believed essential to health. Her secretary Evie Crim once described the place as "a soothing balm for weary nerves."[36] Whether in the city or at Reynolda, Katharine enjoyed celebrating occasions great and small: intimate gatherings in honor of a friend's out-of-town guests; reunions of her father's fellow veterans on Confederate Memorial Day, for which the Fifth Street house was swathed in bunting; or, as in 1916, a Fourth of July barbecue on the grounds of Reynolda, with a program of music and other entertainment, for over four

hundred employees of Reynolds Tobacco.[37] Katharine took particular pleasure in planning special events for which she would bring distinguished performing artists to town. She had included two grass amphitheaters in her landscape planning—an informal one on the north lawn descending from the bungalow to the shore of the lake; another, more architectural in character, completed in 1916 on the slope rising behind Reynolda church, a perfect site for outdoor weddings.

Katharine was also mindful of the importance to her own and her husband's health of restorative time away from the pressures of business, so she continued to plan vacations, sometimes for the two of them alone but usually with the children, at resorts in the mountains or at the shore. Since the early days of their marriage, however, they had shared a dream of embarking once again upon more adventurous trips, especially to see the American West and to visit countries in the Far East.[38] But the demands imposed by years of childbearing, recurring rounds of illness in the family, the expansion of Dick's business enterprises, and Katharine's personal management of Reynolda's development had pushed any hope of exotic foreign travel into what became, with the onset of

the European war, an increasingly uncertain future. They therefore seized an opportunity, in the spring of 1915, to take their
long-awaited western tour.[39] California had become the country's
most popular tourist destination, since two major cities were
hosting international expositions to celebrate completion of
work on the Panama Canal. Luxury tours by train offered travelers a month-long itinerary, with excursions to the Grand Canyon
and to San Diego for the Panama-California Exposition, followed by a stay in San Francisco, which was hosting its own
Panama-Pacific International Exposition. Both expositions included pavilions and gardens reflecting California's historic ties
to Asian culture, so in a curious way such a journey offered the
Reynoldses an opportunity both to see the west and to whet
Katharine's growing interest in oriental plants and gardens, with
little risk to her stamina.[40]

Extensive press coverage of the Japanese installations at both
expositions—San Francisco's six-acre complex was the largest
exhibit of any foreign country—contributed to a growing national fascination with Japanese building and landscape traditions, just as the Japanese pavilion at the 1893 World's
Columbian Exposition in Chicago had so fired the architectural
imaginations of the Greene brothers of California and Frank
Lloyd Wright that their subsequent work owed a debt to that
epiphany. In the same year as the Chicago fair, a scholarly study,
Landscape Gardening in Japan, had been published by Josiah Condor, a British architect who had lived, practiced, and taught in
Japan for many years. A second edition of this book, to which
Condor added a supplement of annotated photographic plates,
reached an even larger audience of Americans when it appeared
in 1912.[41] That year also marked the occasion of a gift to the nation's capital of three thousand Yoshino cherry trees, presented
by the mayor of Tokyo in honor of the long friendship of his
country and the United States (an event still memorialized each
spring when the successors of those trees bloom around the Tidal
Basin).[42]

During the same period of time, Katharine Reynolds had begun her search for someone other than Louis Miller to design the formal gardens at Reynolda. Already curious about the history and culture of the Far East, she would have appreciated the steady stream of magazine articles on Japanese landscape design—including those by Wilhelm Miller published in *Country Life in America*—that illustrated representative garden types, ornament, and planting compositions for the benefit of Americans interested in adapting to their own properties an aesthetic that ultimately influenced both Arts and Crafts and modernist design practice in this country. In some instances, residential gardens created in response to the new fashion aimed at fairly literal renderings of a historic style. At Kykuit, for example, the well-publicized estate of John D. Rockefeller at Pocantico Hills, New York, a 1909 "Japanese Garden," boasting an elaborate teahouse, had been inserted into a terraced hillside landscape that in other respects was an amalgam of Italian, French, and English picturesque landscape traditions.[43] More often, however, and generally with better effect, certain aesthetic qualities associated with Japanese design—a simplified language of forms, a limited palette of natural materials, transparency and craftsmanship in construction, and a heightening of the kinesthetic experience of movement through space—were absorbed and abstracted in the work of American designers intrigued by these effects, particularly among those practicing on the West Coast.[44] Under the instigation of Katharine Reynolds

The Japanese Pavilion, Panama-Pacific International Exposition, San Francisco, from Official Miniature View Book *(1915).*

herself, this subtler and more selective evocation of Japanese garden motifs would find its way even into the European classicism of the formal gardens that Thomas Sears designed for her over the course of the next few years.

For one thing, she must have weeping cherry trees (*Prunus subhirtella pendula*). Her sister Ruth would later recall Katharine's urging her to see the newly planted trees along the Tidal Basin on a planned visit to Washington, D.C.[45] Neither the allées of cherry trees that would line grass paths fronting the greenhouse and the eastern and western perimeters of Reynolda's flower garden, nor the dramatic allée of evergreen Japanese cedar (*Cryptomeria japonica lobbii*) framing the central lawn of its sunken garden, appear on any drawing by Sears, including the set of detailed planting plans

BELOW: *Weeping cherries, formal garden.*

OPPOSITE: *Cryptomeria allée looking toward Palm House, c. 1921.* Photo by Thomas Sears.

❧ *A World of Her Own Making*

for the greenhouse gardens submitted in the fall of 1917, an absence reinforcing the oral tradition that Katharine Reynolds herself introduced these features.[46] Cryptomerias had been grown on the grounds of her Fifth Street house since 1912, and *Country Life in America* had published photographs on the same page of a centuries-old avenue of cryptomeria leading to a royal tomb at Nikko, Japan, and a wisteria-covered pergola in a Japanese garden.[47] The main entrance to Reynolda's formal gardens would bring visitors through doors in the greenhouse conservatory centered on the cryptomeria allée. From there, the vista over the lawn between the trees terminated in a raised rectangular pool and, on the major cross-axis, an elevated screen wall of pergolas and "shelters" separating the sunken flower garden from cutting and produce gardens on the other side. A secondary entrance to the gardens, at the eastern edge closest to the house, was designed for the family's use; here Sears would provide a room-like pergola (balanced by a smaller version on the opposite side of the gardens) on which to support the robust trunks, vines, and annual display of flowering wisteria.[48]

From this eastern overlook, brick stairways on either side of a small octagonal pool would descend to a wide grass terrace walk above the sunken garden. Before the addition of the weeping cherry trees, Sears had planned only mixed herbaceous borders along the edges of this terrace, and between them two parallel rows of narrower flower beds, twelve in all, lining the central path. His choice of plants for these island beds is significant; although he included some summer- and fall-blooming perennials to provide color in those seasons, the beds were dedicated primarily to iris and peonies, two of the flower genera most evocative of Asian culture in the minds of American gardeners. Part of Katharine's fascination with Japan had certainly to do with her admiration for a people for whom the enjoyment of flowers was, in the words of a contemporary garden writer, "interwoven in their minds with poetical and traditional associations" and who had elevated the art of flower arrangement to equality with paint-

OPPOSITE:
*Entrance pergola,
c. 1921.* Photo by
Thomas Sears.

*Pergola on western
end of cross axis,
c. 1921.* Photo by
Thomas Sears.

ing and poetry.[49] (Louis Miller would surely not have suggested enclosing the sunken garden on four sides with a "hedge" of peonies had he not known that his client loved them.)[50] The combination of these iconic flowers, the wisteria-covered pergola, and finally the double row of weeping cherry trees made the eastern entrance and the raised terrace garden a place set slightly apart, poetically equivalent, perhaps—at least for its mistress—to a *giardino segreto* in which graceful homage was paid to a wholly other garden world, romantic and beautiful but very far away.

Together, the allées of cryptomeria and weeping cherry trees, terraced walls and stairs, and the architectural screen of pergolas on the cross-axis would provide the flower gardens with varied and richly textured vertical structuring, reinforced by carefully balanced compositions of sculptural small trees and evergreen shrubs used as hedging or in groups within the borders. Equally sensitive to spatial construction was the decision to balance the visual weight of the greenhouse complex on the north with the strong horizontal line of raftered pergolas and what Sears referred to on plans as "shelters" on the south—five identical ten-foot-square shingle-roofed outdoor rooms, the middle one recessed toward the rear gardens, creating a U-shaped central space. The form of the pergola passage—a sequence of five separate small rooms linked by vine-covered walks—is surprisingly eccentric for a Sears design. What so pleases the eye eventually teases the mind with a question: How, in a practical way, were these spaces meant to be used? The very boldness of their formal exaggeration—not one but five small rooms, to be furnished with tables and chairs—introduces a note of whimsy that enlivens the sedate propriety with which Sears interpreted the conventions of classical garden style.

What is just as puzzling, given the popular fever for *japonisme* to which his client had succumbed, is his consistent description of these structures on the early plans as "shelters" rather than "teahouses," even though their paved floors and supporting columns (more slender than those of Keen, though similar in style and

Teahouse, c. 1921.
Photo by Thomas Sears.

with the same stippled-concrete finish) were refined rather than rustic in appearance. That his "shelters" soon acquired the designation "teahouse" is borne out by his substitution of that term on a later planting plan.[51] Did this bred-in-the-bone classicist try, tactfully, to redirect Mrs. Reynolds's enthusiasm for a design tradition so different from the one in which he was most at home? If such a separation of minds did indeed demand a little polite accommodation on both sides, the gardens only benefited, since in the end the references to picturesque Eastern tradition are seamlessly woven into the familiar patterns and materials of the formal garden style that Sears favored and that Katharine had years earlier determined to be appropriate for the greenhouse complex.

More than any other aspect of her estate planning, including the architectural and interior design services she commissioned from professional firms, Katharine Reynolds could feel confident that she knew enough about contemporary garden design and floriculture—and what she particularly wanted to grow—to stay closely involved in this way as Sears worked to complete the plans for her formal gardens. Moreover, because everything having to do with landscape, and especially the gardens, engaged her mind and imagination in such pleasurable and productive ways, her absorption in this part of his work also served to distract Katharine from a sense of foreboding about the direction the war was taking. She could summon up memories of gardens she had loved completely or in some special part, sharing with Sears her affection for certain flowers—peonies and roses in particular—and her excitement over recent directions in garden and landscape design that seemed inspired by the same aesthetic that had first attracted her to the architecture of Charles Barton Keen. He could also count on her to be quite precise about the things he must avoid. A passing comment to the effect that she might prefer not to have statuary in the garden would, for example, make a critical contribution to a discussion of gardens whose design vocabulary borrowed so much from the Renaissance villa tradition.

An Imagined Garden Is a Perfect World

Sears's task was to give physical form and substance to Katharine's hints and hopes as well as the firm functional requirements she laid down for the formal gardens. With a long rectangular plan as his starting place, he integrated each division and detail of the space within a crisp angular geometry: the paired parallel architecture of greenhouses and pergola-linked teahouses on the north-south axis and single pergolas at either end of the principal cross-axis; the sunken garden "room" with its quadripartite floral parterres, axial allée, bordered walks, and pools; and the screened but accessible complementary space of what he would later label, pointedly, the "Fruit, Cut Flower and Nicer Vegetable Garden," as if to make certain that the physical appearance of food crops grown in close proximity to a fine ornamental garden would be given priority over more practical considerations. For Sears, "good taste" in garden design had nothing to do with the table.

It had everything to do, however, with a discipline of restraint. If not a single thing in this formal garden should be less than pleasing to the eye, neither should any part disturb the delicate equilibrium of the whole by calling attention to itself. The con-

Plan "D" for the formal garden by Thomas Sears.

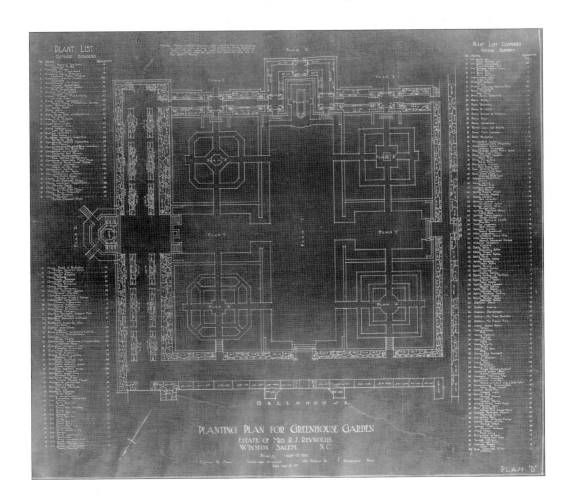

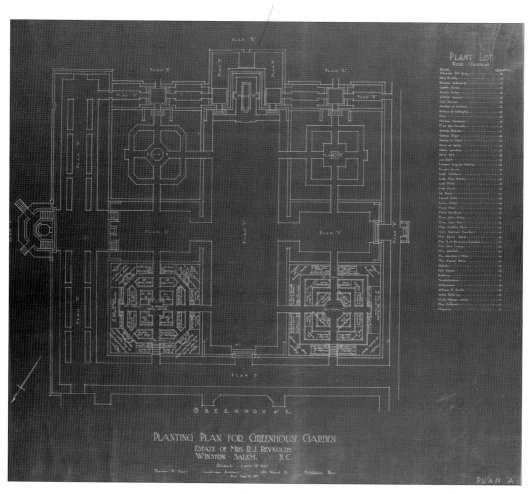

Plan "A" for the formal garden by Thomas Sears.

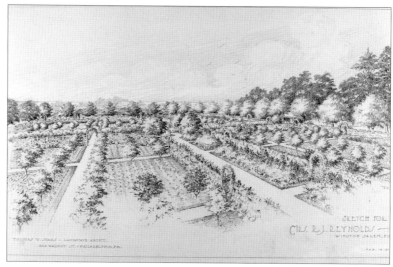

"Fruit, Cut Flower and Nicer Vegetable Garden," drawing by Thomas Sears.

Brick-capped stucco wall and slate path in front of the Palm House, c. 1921. Photo by Thomas Sears.

Path through the Pink and White Garden, c. 1921. Photo by Thomas Sears.

struction materials he selected had to be as familiar yet as fine in appearance as the design features in which they were used: brick-capped stucco for retaining walls and pools; grass paths throughout the flower gardens, except for slate walks bordering the central lawn; crushed stone on the pergola walks and the paths in the vegetable garden; cypress rafters for the pergolas, stained "light brown to imitate natural weathering."[52] Perhaps it is in the character of the flower garden's water features that this preference for understatement seems most apparent, since they were designed as comely but very simple basins. Water enters the larger

Path through the Rose Garden, c. 1921. Photo by Thomas Sears.

Slate path along formal garden border, c. 1921. Photo by Thomas Sears.

pool through a spout with a diminutive lion's head ornament, and a single low bubbler splashes gently near the opposite end. Such fountains are meant to please at close range rather than tempt a visitor to hurry toward them, distracted from the gradual unfolding of spatial and sensual experiences along the way.

Main axis path of vegetable garden, looking toward the Palm House, c. 1921.
Photo by Thomas Sears.

View across the vegetable garden, main entrance pergola in background, c. 1921.
Photo by Thomas Sears.

Water-lily pool with lion's head ornament, c. 1921. Photo by Thomas Sears.

Obviously Katharine's injunctions to her landscape architect had underscored the importance to her of achieving a simple and serene loveliness in the gardens, in keeping with the spirit of the entire place—a working farm that in every detail must be inviting rather than intimidating, homelike rather than palatial. Even a suggestion of virtuous frugality was not to be scorned; everyone in her employ knew that she was both generous in giving and scrupulously careful in spending money.[53] Sears understood precisely the limits she wished him to observe, and embraced them easily, since his personal style was hardly flamboyant. He was able to create gardens for Katharine that elevated quite ordinary materials, traditional crafts, and historic design conventions to a degree of perfection—of scale, structure, texture, incident, and sensuousity—worthy of the venerable epithet "pleasure garden." Because these were not to be private gardens, however, given their location near the entrance to the village and Katharine's wish that they should be available to visitors and townspeople, one of the most important of the pleasures they provided was that gift of welcoming openness. In fact, so much about the gardens seemed familiar and friendly, belonging to a long tradition of southern

View across vegetable garden, church in background to the left, c. 1921. *Photo by Thomas Sears.*

Arch entry to vegetable garden, 2001. *Photo by Carol Betsch.*

View across cut flower garden, 2001. Photo by Carol Betsch.

practice, that more than any other part of Reynolda's landscape, the formal gardens mirrored Katharine's sense of herself and how she wished to live in the world—surrounded by beauty, sweet order, and the delights of nature and of human fellowship.

The only appetite likely to have tempted her to indulge in frank luxury in planning the formal gardens was her passion for horticulture; here she appears to have been less concerned than usual with the costs involved in obtaining a "gracious plenty" of whatever promised to add to the richness and beauty of the floral display. Sears shared her love of flowers and followed the example of Gertude Jekyll in employing in his planting schemes large numbers of species and cultivars (many of them having the added cachet of being only recently introduced to commerce). Yet his fidelity to Beaux Arts traditions of garden-making made him wary of allowing prodigious quantities of trees, shrubs, and flowers to dissipate the dominant visual effect he was after—that of a tightly unified, classical composition of forms, colors, and textures to which both plants and built elements contributed. No American garden designer of his generation could entirely escape the formidable influence of the collaborative garden designs of Lutyens and Jekyll, and Sears was no exception, as his drawings for the greenhouse gardens demonstrate. One sees in them the same strong contrast between a crisply defined architectural geometry in the built elements and the "soft" fabric of amorphous shapes meant only to indicate the approximate edges of living, growing, constantly changing plant masses within the beds and borders, as if the design probed mythic tensions between human making and the world of nature, order and disorder, mind and matter, male and female.

In thinking about the influence of the Lutyens-Jekyll model on the design of Reynolda's formal gardens, we need to remind ourselves that Thomas Sears was young (thirty-six in 1916) and a Yankee newly arrived in an unfamiliar region when he took on a project whose scale and importance had to have made his own heart occasionally race with trepidation. It is easy to understand why he might have been inclined to take fewer chances with his design of Reynolda's greenhouse gardens than he had in his planting plan for the chapel lawn on the opposite side of the road, since the gardens represented the most self-contained and distinctive unit of the estate landscape, the outdoor equivalent of the large reception hall in the center of the main house. Nothing must be allowed to detract from the formal equilibrium or centuries-old stylistic conventions that seemed to offer the surest route to achieving that inviting atmosphere of comfort and tranquility, both physical and psychological, so much desired by his client. He and Katharine had already rejected the easy theatrical impact afforded by opulent materials and ornament. It would be just as important for Sears to modify Jekyll's style of planting to suit his own purposes, particularly her "cottage garden" aesthetic, which aimed to replicate the look of the small rural gardens tended by generations of English householders, in which a spectacular profusion of hardy flowers achieves a beauty that appears artless, owing little or nothing to concepts of design. That sort of informality might be appropriate to the little gardens he was designing for cottages and workshops in the village, but not for the greenhouse gardens.

Sears would instead choose to preserve a desirable association with older traditions of fine gardening, more studied than casual. To this end he planned for a less dense, more meticulous arrangement of plant groups that would help to establish a regime of orderliness, reinforced in the parterre gardens by the sharp linear definition of clipped boxwood hedges—taller common box (*Buxus sempervirens*) to frame each of the four large squares, "truedwarf" edging box (*Buxus sempervirens suffruticosa*) for their interior segments—and by his use of specimen trees and shrubs in balanced sets to mark the four corners of each parterre. The unified visual impression of these four compartments would be further simplified by devoting the two squares on the north, nearest the greenhouse, exclusively to roses, and by narrowing the range of color throughout to mostly pink species in the rose garden and, in the remaining two squares in which herbaceous flowering plants were to be grown, blue and yellow to the east and pink and white to the west.

Louis Miller had made all four of the oval parterres shown on his 1913 plan identical in form; each of the four designed by Sears is different from all the others, yet so much within the same geometric vocabulary that they appear nicely matched without being identical, particularly as pairs, north and south. All such gestures toward more elaboration and complexity in his design of the gardens are modulated with exquisite sensitivity to the need for just enough stimulation to keep the eye engaged and rewarded—as if "not too little, not too much, but exactly right" was his motto—without sacrificing a visitor's awareness that each interlocking

piece is part of an even more beautiful and comprehensible whole. It is precisely this layered accumulation of handsome and well-integrated components that made Sears's plan so vastly superior to that of Miller, with more variety and complexity in its details, more cohesive visual and spatial structure in its totality. If Sears had decided not to test the limits of the design strategies with which he was most familiar, he was still never less than masterly in his orchestration of the garden experience generated by the architecture of the plan, including his use of trees and shrubs to serve essentially architectural functions as green sculpture, walls, or focal points.

He knew from the beginning, however, that as he moved from built elements to natural ones, the same degree of control was impossible, and it was in this area of his design, for an important garden in an unfamiliar region, that he might reasonably have feared that limitations in his knowledge and experience would make it harder to produce work of exceptional quality. In the flower-filled borders and parterres that were the expressive heart of the gardens, he had to deal with the dynamics of biological processes, taking risks with literally hundreds of plant species having different cultural requirements and cycles of growth, blooming, and dormancy. Nor did he have enough space at his disposal to consign areas of the garden to single-season display, as was often done in great country house gardens. Instead, he must choreograph the sequential performance of bulbs, ground covers, flowers, shrubs, and small trees, imagining how they would look in combinations changing over the course of successive seasons. Even the rose parterres, for which he specified fifty different varieties, 1739 plants in all, were planned to ensure "the longest possible period of bloom."[54]

A close look at the planting plan for any one of the four parterre gardens will illustrate some of the problems Sears faced in his dual roles as designer and plantsman, as he struggled to create a reliable three-dimensional composition of living materials that were constantly changing in appearance, from week to week as much as from one season to the next. In the Pink and White Garden, for example, he was working with a ground plan of squares within squares centered on the southwestern pergola, to which one ascended by a stairway set within a narrow walled space framed by a pair of Koreanspice viburnum (*V. carlesii*), a deliciously fragrant shrub whose pink buds whiten as they open in spring; the slope on either side was to be planted with the white-flowered form of evergreen periwinkle (*Vinca minor alba*). Within the parterre, Japanese magnolias (*M. soulangeana*) at the four outermost corners corresponded to identical trees at the corners of the Blue and Yellow Garden to the east. Tree-form rose-colored deutzias (*D. gracilis carminea*) occupied the center of each of four segments making up the middle square, while the small innermost square would be composed only of flowers. By having the rest of the plantings in the beds reflect the same gradation in height from

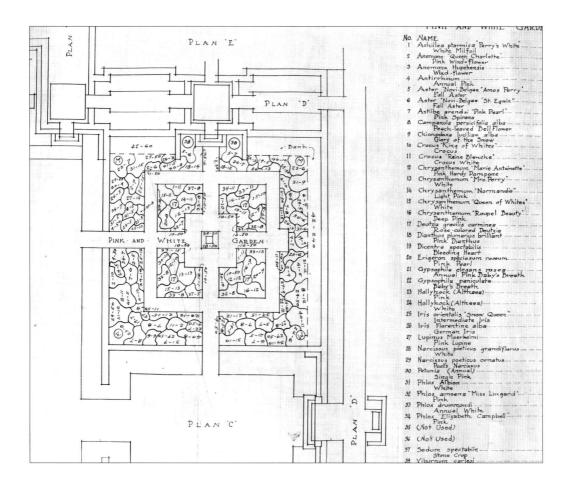

No.	NAME
1	Achillea ptarmica "Perry's White" — White Milfoil
2	Anemone "Queen Charlotte" — Pink Wind-flower
3	Anemone Hupehensis — Wind-flower
4	Antirrhinum — Annual Pink
5	Aster "Novi-Belgae "Amos Perry" — Fall Aster
6	Aster "Novi-Belgae "St. Egwin" — Fall Aster
7	Astilbe arendsi "Pink Pearl" — Pink Spiraea
8	Campanula persicifolia alba — Peach-leaved Bell Flower
9	Chionodoxa luciliae alba — Glory of the Snow
10	Crocus "King of Whites" — Crocus
11	Crocus "Reine Blanche" — Crocus White
12	Chrysanthemum "Marie Antoinette" — Pink Hardy Pompone
13	Chrysanthemum "Mrs. Perry" — White
14	Chrysanthemum "Normandie" — Light Pink
15	Chrysanthemum "Queen of Whites" — White
16	Chrysanthemum "Roupel Beauty" — Deep Pink
17	Deutzia gracilis carminea — Rose-colored Deutzia
18	Dianthus plumarius brilliant — Pink Dianthus
19	Dicentra spectabilis — Bleeding Heart
20	Erigeron speciosum roseum — Pink Pearl
21	Gypsophila elegans rosea — Annual Pink Baby's Breath
22	Gypsophila paniculata — Baby's Breath
23	Hollyhock (Althaea) — Pink
24	Hollyhock (Althaea) — White
25	Iris orientalis "Snow Queen" — Intermediate Iris
26	Iris Florentine alba — German Iris
27	Lupinus Moerheimi — Pink Lupine
28	Narcissus poeticus grandiflorus — White
29	Narcissus poeticus ornatus — Poet's Narcissus
30	Petunia (Annual) — Single Pink
31	Phlox Albion — White
32	Phlox amoena "Miss Lingard" — Pink
33	Phlox drummondi — Annual White
34	Phlox "Elizabeth Campbell" — Pink
35	(Not Used)
36	(Not Used)
37	Sedum spectabile — Stone Crop
38	Viburnum carlesi

Detail of Sears's planting plan for the Pink and White Garden.

the perimeter inward—tallest flowers in the outer square, mid-sized in the next, lowest in the center—Sears accentuated the bowl-like effect and legibility of both southern parterre gardens when viewed from the pergolas and grass terraces.

The bloom cycle in the pink and white parterre began in late winter, when low mounds of white glory-of-the-snow (*Chionodoxa luciliae alba*) dappled the ground. In each location on the plan for which he specified spring bulbs—he also used crocus and narcissus in this garden—Sears indicated how the same area should be overplanted in order to fill the space remaining after the bulbs had returned to dormancy, choosing a single species of herbaceous perennial that would work well with the plants growing around it as the year progressed. In the same way, he chose companion plants for six separate clusters of tall Madonna lilies (*Lilium candidum*) dispersed among beds of the outer square, combining each group of bulbs with a planting of windflowers (*Anemone hupehensis*), astilbes (*A. arendsii* "Pink Pearl"), or some other sturdy perennial that would conceal the void created when the lilies withered into dormancy by early summer. He also used good-sized plantings of hardy annuals and biennials—snapdragons, annual phlox (*P. drummondii*) and vinca, petunias, and hollyhocks—to help create a reliable succession of color (only in shades of pink or white, of course) from early spring until frost. Hollyhocks (*Alcea* sp.), since they commonly attained a height of more than five feet, actually played an important structural role in the garden. Sears repeated them in groups of pink or white around the magnolias at each of the four corners of the outer square, and in smaller groupings interspersed along its outer edge, where, with stands of other fairly tall perennials—phlox, painted daisy (*Tanacetum coccineum*),[55] a white-flowered form of peach-leaved bellflower (*Campanula persi-*

Hollyhocks in the formal garden, c. 1921. Photo by Thomas Sears.

cifolia alba), Michaelmas daisies (*Aster novi-belgii*), and so on— they would help to create a sense of enclosure.

Additional evidence of how much thought Sears gave to working out relationships between individual groups of plants within the garden mosaic emerges as an explanation for what at first glance appears to be a lapse of judgment on his part. Appealing as they might be in form and color, why would he have included two dozen bleeding heart (*Dicentra spectabilis*) and masses of astilbe, both plants requiring moist and shaded conditions for optimum growth, on a list of sun-loving plants for a garden in an open and sunny situation? The likeliest answer to that question has to do with the way he sited these more vulnerable species to take advantage of solar orientation (and milder spring weather in the case of this species of bleeding heart, which goes dormant in summer heat) as well as the screening effect of taller plants in their vicinity to create pockets of shade. The astilbes would bloom during the cooler days of fall, adding their feathery plumes to a fresh flush of glorious color in the pink and white parterre provided by the large numbers of chrysanthemums, fall asters, and Japanese anemones that Sears had specified.

Even if the bleeding hearts and astilbes performed well, however, it is impossible to know with any certainty how close Sears came to achieving that full and fine effect of brilliant color and rich texture, spring through fall, that he and Katharine both wanted. Climate was likely to have been a problem for some of his other choices as well. He apparently knew that *Campanula persicifolia alba* was the only species of bellflower able to tolerate the heat and humidity of a North Carolina summer, and he included among various phlox he specified a more heat-tolerant and mildew-resistant cultivar, "Miss Lingard," although some confusion on his plant list with regard to its nomenclature and color suggests that he may not have had prior experience of this relatively new introduction.[56] But he also gave a substantial amount of space to four separate clusters of a pink cultivar of perennial lupine (*Lupinus polyphyllus* "Moerheimii"), a stately and spectacular flower that, with delphinium (which he used in the blue and yellow garden), was most emblematic of the glories of English perennial borders. At the very time that Sears was designing Reynolda's parterre gardens, there was a good deal of excitement among serious American gardeners about recent efforts of English horticulturists to hybridize this species of lupine, which is actually native to the American West and Canada. If Sears had not expected these important components of his design to remain attractive throughout the summer (two of his four stands of lupine occupied prominent places at the front edge of a bed), he would have specified a second plant group for the same spot. Since he did not, we must assume that this is one of the times when he failed to anticipate the effect of warm summer temperatures even in the North Carolina Piedmont on a plant that demands cool and moist conditions. Southern gardeners have since learned to treat lupines as a hardy annual, usually planted in the fall for a breathtaking show in spring, then discarded. Sears would also misjudge the effect of winter cold on certain tender plants included in his planting plans.

Still, in these situations he may have been aware of the potential for disappointment but willing to experiment. Perhaps Katharine, anticipating any gardener's delight in growing and showing a rare and difficult plant so worth the effort as her pink lupines would have been, not only approved of his choice but suggested it. Imagined gardens are irresistibly perfect.

"My happiness is complete"

Two long and horrific battles, Verdun and the Battle of the Somme, contributed over the course of 1916 to a steady erosion of hope that the United States might yet escape involvement in the great war that raged on the continent. Had it not been so, Katharine Reynolds would have been able to savor more fully her delight in having Charles Barton Keen busy at work on drawings for finishing the interior of the bungalow at the same time that Thomas Sears was regularly submitting plans—at least twenty-two between January and December of that year—for grading and developing various parts of the estate landscape, including construction drawings for walls, stairs, paving, and pergolas in the greenhouse gardens as well as several planting plans for areas surrounding the bungalow. In spite of delays occasioned by the war, intensive building and planting continued throughout the year. Katharine followed these and other projects with her customary tenacity and attention to detail. Writing the company that was supplying materials needed to complete the new dairy building in October, she not only described the three shades of additional green ceramic roofing tile she wanted, but also ordered roofing paper "with nails, etc." and enclosed her check.[57]

Earlier in the year Sears had done a masterly job with a plan that assembled a rich variety of trees and shrubs, most of them native, to form a layered woodland enclosed within the two arms of the arrival drive where it divided as it neared the bungalow, one arm curving up along the west wing to the wide entrance porch with its garlanded columns, the other moving in a long arc that ended in the service court at a lower elevation on the other side of the house.[58] At year's end he presented his plan of a more formal but equally complex and beautiful small terrace garden on the north side of the east wing, where an office "den" for Mrs. Reynolds and a slightly larger one for her husband occupied the first floor. Stairways from open porches outside Dick's den and the living room in the central block of the house led into this garden. Within it, slate walks triangulated the space in a way that suggested the character of a strolling garden, especially since the plantings were mostly a collection of native *Ericaceae*, strikingly lovely and in many cases fragrant in flower—rhododendron, mountain laurel, and azaleas. He complemented these with four

Woodland along the entry drive, 2001.
Photo by Carol Betsch.

*View to bungalow from
the woodland, 2001.*
Photo by Carol Betsch.

*Porte-cochère with
rose-garlanded
columns.* Photo by
Thomas Sears.

OPPOSITE:
*View to woodland from
the bungalow, golf links
beyond, 2001.* Photo by
Carol Betsch.

*North facade of the
bungalow with lake
porch.* Photo by
Thomas Sears.

266   *A World of Her Own Making*

species of small- to medium-height flowering trees, remaining attentive to the same color harmonies in the range of pink, rose, pale lavender, and white that he used in the shrub layer. Three of these tree species—Yulan magnolia (M. *heptapeta*), native sweetbay magnolia (M. *virginiana*), and crape myrtle (*Lagerstroemia indica*)—are distinctly upright in character, at least until maturity, while the fourth species, a pink-flowered cultivar of flowering dogwood (*Cornus florida rubra*), reinforces human scale in a similar way, bringing the show of blooms, bracts, or berries up close in a garden of this scale. The wider of the walks, coming from the library porch, was intersected by a circular terrace enclosed by a low retaining wall, an inner ring of planting beds, and two stone benches carved to match the same arc. The four beds were to contain an evergreen Japanese pieris (P. *japonica*)[59] at either end, and between them plantings of spring and summer bulbs—pale yellow narcissus "Queen of Spain" and regal lilies (L. *regale*)—that would emerge in turn from under a carpet of foot-high evergreen *Paxistima canbyi*. A small round pool—once again, subdued in its effect, with a single low bubbler—occupied the center of the terrace.

Stone bench and pool in the terrace garden, woods beyond. Photo by Thomas Sears.

OPPOSITE:
The terrace garden and pool. Photo by Thomas Sears.

Rhododendron and retaining wall, terrace garden. Photo by Thomas Sears.

Sears finished the plan for this sequestered place of passage to the hillside landscape above Lake Katharine a week before Christmas 1916. That same week Tiffany and Company received an order for an $8,000 sapphire ring that must certainly have been Katharine's Christmas present from her husband in celebration of a very good year in their fortunes and as a token of his abiding love for the woman whose wisdom, goodness, and energy had brought him so much joy.[60] It is fair to say that at this point in their married lives, these two had a right to feel "on top of the world," no matter what the future might hold.

One aspect of that future was certain—1917 would be a very busy year, during which Katharine was involved with a number of organizations. She was already serving as president of the local chapters of the YWCA and of the National Civic Federation, for which she hosted a January luncheon attended by the state chairman and gave a talk reporting on the local group's recent activities.[61] Although Woodrow Wilson had won reelection in the fall with the slogan "He kept us out of the war," German intransigence so forced his hand in the early months of the new year that on the second of April he asked Congress for a declaration of war. The Reynolds family had just returned from a ten-day Florida vacation when the news came,[62] and Katharine responded, typically, with action, joining forces with a small group of women friends to set up a local chapter of the American Red Cross. She shortly thereafter accepted appointment as North Carolina chair of the Woman's Liberty Loan Committee of the Council of National Defense, and in that capacity would travel to Raleigh in September to attend a meeting of the council's executive committee. In the same month, she was one of twelve North Carolinians appointed by Governor Bickett to the newly formed Library War Council, a state group working under the War Service Committee of the American Library Association to supervise a campaign to provide books for members of the armed forces.[63]

Katharine was also a member of the Woman's National Farm and Garden Association, founded in 1914. Her farm had from the

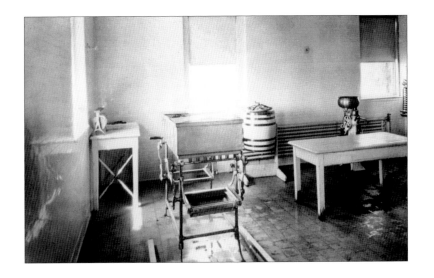

The state-of-the-art dairy with butter press in the corner, bottling machine, churn, cream separator, and testing table.

very beginning been planned as a model useful to the farmers of her state and beyond. Its greenhouses held over a million vegetable seedlings ready for the spring's planting. With the nation now at war, the supply of food was a matter of increasing concern, as thousands of young men left farming to serve in the army, threatening domestic production at a time when additional agricultural products were needed to supply American forces and for European relief. Katharine's dairy had a state-of-the-art sterilizer, and she decided to put it to use immediately in helping local families preserve the summer's coming harvest. In June the Winston-Salem paper noted that a state agricultural extension agent was about to take "a group of farmers and dairymen to visit the dairy of the Reynolda farm . . . to see how Mrs. Reynolds will aid her neighbors to can perishable products during the summer, using the steam sterilizer."[64] The men did the research, the women did the canning; at Reynolda, women and girls put up more than 40,000 quarts of fruits, vegetables, and soup over the course of the summer.[65]

Katharine so loved the feeling of being efficient and useful to others that the prospect of dealing with the challenges presented by the war, when it finally came, left her unruffled. Her lifelong passion for making things function smoothly toward a desirable outcome may have had its roots in an unconscious longing to control the course of events, to ward off by intelligent management whatever threatened her health and happiness or that of her loved ones. It was natural for a woman who had known the death of a sibling at five and the loss of many friends in adolescence, who lived every day conscious that her weakened heart posed a danger to her life, to fear crises that seemed to come out of nowhere, as illness so often does. She had made sure that Keen's design for the bungalow included a large room on the second floor of the west wing identified as "hospital."

If she had ever given in to worry about her husband's being, in his late sixties, well past the average age of mortality for men of his generation, she had good cause to do so in the summer of 1917. In June, Dick developed symptoms of an ailment for which his doctors had no ready diagnosis, but at least two actions he took in the following month suggest that he understood his condition to be serious. One was to arrange for a new or revised version of his will to be drafted and signed. The other was to be formally received into the Presbyterian Church on the first Sunday in July, at the same time as his three eldest children, Dick Jr., Mary, and Nancy. Katharine shared the good news with family and friends, writing the Reverend Neal Anderson, vacationing with his family at a retreat in the mountains, just two lines: "I wanted you to know that my happiness is complete. Mr. Reynolds joined the church this morning."[66] Anderson's response followed quickly, thanking Katharine for "the best news I have received in years. . . . It is a great thing for Mr. Reynolds, who long belonged with God's people," and assuring her that her husband's conversion "will always stand in your memory for a promise fulfilled." He referred her to two passages in the Book of Psalms: "Delight thyself in the Lord; and he shall give thee the desires of thy heart" (37:4) and "The Lord hath done great things for us, whereof we are glad" (126:3).[67] The president of Davidson College, a Presbyterian institution to which Katharine gave financial support, wrote that he too rejoiced with her, knowing that her own example had "much to do with this."[68]

There was good news of a different order that Katharine had apparently been too modest to share with her friend and counselor. In July, the *Winston-Salem Journal and Sentinel* devoted its front page to a long article, illustrated with photographs, under the banner "'Reynolda Farm,' Splendid Country Estate of Mrs. R. J. Reynolds; Its Origin and Development, and the Aims of the Owner," followed by a summary of the article's contents:

An Experiment Station for This Section is Shown
Mrs. Reynolds Proves How Impediments Can Be Converted Into Assets
Utilizing Materials at Hand Effects Economies
Scientific Study of Soils and Crops Improves Fertility of Land and Increases Production—An Interesting Story[69]

The introduction that followed stressed the important difference between Reynolda and countless numbers of country estates, lavishly illustrated in popular magazines, that were "only a creation of individuals who have expended millions in the development of pleasure grounds to satisfy their own whims, or those of a narrow circle of friends." Reynolda, by contrast, was "destined to become one of the great factors in the development of the rural life, not only of Forsyth County but of the entire Piedmont section of North Carolina":

It is already the model of progressive farmers and their families throughout this section of the state, and many have made the trip from distant states for the sole purpose of looking over the splendid development and study[ing] its methods.

Though yet incomplete, through the splendid spirit shown by Mrs. Reynolds in her interest in the progress of this section, Reynolda is becoming the "experiment station" to which students of agriculture, domestic science, dairying, livestock raising, etc. look for reliable and authentic information on farm problems. Mrs. Reynolds has consented that a series of demonstrations shall be conducted on her estate, and these are proving of great value to the farmers and their wives who attend.

The article is essentially an eyewitness account—amplified with quoted remarks by Katharine, her superintendent A. C. Wharton, "a scientific agriculturist [and] graduate of the North Carolina A.&M. College," and other employees—that describes the physical character and operations of the estate in considerable detail. We learn about the exact numbers of acres committed to various food crops, how soil fertility was maintained by the use of cover crops and crop rotation, and the exceptionally fine pedigrees of Katharine's prize herd of Jersey cows and handsome Percheron horses. Just as illuminating for the way they reflect Katharine's personality as well as her hand everywhere at work are

Three of the prize Jersey herd.

such incidental observations as mention of the "reading room" at the rear of the superintendent's office, "in which all the magazines

of current events, fiction and agricultural papers and magazines are kept for the use of the men of the village," or the authoritative tone of such comments of hers as, "Eliminate the stray dog and sheep will yield a good profit to the farmer in this section," or "Quality rather than quantity [was] the deciding point" to explain her selection of stock for the dairy herd. We hear her excitement communicated to the correspondent: "Mrs. Reynolds declares that the greatest future awaits the guinea hen raiser. They sell for a higher price than chickens, and are strongly demanded by hotels and cafes of the north and east. It is a splendid fowl." There is as well the telling heading "A Happy Community" over an account of the advantages enjoyed by the twenty families living in Reynolda's village in "large and airy cottages," well designed and "attractively decorated inside and out," each with a garden to be cultivated as its owner wishes, with spring and fall tilling and seeds supplied free of charge through the superintendent's office.

Most important, the landscape of Reynolda, as it appeared to an interested and sensitive observer, occasionally takes on life in this account in a way that even extant photographs may fail to convey. In describing his impression of arriving at the entrance to the estate, with the "beautiful scene" of clustered community buildings to his right and Reynolda's chapel and manse "nestled in an open lawn" to his left, the reporter is struck by the effect of the "attractive cove" surrounding the chapel, manse, and superintendent's residence, its background "formed by woodlands broken only by beautiful orchards and garden plots," including a flourishing vineyard immediately behind the chapel. Entering the estate through the main entrance on the opposite side of the road, past the monumental stone fountain that provided drinking water "running fresh at all times," then moving on between the greenhouses and the head gardener's cottage, he observes in the distance to his left "the splendid concrete feed barns, silos, and the most modern dairy building to be found in the nation." Continuing along the winding road leading up to the unfinished house, as sounds of building fill the air, he finally surveys a pastoral land-

scape that he recognizes as a work not of nature but of landscape architecture. The vista might on any day include a "splendid flock of Shropshire sheep grazing on a forty-acre section of the farm containing the golf links," watched over by a shepherd and working collie. The description of the sixteen-acre lake stretching below the house to the north, "circled by a drive through a picturesque woodland for more than two and a half miles," confirms that Katharine's research had resulted in exactly the combination of beauty, pleasure, and ecological health she had sought. An accompanying photograph shows the lake—"well stocked with little-mouthed black bass"—with its boathouse, springboards for swimming, and a visiting flock of wild geese. Perhaps it is significant, too, that the reporter used the expression "magnificent English gardens" to describe the gardens then under construction in the greenhouse complex.

What must it have been like for Katharine to have Reynolda interpreted in a way that highlighted her motivations in conceiving and executing a project of such scope and potential significance, that explained to her fellow citizens and to the world at large—for the record, as it were—the educational and social goals

Bungalow under
construction,
c. 1915–16.

Shropshire sheep graz-
ing on the golf course.
Photo by Thomas Sears.

OPPOSITE:
Dairy barns, stables,
and silos. Photo by
Thomas Sears.

View across Lake
Katharine toward the
bungalow on the hill
at right. Photo by Thomas
Sears.

View of drive along Lake Katharine over the dam.

Daffodils in the woodland. Photo by Thomas Sears.

that were so essential to this undertaking? There can be no question about the extent to which Katharine had prepared herself for the visit of the newspaper's representatives, and that it was she herself who told the story: the difficult clearing of the land; the purity of the water in its artesian well, "never [reaching] the surface until it is drawn from the hundreds of faucets on different parts of the estate"; the gathering of "well known experts, each an authority in his line," to help her transform rocky and eroded land into "one of the most productive farms in the Piedmont." How many women of her day, much less within her own community, would ever experience the thrill of having their life's work validated in such a public way? Nor was Reynolda any longer merely the landscape of her imagination—her dream of rolling green lawns, pastures, and manicured fields, a picturesque lakeside carpeted by daffodils in spring, streams and waterfalls, shady wood-

Daffodils in bloom on the lake bank.

land paths, a village of pretty homes, bustling workshops, pristine farm buildings. It was already here, real, happening.

To have come this far, with so much already accomplished and the long-awaited move to the estate now close at hand, and to know that her husband had finally come to share the religious faith that meant more to her than anything the workaday world could offer—what could so much happiness mean, she might well have wondered, except that the Lord truly had, as Neal Anderson suggested, seen fit to fulfill the desires of her heart?

"Whom the Lord loveth, he chasteneth"

All through that summer and into the fall, Dick's doctors at the Johns Hopkins Hospital in Baltimore and at Jefferson Hospital in Philadelphia treated his symptoms without being able to determine the cause of his illness, an uncertainty that may have helped to sustain both his and Katharine's hopes for a recovery.[70] They spent as much time as possible during July and August in Atlantic City, a familiar and well-loved vacation spot close to his doctors. Their situations were now reversed, however; it was Katharine who had to travel back home or to New York on business, while her husband remained at their hotel with the children, Bum, and a maid. "Can't leave just yet on account of some work at the bungalow," Katharine wrote him during one of these separations, and during another: "Am attending to matters on both your farm and mine. Crops exceedingly fine."[71] She appears to have been occupied as well with a good many financial matters in these months, transacting business regularly with bankers and her broker.[72]

September brought no improvement in Dick's condition. Not long after coming home from a stay at Jefferson Hospital, he had to leave again for tests and treatment at Johns Hopkins, where his stay extended into November with only occasional respite from increasing debility. Construction and interior painting of the bungalow were finished by September, and Wanamaker's in Philadelphia shipped two railroad carloads of furnishings to Winston-Salem early in October. Katharine, meanwhile, traveled to Philadelphia, Baltimore, and New York City, making frequent visits to her husband in the hospital and devoting the remainder of her time to other business. Bum kept her informed about the children's activities and the progress being made in finally getting the house ready for the family's upcoming move: "Carpet and drapery men got to work in earnest this morning. . . . Telephone men hope to finish downstairs tomorrow."[73] There was no way that Katharine could keep up with the steady stream of invitations and requests for help that inundated her desk during these stress-filled weeks—among them, an invitation to attend, as a member of the North Carolina Agricultural Society, the dedication of the new Women's Building at the State Fair Grounds in Raleigh (Jeannette Rankin of Montana, the first woman elected to the House of Representatives, was to be the speaker) and an urgent letter from an officer of the National Woman's Party, headquartered in Washington, D.C., asking her to participate in a woman's suffrage meeting to be held in Winston-Salem on October 12.[74]

Katharine returned home in mid-November burdened by an almost unbearable request. The doctor in charge of Dick's care at Johns Hopkins, Thomas R. Brown, had asked her to censor her correspondence with her husband and to refrain from visiting him for an unspecified period of time. Dr. Brown's explanation could hardly have brought much comfort:

> I was very sorry to have to isolate Mr. Reynolds, but worry in regard to his business was so definitely inhibiting his recovery, that I felt he must have complete mental rest. It seemed necessary with the unsettled condition of certain of his affairs that he should see his business associates, and you, with your great knowledge of his business and his supreme confidence in your judgment could not fail to keep his mind more or less active along business channels. This morning he tells me that he feels better than he has

for many months, and I am sure the rest is doing him good, although I know how hard it is for you. Will you write him short, cheerful letters, without any reference to his business affairs?[75]

Katharine wrote her husband a cheerful letter almost at once telling him, "The house is finished and ready to move into," but she also expressed her longing to see him.[76] Dr. Brown wrote her again to say that while he had allowed Mr. Reynolds to read her letter, "I still feel that his real rest should be carried out a little while longer. I know how hard it is on you as well as on him, but I am quite sure I am right."[77]

The doctor may not have anticipated how much the regime he had imposed would upset Mrs. Reynolds. By the time she received a telegram from him at the end of the month, reporting that her husband "has been unquestionably feeling and seeming better the last few days. . . . I feel sure you can pay him a short visit early next week when I should talk over the case with you,"[78] Katharine had to have Bum wire back in her behalf: "Mrs. Reynolds just received message. I have made plans to go with her to Baltimore to consult specialist. Heart giving much trouble. Wire whether or not Mr. Reynolds knows you expect to allow her to see him next week. If so she will delay entering hospital. Does not want Mr. Reynolds to know but what she is perfectly well. She is most eager to talk with you concerning him."[79] Assuming that "H. van den Berg" must be a doctor, Brown wired immediately to say that he had already told Dick that his wife would be coming to see him the following week.[80]

Having decided that she would not yet be hospitalized herself, Katharine left the children in Bum's charge and went to Baltimore alone, for a visit with her husband and a discussion with his doctor that produced a sudden change in their plans. Apparently Katharine had hoped to bring her husband home with her after so many months of hospitalization—and to Reynolda, not the Fifth Street house. But now she wired Bum shortly after her arrival: "Not permitted to go home but ordered to Hot Springs for rest."[81] She and Dick were at The Homestead inn by December 7, when Katharine wrote nine-year-old Mary: "I hope you are enjoying your pretty room. There is deep snow here and Father and I go sleigh riding each day. Wish we were at home with you. Best Love, Mother."[82] She wired instructions to Bum for the placement of furniture in the bungalow, referring to various rooms by number: "Try suite from room 51 in your room and suite from 44 in 51."[83] Bum had her hands full during the next week or so, reporting to Katharine about the children's gradual recovery from winter colds and sore throats, the status of still more furniture shipments, holiday decorating, and the last-minute activities of carpenters and other workmen hurrying to have everything in order before their return. After a brief excursion to Baltimore for consultation with Dick's doctors, the Reynoldses finally made their way home to Winston-Salem less than a week before Christmas, grateful that the family was at last together in their new home.

Their lives had turned a corner by the end of the year, and the customary promise of a new year's beginning was shadowed not just by Dick's illness but by the threat to Katharine's own health posed by concern for his suffering and the continuing pressure of multiple responsibilities that were now difficult or impossible to fulfill in a way that met her expectations. She had been unable, for example, to present a promised paper, "Edgar Allen Poe: The Prince of American Literature," scheduled for the December 12 meeting of the local chapter of Sorosis, a literary club for women to which she belonged.[84] A small thing, weighed against the import of all that had happened in recent weeks, but she had to have wondered what sort of day-to-day accommodations she would have to start making in response to the overwhelming new reality that her husband was, at least for the foreseeable future, an invalid, that she might even lose him. In the third week of January, Katharine resigned from her position as state chair of the Woman's Liberty Loan Committee, explaining that "I have been taking care of [Mr. Reynolds] myself at night." Reynolds Tobacco had already purchased, in response to her appeal, the largest single subscription of bonds—a million dollars' worth—obtained anywhere in the country.[85]

Her task, she knew, would be to put her trust in God, then to keep busy and present a brave face to the world, which is exactly what she did in the months that followed. There was no end of details that needed to be completed or changed in the house, things as minor but time-consuming as having the lampshades in the reception hall replaced by others that would screen the view of bare bulbs from the gallery above, or pressing the company from which she had ordered an organ for the house to have it shipped, installed, and "voiced" before the Easter season, "which is a great one for us, with many visitors to the town, and I have plans to use the organ by that time."[86] An exchange of February letters between Katharine and Thomas Sears affords testimony to her calm perseverance in pursuing whatever seemed to her the right course of action in difficult circumstances. When a government embargo on nonessential freight shipments held up an order of slate needed for construction of garden walks and seats, Sears suggested to her that the R. J. Reynolds Tobacco Company could probably obtain a permit for a special railroad car to bring the shipment to Reynolda. "It seems to me wise," he added, "to get the slate here at the earliest possible time."[87] Katharine replied that she "would not like to take any action in the matter to push it through earlier than the [supplier] themselves can do, for with the food situation in the east in the condition that it is, this being something that I can do without, I do not feel that I have a right to push the matter."[88]

The same letter reports on the flurry of planting in accordance with Sears's plans being carried out in various parts of the estate under the supervision of Robert Conrad, a bright, articulate young man, eager to pursue a career in horticulture; Katharine could not have been more pleased with him. But within just a few months Robert would leave for service in the Marine Corps after spending his last afternoon "pathetic[ally] . . . stooping over different plants and flower beds at Reynolda for the longest time."[89] Another young man, a professional trained in forestry and engineering who "had worked out in the office" the plans that guided extensive planting at Reynolda in the fall, kept in close touch as he prepared to go overseas with a "gas defensive measures" unit of the army, and would later write Katharine a lovingly detailed description of the landscape and gardens he saw while stationed in Bordeaux.[90] The first supervisor of her greenhouse operations, an Englishman, left his young wife living at Reynolda when he went to war, only to be killed on his first day of fighting.[91] Hearing from a friend or correspondent of a loved one's death in combat would soon become a sadly familiar experience for Katharine. Later in the spring she would be faced with Bum's growing conviction that she, too, must leave the family she had come to love as her own in order to answer her country's call for badly needed nurses. Both of Katharine's brothers would soon be serving with the American Expeditionary Forces in Europe.

When Dick rallied for a short time in February, Katharine wrote their nephew Hardin, vacationing with his wife in Florida, to say that Dick seemed to have been helped by following the advice of his doctor in Winston-Salem that he should eat whether or not he was hungry and spend as much time outdoors as possible (he even rode along on a rabbit hunt). "Should he have another downward turn," she added, "I shall probably wish you to engage rooms for us and we will try Miami and see what it will do. . . . The country is beautiful now, and I assure you it is quite a sacrifice to leave Reynolda."[92] As it turned out, once his symptoms recurred Dick had neither the stamina nor the time for such a trip; the only one to be considered must take them to Philadelphia, where he was admitted to Jefferson Hospital on or about the fifth of April.[93] Katharine stayed at his side for three weeks before returning home, not well herself. A letter arrived just a few days later from Jessie Hill, the private nurse in charge of her husband's care, saying how sorry she was to hear that Katharine was sick. Katharine, who probably had not wanted Dick to know that she was ill, swiftly communicated as much to the nurse, who wrote the next day to say that "Mr. Reynolds . . . is glad you are feeling better and will be delighted to see you, but does not want you to come until you are feeling all right. He is keeping your room for you. . . . Take care of yourself and do not hurry back until you are perfectly strong."[94]

Katharine was back at the hospital within three days. (A room was being held for her, perhaps in or near the building in which her husband was staying.) She had access to a typewriter and kept herself busy with correspondence, but the days were long. Dick was growing steadily weaker, and it was hard to cling to hope that he would recover. She received detailed progress reports from her staff on what was being accomplished at Reynolda, within the house and on the grounds, and continued to be engaged in a rather trying exchange of letters with a North Carolina teacher who was supposed to be helping her organize and staff a small primary school that Katharine hoped to open at Reynolda in the coming fall. Within just a few weeks of having agreed to head the school, the woman reconsidered her decision (there was too little time, and she had "a fine offer" from Salem Academy), then changed her mind once more and accepted Katharine's offer.[95] Senah Critz, a niece planning to be wed in the amphitheater of Reynolda church on June 15, sent anxious bride-to-be notes: Katharine must please do her best to make it home for the wedding, but perhaps not try to provide the floral decorations as she had offered to do, for "I do not want you to work when you are not well."[96] By the end of the month, Bum noted that Katharine was "tired and discouraged."[97]

Family and friends tried to reassure her. A fellow board member of the YWCA wrote to say that although their most recent meeting was "interesting," she would be glad when Katharine was able to join them again:

We need your council [sic], for so many things are continually coming up that I feel unable to cope with. The work there and the building are great tributes to your faithfulness and efficiency.

Winston is proud to claim such a woman as you—for you are wonderful and so modest and direct. I don't know how you manage to be and do so much.[98]

Katharine's secretary Evie Crim wrote to say how serene and lovely Reynolda had seemed to her on a fine morning: "I know that you and Mr. Reynolds would love it if you were here . . . [it] is so sweet and homelike. . . . The family are all well, the children are settling down to vacation regime, and all seem happy."[99] Maxie's husband wanted Katharine to know how much she was missed at the Reynolda Sunday school exercises on the second of June, at which her daughter Nancy had recited, and that everything at the farm seemed to be thriving.[100] And in a thank-you note for a wedding gift Katharine had sent, Senah Critz described how she, too, had been struck by Reynolda's beauty when she visited one evening: "There were so many flowers blooming and the box bushes so green and healthy looking. The porches were lighted and the children were out there studying and they made quite a pretty picture—I wish you could have seen them."[101]

Katharine was not able to attend the wedding, but she and Dick did begin preparations to go home together. He had undergone surgery of an unspecified nature in the middle of June,[102] and soon after started to make arrangements with the Pennsylvania Railroad Company to provide a private Pullman car for a party of six to be added to an overnight train traveling between Philadelphia and Winston-Salem. In the weeks of recuperation and waiting that followed, some or all of the children were brought to Philadelphia for a visit, and there are other indications that Katharine was beginning to feel more hopeful. She had certainly made up her mind that her husband could receive the same quality of care at home that the hospital provided (Katharine described it as "hot, dusty, and noisy"[103]). Since Dick's doctors were allowing him to return home despite his severely weakened condition, however, they may very well have advised the Reynoldses that all medical options were now exhausted.

Their departure was set for five in the afternoon of July 18; Dick would be transported on a cot to the train and accompanied on the trip by a doctor and two nurses. Katharine spent a good part of that morning typing letters to her secretary and a number of friends. She tells each one how happy both of them are at the prospect of returning home at last, how grateful to have obtained a private car in order to insulate Dick as much as possible from discomfort on the journey, and that although very weak and thin, Mr. Reynolds was nevertheless a little better. The letter to Evie Crim resonates with Katharine's understandable longing for the routines of a normal life: "I am delighted to know you have the files all in shape, the catalogs arranged, the keys and the safes marked and everything in good shape for me, so that when I have an opportunity on our books we may get into it in earnest."[104] Another letter was to Robert Conrad, now stationed at the marine base at Parris Island, South Carolina. He had recently written Katharine to thank her for a gold watch she sent him in appreciation of the work he had done installing landscape projects on the estate before leaving for the service. Conrad told her that the inscription "Reynolda" on the back of the watch made him "begin to get the blues right off. It seems that it is harder for me to leave than anyone else, as . . . I have to leave two homes rather than just one." Nothing he wrote could have pleased Katharine more. Her warmly affectionate response reassured him that "we are simply holding [your] place open until you come back . . . and I trust you will always feel this way, for I want you to look upon 'Reynolda' as your second home."[105]

Only a letter to Neal Anderson mentioned how hard the time at the hospital had been for her. She wanted him to understand why she had not been able to write until this day of departure: "I have postponed writing to you feeling that I might get the time in which to do it myself, but have found this an impossibility as all of my time for the past six weeks has been taken up in the care of

Mr. Reynolds and trying to keep him happy, cheerful, and contented. I have been on duty each night until one o'clock and frequently until three—consequently, [had] to spend a greater part of the day trying to make up in sleep." More than a year earlier, when Dick had first developed symptoms of his disease, Katharine had asked Anderson to prepare a brief article summarizing her husband's life and achievements (another indication that both she and Dick understood that the illness might be life-threatening). Now she was able to thank him for sending the recently finished piece for their consideration: "I wish I could express to you how delighted Mr. Reynolds was over the sketch. . . . He felt it was beautifully done and had only a very few slight corrections to make; [we] so deeply appreciate your writing this article."[106]

They arrived home the next morning, just a day before Dick's sixty-eighth birthday. He had spent barely three months living at Reynolda after the family's move into the bungalow at the end of December; now he would live there just ten days more. He revised

View to Lake Katharine from the bungalow. Photo by Thomas Sears.

his will in that time to provide for construction of two new hospital buildings on the grounds of Winston-Salem Hospital, one for white and one for "colored" patients, each to receive the sum of $120,000 to cover costs. Neal Anderson had used the present tense in his piece about R. J. Reynolds. He would now simply append a note: "Mr. Reynolds died at his home at Reynolda, North Carolina, July 29, 1918."[107] Katharine's heart might be broken, but she must have felt a measure of relief and gratitude that they had been able to come back home to say their last good-bye.

FIVE

Changing Seasons, A Vision Renewed

FEW AMONG THE HUNDREDS OF MEN AND WOMEN around the country and in distant parts of the world who sent expressions of sympathy to the widow of R. J. Reynolds in the weeks and months following his death could have grasped the full dimensions of the loss for Katharine. With apprehension about the future on her mind, she bore the dead weight of grief on her heart. Most no doubt assumed that she had always known she was likely to outlive a husband thirty years her senior, and that his long illness had provided plenty of time in which to anticipate her financial needs and those of the children after his death. Those close to the couple knew what a good marriage it had been; these two clever, attractive, and ambitious people had remained passionately devoted to each other, grateful for their own happiness and for the extraordinary prosperity that had graced the thirteen years of their life together. While it was natural for Katharine to mourn for a time, she was expected to take comfort in her faith, in happy memories of her husband and the life they had shared, and in the four children for whose sake she must now carry on alone. Neal Anderson's note of condolence tried to reassure her that although the days she was living through right now would be the saddest of all, "you have had so many tokens of God's love and goodness you can lean hard on him when you need him most."[1] Moreover, because Katharine epitomized within her own society the still novel notion of the "New Woman," she was presumed to be far better prepared for the adjustment to widowhood than a more traditional wife and mother.

"A time to mourn . . ."

What people failed to take into account was the extent to which her husband had made Katharine's life possible. It was not so much the indulgence that had allowed her to manage large sums of money and occupy herself in a host of projects and causes, but rather Dick's manifest pleasure and pride in whatever his wife did that had enabled her to move freely and act with authority. He had, in a real sense, bestowed power on her. Katharine's formal education may have instilled the values that helped decide what she wanted to accomplish in life, but it was Dick who taught her how the world of business and finance worked. She had started with native intelligence, curiosity, and unabashed awe of her husband's entrepreneurial genius. He became her tutor, helping her to achieve a sophisticated understanding of the business world, then encouraging her to become a player in her own right by investing and trading, planning and managing. Katharine Reynolds came to derive the same satisfaction from success in a business deal that her husband did.[2] With Dick gone, she had no illusions about the extent to which his brother Will and his other successors would involve her in the affairs of the industrial empire they now controlled.

For Katharine, therefore, the rituals of mourning represented more than a public expression of sorrow over the loss of a cherished husband and her children's loss of their father. Dressing only in black and absenting herself from most social activities for at least a year, as custom required, would also serve as a daily reminder that her former life—challenging, fulfilling, and suffused with love and enough shared happiness to sustain her through every crisis—had ended with Dick's death. She knew, of course, that she must go on, staying as busy as ever. The year ahead would place even more demands than usual on her time, since she needed to establish a suitable memorial to her husband's memory, travel to northern cities on business, and supervise her farming operations and the continuing development of the estate. But Reynolda was meant to be the joyous heart of a vibrant family and community life over which she and Dick would preside. What kind of a future could she possibly imagine having there now, beyond keeping herself busy? A letter written to a Philadelphia dressmaker eight days after her husband's death speaks with a voice that scarcely resembles Katharine's own:

> You have undoubtedly heard of my sad bereavement in the loss of my husband. I have not had time or heart to think of clothes before, but am coming to the realization that I must have something, consequently, I am going to ask you to make for me right away two simple, neat dresses, both of light weight material suitable for our warm climate—one to use especially for morning or street wear, and one a little more dressy, for afternoon and house wear. You understand, of course, that I wish both of these in dull black.
>
> I also want you to select for me the proper light weight hat and veil. I will not set any price on these, but will only say that I desire good quality, but nothing about them to cause an unusual amount of expense.[3]

What is familiar in this communication is Katharine's insistence on simplicity, practicality, and reasonable cost—as if she were placing an order with a company supplying some item for the house. What is new is the tone of leaden indifference to the style of the garments she would be wearing for an extended period of time. She had apparently decided not to bother waiting to see fabric swatches or sketches. Her tone suggests that, at least for the present, she had no interest in a form of self-expression that had always meant a great deal to her. Katharine loved fine clothes and had always made a point of dressing with considerable flair as well as impeccable taste. Though understandable under the circumstances, this subtle but poignant erosion of her vitality to the point where she appears to be "not herself" deserves the attention for which Virginia Woolf would argue eloquently in the following decade. In *A Room of One's Own*, Woolf insists that "the values of women differ very often from the values which have been made by the other sex . . . yet it is the masculine values that prevail." She writes: "Speaking crudely, football and sport are 'important'; the worship of fashion, the buying of clothes 'trivial.' . . . This is an important book, the critic assumes, because it deals with war. This is an insignificant book because it deals with the feelings of women in a drawing room. A scene in a battlefield is more important than a scene in a shop."[4] Woolf believed, and demonstrated in her own work, that the minutiae of a woman's life, including her "relationship to the everchanging and turning world of gloves and shoes and stuffs,"[5] may possess an expressive value and meaning equivalent in significance to the larger subjects that dominate narratives about men's lives.

Had the course of the fateful year following her husband's death been sufficiently uneventful to allow Katharine Reynolds the quiet time she needed for rest, reflection, and healing, her story and the story of Reynolda might have turned out differently. As fate would have it, however, events conspired to hold her in the grip of old and new fears in spite of her strenuous efforts to seek distraction in productive and important work. Having given Charles Barton Keen the task of designing an appropriate building for her new school,[6] she decided that in order not to delay the beginning of the 1918 fall term, she would install classrooms in another cottage that would be finished in time. This "very convenient and attractive" addition to Reynolda village was the work of an English architect, C. Gilbert

Humphreys, whom Katharine may have discovered when he was awarded the commission for a major office building in downtown Winston-Salem—an automobile dealership and parking garage, touted as being "the most modern in the South," completed the following year.[7] On the tenth of September she wrote both to Humphreys, saying how "very much pleased" she was with his design of the cottage, and to her principal, Minnie Morrison, whom she advised about the school's temporary location and urged to come to Reynolda as soon as possible. Her note to Miss Morrison was a masterpiece of subtle command: "I think it would be wise for you to come over just as soon as it now suits you so that you can get your own house in good order" (a cottage had become available in which Miss Morrison and another of the arriving teachers might be comfortable accommodated). "You understand there is no particular hurry, just so everything is ready by the first of October." Katharine added that her children were looking forward to the start of school "as if it were going to be a picnic," and seemed no less excited herself as she supervised the purchase of desks, books, and supplies and solicited additional students for the upcoming term.[8]

What would come to be called the Great War continued to slow the pace of both building construction and implementation of the landscape plans that Thomas Sears had developed in 1917, although news from the front improved after the arrival of American troops in Europe late in the spring of 1918. They had helped to turn back and counter a massive German offensive in Flanders, so that by July a turning point had been reached, although engagements resulting in horrific losses on both sides would continue throughout the month of October until the November armistice. Henrietta van den Berg, the family's indispensable nurse and caregiver, who had postponed her departure for army service in the months before and after Dick's death out of consideration for Katharine and the children, finally did leave in the fall, at about the time the new school opened—anticipating, no doubt, that Katharine would be able to manage without a trained nurse in residence.[9] Dick Jr., now twelve, would be attending a private boarding school in another state, while Mary, Nancy, and Smith joined children from the village and the town in the three primary grades being instituted at the Reynolda School.

In the first week or so of the new term, Nancy came down with an illness serious enough to prompt Katharine to obtain the services of the same Baltimore nurse she had retained to care for her husband in the months before his death—Miss Jessie Hill, whom Katharine had come to consider a dear friend.[10] Miss Hill herself became ill within days of her arrival, and died at Reynolda before the month was out,[11] a chilling introduction for the family to the epidemic of Spanish influenza. It seemed to have struck without warning. By November, less than four months after Dick's death, there were enough active cases in Winston-Salem to prompt many townspeople to seek refuge in other parts of the country.[12] Katharine apparently hoped to take the children to Florida as soon as possible, but illness or other problems intervened until late in December. They would spend the Christmas holidays—their first without their father—at Pinehurst, and then go on to Jacksonville early in the new year, stopping on the way in Savannah for a visit with Neal Anderson, who had moved there a year earlier to serve as pastor of the historic Independent Presbyterian Church.[13] Katharine was "really ill" during her stay in Jacksonville, probably from the flu.[14] We know that Anderson contracted the disease early in February, and that Savannah was by that time under a "flu ban," which prohibited all church services.[15]

It must have seemed impossible to escape the risk of contagion, and indeed it was. The flu pandemic of 1918 caused more deaths than any other disease in human history—at least 50 million worldwide, possibly even twice that number—more than the Black Death, more in twenty-four weeks than the AIDS epidemic would take in as many years. One out of four Americans contracted the disease, and 675,000 died; average life expectancy in the United States dropped by 10 percent in a single year. Symptoms could range from relatively mild to severe, but in the worst cases—up to one in five—victims endured indescribably painful physical suffering.[16] The cause was unknown and there were no vaccines, not even an effective medication. Doctors were helpless, and the public lived in constant fear, afraid of a handshake as much as an embrace, a loved one as much as a stranger. Having survived epidemics of malaria and typhoid, Katharine Reynolds had come to place her trust in the modern scientific understanding of germs and infection, and had pursued almost obsessively the pure water, clean air, wholesome food, and sanitary practices that promised protection from such diseases. Reynolda was supposed to set an example of how effective such strategies could be. Now she had to accept the reality of a mysterious killer—for which there was no explanation, no control, and no effective treatment—that had swept over the entire nation and the world beyond, suddenly and with ferocious force. No one old enough during the flu years to understand what was happening would emerge unscathed by the experience, and Katharine, still trying to cope with the aftershocks of her husband's undiagnosed illness and death, could not possibly have escaped being changed by the scale of the dangers endured.

"A time to heal . . . and a time to build up"

Although she had begun the new year in a state of physical and emotional exhaustion, as the crisis in her health passed and she began to feel stronger, Katharine was able at least to savor the relief of having once again survived, having been spared to live out what she now knew, more profoundly, to be a future beyond her control. Never a person inclined to self-pity—quite the opposite—she realized that she must bring all the strength and spirit she could muster to the task of finding her way out of the morass into which grief and illness had plunged her. Fear must finally yield to a resurgence of the confidence and common sense that were so much a part of her nature. Well-wishers were right: she was a woman of means, still young, her children needed her, and there was plenty of rewarding work to be done. If her future was not to be as she had imagined it, she would do her best to find fulfillment in the gift of each precious day. In the aftermath of war and plague, the whole country was ready to live in the spirit of *carpe diem.*

It helped that she had come home to Reynolda in spring, with Thomas Sears back at work after a long hiatus,[17] Robert Conrad returning from the war, and the new gardens bursting into life. In addition to supervising the continued development of the formal gardens, Sears would produce at least a dozen new plans in 1919 and almost twice that number the following year, a good indication of Katharine's commitment to achieving the fullest possible realization of her original landscape vision. Perhaps nothing illustrates that intention better than the evidence that Sears was expected to approach the planting plan for individual cottages, such as those designated for the chauffeur, the poultryman, and the electrician, as if each was an important residential commission. No expense was spared to provide each yard with handsome trees and shrubs and interesting compositions of flowering plants, woody and herbaceous, in styles ranging from informal open lawns and borders to quite formal enclosed gardens.

A cottage near the blacksmith's shop, for example, was set within a spacious grove of more than forty trees, including large-canopied species, fruit trees, and smaller ornamental types, with shrubs, perennials, and flowering vines used as foundation plantings and massed in beds.[18] He used a completely different approach in the landscape of the teachers' cottage, which was to be framed within a geometric arrangement of walks and planted beds. At the rear of the house, a flight of stairs ascended to a spacious quadripartite vegetable garden defined by gravel paths and enclosed on all four sides by a "cut-flower border" and an outer hedge. The central path terminated in a covered exedra with a shaded seat from which to enjoy the view looking back over the garden toward the cottage—a charming echo of a similar feature Sears would use in the "Cut Flower and Nicer Vegetable Garden" planned for the greenhouse complex, for which he submitted a preliminary study in February 1919.[19]

It helped Katharine, too, that so many people, fully aware that she was in mourning, still did not hesitate to request her participation in one or another worthwhile cause. A letter that reached her at Pinehurst in December had urged her participation in a suffrage conference to be sponsored by the Raleigh Women's Club early in January, promising that she would get "suffrage inspiration" and declaring, "We would love to have you with us." She also agreed to serve that spring on a standing committee of the first Women's Club of Winston-Salem, which was to be affiliated with both the state and national federations. The new club "immediately entered upon its policy of promotion of matters of community interest" by communicating "a strong resolution of protest" against the site selected for the city's union passenger station.[20] The Woman's National Farm and Garden Association had asked her to serve as its delegate to the Southern Congress for a League of Nations, meeting in Atlanta at the end of February, and to consider writing an account of her dairying operation for the benefit of its membership.[21] In March, Governor Thomas W. Bickett of North Carolina appointed her to a committee charged with soliciting funds for and erecting a building to serve as a memorial to those who served in the recent war.[22]

In addition to her involvement with planning for the two hospital buildings her husband's will had funded, Katharine was exploring the possibility of establishing a larger elementary school at Reynolda, since the first year's enrollment had exceeded her expectations.[23] This was one of several projects, including her recent election to the board of directors of the Alumnae and Former Students Association of the North Carolina College for Women (formerly the State Normal School), that reflected a rekindling of her passionate dedication to the cause of improving education in

North Carolina.[24] For that reason, she was also pleased to respond favorably to an appeal for help from the superintendent of the Winston-Salem public schools, whose "great problem" was to find a site outside the city center for a new high school being planned to accommodate more than a thousand students.[25] Katharine immediately offered to pay for whatever site was selected, and to fund as well the design and construction of a large auditorium for the school as a memorial to her late husband.[26] Once her offer was accepted, Charles Barton Keen was given the commission to design the whole building.[27]

She was particularly excited, however, by the potential of her own school, now renamed the Richard J. Reynolds Memorial School for Boys and Girls, to become a state-of-the-art educational facility. After closing for a brief period of time during the flu scare of the preceding fall, the school completed a successful first year, climaxed in June by the students' presentation of a pageant staged before a large audience in the Reynolda church amphitheater.[28] One of the first things Katharine had done early in the year was to write the federal Bureau of Education in Washington, D.C., for advice in planning the new school building. The agent who replied advised her to hire an architect (which she certainly intended to do), while expressing admiration for a letter so "unusually explicit and full of helpful data."[29] She did not stop there, of course, but continued her research as part of a dialogue with Charles Barton Keen about the innovations she hoped to incorporate in the new facility. Early in March an article had appeared in the local newspaper describing her intention to expand the school, moving it into a building and an outdoor environment designed in accordance with the most progressive scientific, educational, and architectural theories of the day. Programs would now include opportunities for vocational training as well as academic subjects and physical education. "I want to erect a monument to Mr. Reynolds," Katharine had told the reporter, "other than in stained glass or stone. While he lived the welfare of his employees and his fellow men and women . . . was one of the things nearest his heart. So I shall build this school [offering both grammar and high school programs, liberal arts and industrial education] to train boys and girls into the men and women who will help make this country not only great but homelike, moral, and enduring."[30] Here was a project even more challenging, perhaps, than building a model farming estate and community. Less than a year after Dick's death, Katharine had recovered enthusiasm and renewed purpose, her earlier vision greatly expanded. Through the establishment of a much larger progressive educational institution on the grounds of the estate, generations of graduates might be prepared to go forth, like so many missionaries, to make the nation and the world more "homelike," in the spirit of Reynolda's community.

The account of this proposed development published in the Winston-Salem newspaper represented another instance of Katharine's providing carefully structured information to reporters in order to explain her educational agenda and attract support for ideas and values to which she was committed. The strategy worked. The superintendent of schools wrote to say how glad he was to learn that she was developing "a school plan which will be a model for [other] schools to work towards. It will encourage us in the city to plan along similar lines. . . . I would appreciate an opportunity, at such time as is convenient to you, to look over the [plan] so that when the time comes we may incorporate in our own building plans and course of study the ideas which you are working out at Reynolda."[31]

The wellspring of her new vision was Fletcher B. Dresslar (1858–1930), a professor of school hygiene and architecture at the George Peabody College for Teachers in Nashville, Tennessee, author of influential government publications on rural school design, and the same special agent of the Bureau of Education who had responded so favorably to Katharine's recent query.[32] One can understand the appeal of Dresslar's work for her, since he pointed to essential connections between good pedagogy and environmental factors such as lighting, air circulation, and sanitation, stressing the relevance of modern architecture and engineering to life experience and educational goals from an aesthetic as well as a practical perspective. The aesthetic values he favored were Katharine's own, aimed at the creation of well-equipped, smoothly functioning, cheerful, and health-promoting buildings and playgrounds. She hoped to have him come to Winston-Salem for a visit and consultation, and apparently succeeded in doing so.[33]

If the existing school, as much as the rest of her estate, was to become a regional model for progressive theory and practice, the quality of its programs would be just as important as its physical facilities. Katharine decided that she needed to think not just about adding teachers but about finding a new director for the school, ideally someone already aware of the nascent movement with which Dresslar was associated and eager to explore the full potential of the educational resources that Katharine was bringing together. She may very well have asked her friend William Martin, president of Davidson College, for a recommendation. In any event, she filled the position in time to publish an announcement late in July that the fall term of the Richard J. Reynolds Memorial School would begin at the end of September 1919; parents wishing to enroll their children were "requested to communicate with J. Edward Johnston, Superintendent, by letter . . . for information regarding tuition and transportation."[34]

The new superintendent was Lieutenant Edward Johnston, a 1914 graduate of Davidson recently returned from two years of service overseas with the army's Fifth Field Artillery Battalion, First Division. He was twenty-five years old, a South Carolinian by birth, suave, intelligent, well spoken, and strikingly handsome. If Katharine needed further proof that the course of human lives—or, if she preferred, divine providence—moved in sudden and mysterious ways, Ed Johnston provided it on the day, fortuitously close to the one-year anniversary of her husband's death, when he arrived at Reynolda, still in uniform, for an interview.[35] Her first emotion was bound to be relief at finding a

J. Edward Johnston, 1921.

candidate who appeared so well suited to the position she was offering. He was young, but his education and war experience had obviously had a maturing effect. He had excellent teaching credentials, having served for two years as a high school principal in Washington, North Carolina, and the following year, before entering the service, as principal of the graded schools in Davidson.[36] Once she got to know him better, Katharine discovered his gift for the same kind of good conversation and exchange of ideas that had been such an important part of her life with Dick. She admired and liked this man, and no aspect of her widowhood was likely to have been more difficult for her to bear than her loneliness.

"To laugh . . . to dance . . . to embrace"

By the end of August she was able to announce the completion of Charles Barton Keen's plans for the new school building, which was to be sited "on a beautiful knoll just back of the Reynolda Presbyterian Church" and expressly designed in accordance with the environmental theories of Dr. Dresslar: "The problem of heating, lighting, and ventilation has been given particular attention and a distinct effort has been made to create an artistic whole to surround the child with beautiful architecture, equipment, and landscape. The latter will be carried out under the direction of Mr. Thomas W. Sears."[37] Katharine was able to claim as well a "splendidly trained faculty," since she had sent Ed Johnston and two of her women teachers to take summer school courses at Columbia Teachers' College in New York City.[38]

One of the women, Lucy Hadley Cash, later recalled that Katharine had come to New York on business during their time there, staying as usual at the Plaza, and had invited the three teachers to dinner on her first night in town, then to the theater on the following night. Mrs. Cash remembered what a good dancer Ed Johnston had shown himself to be when, at Katharine's request, he had escorted his fellow teachers to a hotel for dinner and dancing before joining Mrs. Reynolds at the theater.[39] Dancing had become something of a rage all over the country. Katharine, of course, had gone out very little and done almost no entertaining during her first year of mourning, so the chance to interact with these young people coincided with the beginning of a welcome relaxation of the strictures associated with her bereavement. When the newly enlarged staff of single women teachers gathered at Reynolda in preparation for the start of the fall term, she arranged for them to stay at a small hotel in town until housing on the estate was ready for them.[40] The younger ladies often invited eligible bachelors for an evening of dancing to the music of records played on a Victrola (the jazz tune "Wang Wang Blues" was a favorite[41]).

Katharine had already had her hair bobbed and raised her hemlines, although those "dull black" dresses of her first year of mourning may have been longer than was now the style. Townspeople could not have failed to notice, however, that over the course of the next several months the widow "abandoned the

Katharine Smith Johnston, c. 1921.

veil" and changed from black to lavender, then to blue, with each new dress or suit fashioned, as before her husband's death, to flatter her appearance.[42] At the end of this process, a society columnist for a Philadelphia newspaper would observe that Mrs. Reynolds, newly appointed by President Wilson as the only woman serving on the 1921 Annual Assay Commission, had made a stunning debut at the first meeting she attended: "When seen at the mint yesterday noon, between sessions, Mrs. Reynolds wore a smartly tailored suit of Joffre blue. The hat was of the same soft blue material and tilted at a piquant angle most becoming to the fair Carolinian."[43]

In the spring of 1920, Katharine endowed the first chair in biology at Davidson College in her husband's memory.[44] She also sponsored a research trip of several weeks' duration for a party of six, the purpose of which was to study high school facilities in at least seven northern cities in the East and Midwest, as preparation for the development of a design program for the new secondary school in Winston-Salem. Besides herself, the group included Ed Johnston and Ethel Brock of the Reynolda School; Charles Barton Keen; R. H. Latham, superintendent of the Winston-Salem school system; and W. L. Engelhart, a member of the faculty of Columbia University.[45] The trip had to have been gratifying for Katharine, an endorsement of her own credentials as an educator and hence the symbolic fulfillment of her long-ago promise to the Normal School. It also appears to have contributed to a major change of plans, however, since as soon as the school year ended in June, Ed Johnston resigned his position as superintendent.

A strain in the relationship between Katharine and her employee had come about not through any falling out, however, but because they could no longer conceal their growing attraction to each other. Her husband had been dead less than two years, and she had already developed a romantic relationship with a man thirteen years younger than she. She found herself in the proverbially inappropriate situation of the rich widow being courted by a relatively impecunious but charming younger man. If either or both of them suffered embarrassment—he for fear of being cast as a predatory fortune-seeker, she for appearing scandalously naïve and foolish—they did not allow gossips the satisfaction of knowing that they did.

Katharine had never permitted herself to be reckless. She had since childhood been mature beyond her years—serious, responsible, achievement-oriented. Eventually, adolescent curiosity and a sharp intelligence had opened her mind to modernity, to a fascination with new ideas, new science, new fashions. Now the postwar decade—the "Roaring Twenties"—introduced the same modernity into previously sacrosanct social and cultural spheres. The Nineteenth Amendment to the Constitution, giving American women the right to vote, won ratification by the states in August 1920, and in 1921 the notion of family planning gained respectability among middle-class women when Margaret Sanger founded the American Birth Control League. Katharine Reynolds did not need the popular film series *Perils of Pauline* to inspire her to challenge social expectations of what a woman could do; she was already accustomed to moving gracefully within traditionally male spheres of action, and took pride in her autonomy and competence.

In other ways, however, her pride made her vulnerable. She would be forty in November, at a time when fashion and the media were exalting youth and the slender, short-skirted, flat-chested "flapper" as the feminine ideal. Changes in sexual mores placed a new emphasis on romantic love and self-fulfillment rather than self-sacrifice in marriage. Katharine, the long ago "Ruler of Hearts," now had to face the fact that she had been swept off her feet by a man as handsome as the new screen idol Rudolph Valentino, but also tender, wise, witty, elegantly sophisticated—and still in his twenties. Ed Johnston seemed to be in every way an answer to the question of what her future was to be, for she could imagine it now as full of love and excitement. She had only to throw caution to the winds and surrender—and she did. Sensitive to the potential for embarrassment she might face because of their relationship, he had offered to resign and go away as early as November of his first term at the school. "If you had left me [then]," she later assured him, "I do not doubt in the least that I would be wearing black today. What could I have cared for colors or brightness in my life when my life was gone? Edward mine, it was you who brought happiness to me when I'd never thought to have it again."[46]

Once he did resign seven months later, Katharine and he waited a respectable year, doing their best to convey to the world at large an impression of preoccupation with other concerns. She had been immersed for a long time in business transactions aimed at increasing her holdings and potential influence in the R. J. Reynolds Tobacco Company and solidifying other financial resources, several involving court settlements. Her expectation that her late husband's family and other interested parties would disapprove of her marriage to Ed for any number of reasons, ranging from the question of propriety to the prospect of his (or an heir's) claims on the corporation, helped to focus her mind on finding ways to increase her own leverage. Since the firm had always been a "family" business, she sought the advantage of having her future husband become part of the company, and succeeded in persuading Will Reynolds and his associates to offer Ed a job. Shortly after he had begun his employment that fall in the Wilson, North Carolina, offices of Reynolds Tobacco, he was hospitalized for more than two weeks following emergency abdominal surgery. During that time Katharine made at least two trips to see him, confirming the growing suspicion of family members and friends that she was romantically involved with the former school superintendent. He wrote her from the hospital almost daily, thanking her for the gift of "a huge block of 'A' stock" as well as food sent from the farm, and expressing his distress that she was "coming in for so much criticism" on his account. On his release from the hospital, Ed went home to Davidson to recuperate and to give Katharine time in which to share news of their intention to wed with those closest to her, at her own discretion.[47]

She was able, now that Bum had returned from military service, to spend longer periods away from home on business, traveling between New York, Washington, and Baltimore. Since Dick was attending the Tome School for Boys in Maryland, she took advantage of opportunities to visit with him when she was staying nearby. "He seems improved in every way," she confided to Ed, noting how strange it seemed that her son was now "old enough to be traveling around by himself."[48] Mary, Nancy, and Smith were still students in the Reynolda School, its original name having been restored in the 1920–21 school year after the city fathers decided to name the high school then under construction in honor of their father. To the distractions afforded by business and travel, Katharine also added more frequent entertaining, from small dinners to quite ambitious gatherings. Even when she had to be away from home for weeks at a time during the early months of the new year, her sister Maxie and her husband, her sister Irene, a few of the teachers, or close friends of the family often "came to supper," as twelve-year-old Mary regularly recorded in her diary. In January Katharine hosted a large gathering at Reynolda of alumnae and faculty (including several of her former teachers) of the North Carolina College for Women.[49] She was also bringing to completion a few small construction projects on the estate, writing Ed that "our buildings are all about finished now. . . . I hope to have everything entirely finished and in beautiful shape by the middle of April."[50]

She was particularly apprehensive about telling her parents that she had decided to marry Ed Johnston, and postponed the conversation on several occasions because she thought the moment might not be right. When severe weather forced cancellation of a planned trip to Mount Airy at the end of January, she decided simply to write them the news, then shared her relief with Ed: "I told them how I'd worked and planned for the happiness of others, but now I was working and planning day and night for my own—of how I loved you. I told them all about you, giving something of a historical sketch. Then I told them what a wonderful and splendid man you were. I told them I didn't ask them to love you because I did—I only asked them to trust my judgment in this matter—when they finally knew you they would love you for your own sake. Finally, I asked for their blessing for me and for you whenever you should write."[51]

Given the emotional and physical strain of these months, it is not surprising that Katharine became ill toward the end of a February trip to Philadelphia that included participation in the three-day meeting of the Assay Commission. She went to Atlantic City for a brief recuperation before returning to Reynolda on March 7, only to leave again for New York three days later. The three youngest children joined her and Bum there for a fast-paced holiday that included, Mary duly noted, "fittings"—undoubtedly related, although the girls did not know it, to a wedding for which their mother was preparing.

"Hiawatha, An Indian Passion Play," performed on the shore of Lake Katharine, May 25, 1921.

They did anticipate the excitement of attending the wedding in Raleigh of their uncle Gene, Katharine's brother, just a few days after their return to Reynolda, and rehearsals for another end-of-the-school-year pageant, this time "Hiawatha," based on

The playhouse, 2001.
Photo by Carol Betsch.

Longfellow's poem but probably chosen because Smith and Mary had tried to write an "Indian play" of their own in January.[52] This lavish production was to be staged not in the church amphitheater but on the shores of Lake Katharine, below the grass amphitheater of the north lawn. As if that were not thrilling enough, construction was almost complete on the girls' playhouse, tucked away in a spot overlooking the new fruit and vegetable garden, and modeled on a tiny cottage for children illustrated in a book by Gertrude Jekyll.[53] (The boys already had an old log cabin in the woods for their own use.) Best of all, however, was the Reynolds children's awareness of their mother's happiness, as if the sad memories of their father's dying, her mourning, and their own grieving were finally giving way to brighter days. Their brother Dick, now fifteen, may have observed the same change in his mother with more trepidation when he arrived home for spring break in March; Ed Johnston's mother arrived for a visit during the same period.

Earlier in the spring Thomas Sears had completed his design of the greenhouse garden complex by furnishing Katharine with the final version of his planting plan for the "Fruit, Cut Flower and Nicer Vegetable Garden."[54] He had outdone himself in elevating its utilitarian purposes in the noble tradition of the paradise garden—enclosed and geometrically ordered, yet intricately tapestried with fruits, vegetables, and flowers of endless variety. The annuals, perennials, and bulbs supplying cut flowers were not to be isolated but integrated in formal beds lining walks that defined larger rectangular beds of herbs, berries, and vegetables. Dwarf apple and pear trees, figs and espaliered varieties of apples, pears, plums, and grapes; tree peonies, climbing roses, and flowering vines provided vertical structuring at different heights. This delightful garden would have the same combination of serenity and sensuous beauty as the pleasure garden that it complemented; the elevated tea houses separating the two spaces reinforced that equality of importance. Katharine's formal gardens were finally ready to receive all the company she was expecting.

On the very day late in May on which "Hiawatha" was to be performed, she returned from a two-week stay in Kentucky, where she and Bum had been guests at the home of R. S. Reynolds, a nephew of Dick's who in his early manhood had been like a son to him.[55] It was almost as if she had gone into hiding among family members she could count on to understand her situation and to shelter her from the stress of the otherwise altogether wonderful event she was about to experience. Mary would note in a diary entry for June 7, 1921, "Mother told us she was going to marry Mr. Johnston." On the following day, Katharine hosted a recital and "informal reception" for five hundred guests at Reynolda; the young American tenor Mario Chamlee was the featured soloist. A columnist for the local paper described the evening's festive atmosphere: "The affair had been planned for a garden party, but showers caused it to be staged indoors and the home rang with music, then mirth and merriment from one end to the other."[56] There was not so much as a hint in the article that Mrs. Reynolds planned to marry J. Edward Johnston three days later, in the same reception hall of her home.

A brief account of that surprising event appeared in newspapers, but Mary's diary captured best the difference between the grand party that had been held a few days earlier and the intimate ceremony witnessed by a small gathering of friends and family: "At about 7:15 Mother was married to Mr. Johnston. The affair was very quiet. Smith was ring bearer and Nancy and myself were flower girls."[57] The couple set out the next morning on a two-month-long European honeymoon, keeping in close touch with family and friends back home as they made their way through London, Paris, and spectacular countryside in between, including visits to the battlefields in the Argonne where Ed had seen action during the war.[58] Their correspondence suggests how much they savored the small perfections of each day as well as many memorable experiences of art, architecture, and landscape. Ed wrote Mary after an excursion from London to Oxford that Katharine and he had spent the afternoon exploring the university, finding the grounds and gardens beautiful. "Brought back some flowers and the feather of a swan. Mother joins in sending lots of love."[59] (Katharine was collecting and pressing flowers encountered in their travels for Mary: "Have quite a little collection of flowers and leaves for you."[60]) When the newlyweds returned to New York aboard the *Olympic*, nine-year-old Smith was at the dock with Ed's mother and a nanny to greet them; the older children were still at summer camps—Mary and Nancy in the Pocono mountains of Pennsylvania, Dick at Greenbrier in West Virginia. Katharine and Ed stopped for visits during the

Mary and Nancy Reynolds, flower girls at their mother's wedding, June 1921.

automobile trip that brought them home to Reynolda by the middle of August.

Once back home, their mutual happiness was apparent to all; one of Katharine's household staff would remember them as "two lovebirds . . . hugging and kissing all the time."[61] An almost constant round of parties in their honor continued for many weeks, as well as two more weddings, days apart, within Katharine's Mount Airy family—her sister Ruth's and her brother Matt's. It is hard to imagine how she found time during that busy late summer and fall to draw breath, much less to manage the operations of her estate and the manifold obligations of her civic activities as she had in the past.

"A time to keep . . . and to cast away"

Adding to these pressures during the time that Katharine, Ed, and the children were beginning their life as a family was a set of circumstances occasioned by the marriage that required important decisions to be made and acted upon without delay. Since his brief experience in the Wilson office had convinced Ed that he was unlikely ever to feel welcome within the corporate offices of Reynolds Tobacco, he had chosen instead to pursue a career in banking and investment management. In doing so, he hoped to make himself useful and knowledgeable in matters of great importance to Katharine, while proving to the world at large—and in particular the relatives and associates of her late husband—that he could earn professional success by his own wits and hard work.

That work started little more than a month after the Johnstons returned from their honeymoon, when Ed, encouraged by the offer of a position with Wachovia Bank of Winston-Salem on condition that he obtain additional schooling, enrolled in a training program being offered by Morgan Guaranty Trust Company of New York City. He took up residence there early in September, writing home to Katharine on the evening of his first day at Morgan to say how much he had enjoyed both the orientation—"I think I am going to like my new work very much"—and her amusing letter describing the "ill concealed joy and relief" exhibited by an executive of the R. J. Reynolds Tobacco Company on hearing the news that Ed was leaving the firm.[62] Yet no matter how reassuring Ed's confidence that he was now embarked on a satisfying career, Katharine knew that the months of his internship were going to be challenging at best.

She had now to divide her life between two homes. Although she had been forced to delay for two tumultuous years breaking ground for the state-of-the-art facility that would allow Reynolda School to expand its programs and enrollment, the existing elementary school was flourishing in well-equipped "temporary quarters," using the grounds for all sorts of learning and recreational activities.[63] The primary grades, under the supervision of Miss Morrison, were accommodated in one of the cottages, the upper grades in a spacious building at the entrance to the village which had been designed and adapted to its current use by Charles Barton Keen and would eventually house administrative offices for the estate. The new superintendent, E. M. Campbell, was working out well, an innovative curriculum was in place—such courses as weaving and folk dancing were "unheard of" in the public schools at that time—and the county contributed a modest amount of supplemental funding based on the number of local children in attendance.[64] Katharine had decided in January to use the handsomely furnished manse, newly completed after the setback of a fire during construction, as a house for her women teachers, so that they were now full-time residents of the community.[65] Reynolda was by this time as much a campus as a home, farm, and community. Only her conviction that the family needed to be together could have persuaded Katharine to disturb her children's contentment within that familiar world.

Once Ed had found suitable temporary housing for them in New York—a suite of rooms in the 14 East Sixtieth Street Hotel, "quiet, convenient, near the park and very nice"[66]—the three youngest children joined them in the city, while the search began for schools to which they might transfer later in the year. Katharine need not have worried about her children's resilience to so much change in their lives. Nancy would remember their time in the crowded suite as a delightful adventure: "Ed and Mother had a bedroom on one side of the living room . . . and on the other side there were two bedrooms, where we had my sister and me and Bum all in one room, and Lizzie [a nursemaid] and Smith in the other room. And we had turtles . . . canaries . . . love-birds [and] a monkey." Their youthful stepfather was a loving, willing companion in high jinks and play of every sort, even to allowing basketball in the living room: "One night the basketball went out the window into the back alley, and my stepfather had to go down and get it out of there. We were holding lamps out the window ten floors above so he could see us."[67] On one of several occasions when Katharine had to be away attending to affairs at Reynolda, Ed reported faithfully on the children's activities—Smith's ball game, Mary's tennis—then added, "Mary says be sure and not forget the sausage. Katharine, sweetheart, do hurry and finish your work and come on back here, first stopping by Baltimore, though, to see that doctor."[68]

The visit to her doctor in Baltimore probably intensified Katharine's sense of urgency in working out their new living arrangements, since traveling back and forth between their two homes was soon to become more difficult for her. She was expecting a child, in spite of her doctors' admonitions not to attempt another pregnancy. She was fully aware that it was not so much her age—Katharine's mother had been forty-three when Ruth was born—as the weakened condition of her heart that put her at risk. Nevertheless, in desperately wanting to give her new husband the gift of his own child, she had formed a dangerous resolution, forged from an amalgam of happiness, hope, and raw will that steeled Mrs. J. Edward Johnston against reasoned argument. There was probably another motivation as well, a fear of humiliation that had found a voice in innuendo scarcely concealed beneath gossipy chatter in a letter sent by a close friend while Katharine and Ed were still on their honeymoon: "A woman at the club here, the other day, asked me if it were true that you were *forty-eight* and Edward *twenty-two*! Well, I was able to answer her. But [with] another who told me she thought it was fine for you to marry the man who was at the head of the R. J. Reynolds Tobacco Co. and that you'd made over all your property to him, I took the position that she knew more than I did."[69]

At some point in the spring of 1922 the Johnstons took a suite at the Plaza Hotel, perhaps to provide more convenient and comfortable quarters for Katharine and to accommodate occasional guests; Mary and Nancy were allowed to bring two friends along when they returned to the city after a visit to Reynolda and their Mount Airy grandparents during spring break.[70] A few weeks later, on the first of May, Katharine gave birth prematurely to a daughter, given the name Lola for Ed's mother before the infant died the following day.

It was a painful loss, another death to be accepted in the spirit of "God's will is not our own." Katharine left New York toward the end of the month with Ed and Bum (who had attended her during delivery) for a recuperative three-week stay at the Marlborough Blenheim in Atlantic City. The children returned to Reynolda, where they would soon be joined by their brother Dick, who had written his mother from school to say how much he was looking forward to spending the summer at home.[71] Katharine arrived back just in time for the happy distraction of a house filled with teenagers, a "house party" reunion of Mary and Nancy's Camp Tegawitha friends before the start of another camping season in mid-July. The entertainments at Reynolda included an evening garden reception, illuminated by Japanese lanterns, for more than a hundred young people.[72]

A year earlier, Thomas Sears had done a plan for a woodland walk, extending beyond the fruit and vegetable garden, that came to be called the "cedar walk" for the eastern red cedars (*Juniperus virginiana*) lining the path on both sides.[73] These fast-growing native trees promised to achieve an effect of stately green enclosure more rapidly than the allée of Japanese cryptomerias bordering the central lawn of the flower gardens. Like that feature, the cedar walk was almost certainly inspired by photographs published in *Country Life* and elsewhere of the famous avenue of 15,000 cryptomerias leading to the seventeenth-century shrine of the founder of the Tokugawa shogunate at Nikko, Japan, and hence reflects Katharine's continuing fondness for allusions to eastern landscape traditions. Before the summer was out, Sears would submit a plan for compositions of spring bulbs to be planted along the borders of the walk.[74]

For now, on this June evening when she found herself surrounded by the unfolding loveliness of her gardens and the gaiety of the gathering, and no doubt pleased to see how gracefully fifteen-year-old Mary performed as hostess, Katharine would of course take heart. No less than her son Dick, she looked forward hopefully to this summer at home. In just a few weeks, the local paper published the announcement of J. Edward Johnston's appointment as an assistant trust officer at Wachovia specializing in corporate trusts and taxes.[75]

R. J. Reynolds had been a man obsessively preoccupied throughout his life with the business of building a financial empire, and Katharine had contributed to their marriage by understanding and sharing his passion. Instead of narrowing her own opportunities, that investment in her husband's affairs had made possible the pursuit of her own vision, a rich and challenging career of her own. She knew very well that in marrying her, Ed had made his own pursuit of a rewarding occupation more problematic; for one thing, whatever he earned was unlikely to make a significant difference in their fortunes. But Katharine had coped with illness and death, and Ed had lived through the terrors of warfare. Basking in the sweetness of the life they had found with each other, neither was inclined to fret about the future. Rather, they were determined to make each single day, each single trip or party as perfect as it could be. "Doing my best," as Katharine had once explained to Burn in her own defense, now included taking more time to savor small pleasures.

Even the children, privileged in so many ways, had by this time absorbed the chastening lessons of mortality and fate. Each of them was aware that no matter how vibrant and confident a person their mother appeared to be, she was never out of danger from a possibly fatal heart attack. Searching for words to describe how she and her siblings responded to this reality, Nancy would later observe: "We didn't feel that she was securely in life . . . that she was healthy."[76] They had already shared at close hand the experience of their father's illness and death, the death of the nurse who had come to care for Nancy, and the recent loss of the baby their mother had been carrying. Then, less than a month after the garden party honoring the girls' camping friends, the family had to deal with another, more shocking death of a loved one. The children's thirteen-year-old cousin Jimmie Dunn, Maxie's son and a special chum of Smith's, died suddenly from an acute infection while attending camp in West Virginia.[77] The early promise of that summer of 1922 suddenly gave way before a terrible grief.

The boys spent most of the summer at home, although Dick accompanied his mother and stepfather on an August motor trip to New York and Pennsylvania that included stopping to see Mary and Nancy at Camp Tegawitha. Mary was to attend Miss Mason's School in Tarrytown, New York, that fall while Nancy finished elementary school at Reynolda and Smith attended West End School in Winston-Salem. The reassuring order of familiar routines on the estate provided Katharine with a welcome change of pace after months of hotel living, and allowed her to extend comfort and help to her sister and brother-in-law, devastated by the death of their only child. Ed's mother, who had been living in Statesville, North Carolina, now joined the family circle on a more permanent basis, as work began on a house for her on the estate. By fall, Katharine was once again involved in a whirlwind schedule of social events, including a dinner honoring Mrs. George Vanderbilt of Biltmore and her daughter Cornelia, guests at Reynolda in September.[78] She also managed to squeeze in back-to-back trips to New York in November that combined business, shopping, and—on the second trip, when Ed accompanied her—visiting Mary at her new school.

Katharine had just turned forty-two. Looking back over a year shadowed by two deaths, she would want the upcoming holiday season to be especially happy and restorative, confirming bonds of affection within the family and Ed's belonging there as husband and father, loving and loved. Nothing else, not even the evidence that the estate was now operating at a significant financial loss, disturbed her equanimity as it might have done in years past. Living with a man so much younger than she, and so different from her first husband, had to affect the way Katharine dealt with any number of issues. Besides caring less about business success than Dick had, Ed is unlikely to have fully grasped, in the relatively brief time that Katharine and he had been together, the extent to which she identified Reynolda with the essential meaning and purpose of her very life, her mission to work toward the transformation of a community, a people and place dearer to her than any other ever could be.

A series of small projects on the estate continued to move toward completion, but not the ambitious plan for a much enlarged "model school." Early in the spring of 1923, Charles Barton Keen had instead been developing plans for additional expansions to the school's existing quarters in the cottage designed by Gilbert Humphreys.[79] Then, at the end of March, the Johnstons unexpectedly announced that Reynolda School would close "temporarily" at completion of the current term, although they and the school's patrons hoped that a suitable building "may be erected in the not distant future."[80] Katharine and Ed may actually have needed time in which to reconsider educational projects involving such substantial long-term commitment. In the intervening years Katharine had seen her financial contributions to design and construction of the R. J. Reynolds High School in Winston-Salem begin to bear splendid fruit; the school had begun operation even before completion of Keen's Academic Arts Building, after a fire the preceding January gutted the old Winston High School. In her original 1919 offer to fund the project, Katharine had spoken of her "earnest desire" that "this great school . . . may be a success down through the years,"[81] and since the dedication of the high school's Richard J. Reynolds Memorial Auditorium was still a year away, she and Ed may have been opting for caution before forging ahead on another major building project.

As the pace of development slowed, a different, more relaxed tempo suffused the small community that Katharine had brought into being. Thomas Sears continued to work on a number of im-

The boathouse. Photo *by Thomas Sears.*

OPPOSITE:
The outdoor swimming pool, Lake Katharine in the background.

The Winston-Salem polo team (Ed Johnston second from left), 1923.

provements, mostly additions and enhancements to recreational facilities and small planting design projects at various locations on the estate. The lake offered first-rate fishing and boating, and children swam there or in the cooler, shaded swimming pool on summer afternoons. Tennis courts in several locations were kept busy, an athletic field had been added in 1921, and over the course of the following two years Ed Johnston oversaw the creation of polo fields, organized a local team for which he served as president, and began to arrange a regular schedule of matches that drew enthusiastic crowds to Reynolda.

The gardens flourished, especially as a setting for parties and entertainments. The eastern pergola once served as the stage for a twilight performance by Reynolda School students of *A Midsummer Night's Dream*,[82] and at a garden party in July of 1923, hundreds of guests enjoyed the music of Paul Whiteman's orchestra

while sampling delicacies sent by refrigerated railroad car from a New York City catering establishment.[83] Later the same month, Mr. and Mrs. Johnston entertained pupils and teachers from the nearby Children's Home with supper in the same gardens, after an afternoon of outdoor play that included a chance for the older children to attend a polo match.[84]

The culminating social event of that year at Reynolda, however, was a masked ball in mid-November, for which Katharine dressed as a shepherdess and Ed—indifferent to the irony—as Valentino's "Sheik."[85] The "very long and gracefully hooped" blue brocade dress of the shepherdess probably concealed a slight fullness in Katharine's figure that would soon reveal her secret, the new life growing within her. This time she planned to be even more careful with her health; she and Ed spent Thanksgiving at Pinehurst, then a week in Atlantic City before returning to New York. It may have been sometime during those early weeks of December that she obtained from Tiffany's a very small gold-embossed lady's calendar for 1924, with blank pages for "memoranda" opposite the calendar for each month. Katharine's first cryptic entry, lightly penciled in on January 14—"slight movements"—was a record for herself and no one else of the joy she felt on that day.[86]

She returned to Reynolda in February, knowing that she had to prepare herself for just one more trip back to New York, after which she intended to settle in under the close supervision of her doctors there to await the birth of her child in May. She probably was anxious during those last weeks at home; her little calendar noted that Nancy had scarlet fever and Bum was sick as well. Dick, who would be eighteen in a few months and was now attending North Carolina A & E in Raleigh, spent a week with the family.[87] Spoken or not, his misgivings about his mother's pregnancy were bound to have troubled her peace of mind. She left Winston-Salem on March 14, arriving in New York the following day. Ed later joined her there to keep vigil with her doctors at Harbor Hospital during the days leading up to the birth of a healthy son, John Edward Johnston Jr., on the twentieth of May. One can only imagine Katharine's deep gratitude for what was in every sense an extraordinary blessing.

Three days later she died suddenly, of an embolism.

"That which has been is now . . ."

If she had died in giving birth, the shock to Ed, her children, family, and friends would have been less grievous than it now was, coming days after the relief occasioned by a successful delivery. Neither they nor Katharine herself, diligent as she had always been in seeking out whatever knowledge or expert advice might ensure the best outcome in any course of action she pursued, could have anticipated that the bed rest advised by her doctors during the weeks leading up to her lying-in actually increased the risk of sudden death from a blood clot.

She had been deeply mindful, however, of the danger posed by her heart condition, and knew she must provide for her husband and children in the event that the future she had previously imagined for the family could not survive her death, as it did not. She had drawn up a new will in March, bequeathing her estate—except for annuities established for her parents and Henrietta van den Berg, legacies provided to specific employees, and provision for religious and charitable donations—in six equal portions to her husband and five children. Ed was named executor of the will, sole guardian of his and Katharine's child, and joint guardian with Dick's brother Will of the four Reynolds children. While Ed's share of the estate was made available to him "in fee, absolutely free of any trust," the Safe Deposit and Trust Company of Baltimore, which had served as the principal bank for her late husband and currently administered the trusts established by his will, would now continue as trustees under Katharine's will of each child's inheritance until he or she reached twenty-one years of age, "or until all the trusts established by the will of R. J.

Reynolds have expired and become inoperative, whichever shall happen last."[88]

She had been forced as well to address the painful question of how both Reynolda the corporation and Reynolda the place might have to change in her absence. She decided to withdraw from the land owned by the corporation and now to be administered by the trustees a tract designated as "Home Place" on a plan produced by Thomas Sears and attached to the will as a legal document. This core property, which included the house, lake, golf course, gardens, and village, would now function as a separate entity, while all or part of the remainder of the estate might be sold whenever the trustees determined that it was in the best interest of the corporation to do so. Katharine had even anticipated the possibility of conflict: "The Home Place shall continue to be kept for the home of my husband and children as herein provided . . . until the expiration of the trust as above limited. If any child or my husband marry, he or she can not bring his wife or her husband to live in said home without the consent of all other adults living in the home and the guardians of any minor child, and such wife or husband of such marriage may remain only as long as they have the consent of those living at the Home Place."[89]

She had already experienced the resistance of her first husband's relatives and other executives of Reynolds Tobacco to her efforts to increase her leverage within the company through the acquisition of additional shares of Class A stock, which granted voting rights and a generous percentage of annual profits to employees of the company. For the same reason, Will and the others had refused to offer Ed Johnston a suitable appointment within the firm, since to do so would have added to the couple's ability to influence management decisions.[90] Yet in spite of these tensions, Katharine had appointed her brother-in-law joint guardian with their stepfather of Dick Jr., Mary, Nancy, and Smith. She was trying to find a way to perpetuate the family recently formed by her second marriage and to preserve Reynolda as its home, without jeopardizing the existing and potential value of each child's inheritance. She knew that she could count on the Reynolds family to make sure that her children's wealth was managed with great perspicacity, especially since her husband's brother would be among the officers overseeing the trust administered by Safe Deposit and Trust of Baltimore.

It is impossible to know with what degree of candor Katharine and Ed had explored the difficulties he would inevitably face if, as the language of the will seemed to suggest, he continued to maintain Reynolda as the primary home for a household that included his stepchildren and infant son. Katharine obviously had hoped to spare the Reynolds children the added pain, if she should die, of their being separated from a childhood home that had always been a source of secure comfort and happiness, where they were surrounded by a solicitous community of family, friends, and servants who had been with the family for many years. On the other hand, the clause in the will stipulating that if her husband should remarry, his new wife and he could remain at Reynolda only with the consent of every child or child's guardian (namely, Will Reynolds) had to give Ed pause once he was faced with the reality of Katharine's being gone. Now thirty, he had quite recently embarked on a new career, and a commitment to the estate as a family home would probably require him to limit his employment opportunities for the foreseeable future to Winston-Salem.

Moreover, all four of the Reynolds children were by now in their teens—the youngest, Smith, would be thirteen that November—and therefore likely to spend most of every year away at school. Having spent the summer following their mother's death touring Europe for the first time with Will and Kate Reynolds and Bum as chaperons, they were bound to do still more traveling on their own before long. Certainly eighteen-year-old Dick, whose relationship with Ed was strained at best, was already his own man. This oldest son was a lot like his father, not academically inclined but a gregarious and capable man of action with a risk-taking entrepreneurial spirit. Aviation was the new American frontier, and both he and his younger brother were destined to achieve national prominence as pilots and aeronautical pioneers within just a few years, even before their respective twenty-first birthdays. Ed adored his stepdaughters, who called him "Pop," but they, too, would be grown women in just a few years' time. Then, too, how best might he consider the needs of his mother, who lived at Reynolda with him, and of his baby son? If Ed Johnston Jr. were to grow up in Winston-Salem, would he bear the whispered stigma of a child whose birth had cost his mother her life?

It cannot have been easy, but the grace and good humor that Katharine had so loved in Ed undoubtedly sustained him over the course of the next few years. He had nothing in him of the demanding patriarch—he was scarcely old enough to have been father to the Reynolds children—and apparently no heart for challenging those few family members who had never trusted his motives in marrying Katharine and blamed him for her death. He would want to give the children and himself sufficient time in which to recover from her loss and find their way into new and, as anticipated, very busy lives spent mostly away from Reynolda. Dick moved to New York City in the year following Katharine's death and subsequently started his own company, Reynolds Aviation, at Curtis Field on Long Island. In a way, it was he who gradually assumed the role of head of the family while the girls finished secondary school and Smith came under his mentorship, getting his pilot's license and his first airplane. On the occasion of his auspicious twenty-first birthday in 1927, Dick initiated a petition, later granted, asking that the Safe Deposit and Trust Company of Baltimore increase the yearly allowance received by each of the Reynolds heirs from five to fifty thousand dollars. In spring of the following year, Ed Johnston, by then a resident of Baltimore, transferred his share of the joint guardianship of the three younger Reynolds siblings to Robert E. Lasater of Winston-Salem, their father's nephew by marriage and an executive of Reynolds Tobacco. Ed remarried the same year.[91]

Although most staff was retained at Reynolda and the property routinely maintained, Katharine's "home place" now func-

Ed with John Edward Johnston Jr.

tioned more as a traditional country house, drawing the children back for visits as if to a hearth of memory and kinship. In anticipation of her return there after her June 1927 graduation from Miss Wright's School in Bryn Mawr, Pennsylvania, Mary planned a party with friends; she wanted "small tables down at the playhouse in the yard, 2 couples to a table, and afterwards play the vic, dance in the playhouse or walk and talk, very informal." Nancy hosted a "shag"—the latest dance craze—when she visited later that summer before returning to Paris, where she, Mary, and a chaperon had shared an apartment in the Hotel Plaza Athenée the preceding summer. The three women had the same living arrangement at the Barclay Hotel in New York City in 1928–29, while Mary and Nancy took courses at Columbia University.[92] Each of the sisters began a courtship during this period that would end in marriage, although Smith was the first of the Reynolds children to wed, less than two weeks after his eighteenth birthday in November 1929. Dick had recently moved the headquarters of Reynolds Aviation to Winston-Salem,[93] so Smith and his new wife took an apartment in town. Then, at weddings two weeks apart during the winter of 1929–30, the girls were given in marriage by their brother Dick in the same reception hall at Reynolda in which their mother and Ed Johnston had exchanged vows.

This was the winter following the October 1929 collapse of the stock market, a defining event that brought an end to the exuberant era of the American country place. The trustees of the Reynolda corporation had been trying for several years prior to this debacle to keep annual expenditures for managing the estate under control, by gradually scaling back unprofitable operations and selling land, livestock (including, in 1926, Katharine's herd of prize Jerseys), and other assets. Katharine had literally counted pennies in her zeal to prove that scientific methods and good management could improve the profitability of southern farms and restore beauty and health to a neglected rural landscape. The trustees counted in tens of thousands of dollars, striving simply to keep what remained of the original property in acceptable condition, without unnecessary sacrifice of capital.

The years of the Great Depression exacted a heavy toll from the lives of all Americans, even those spared poverty, hunger, and joblessness. No matter how insulated the Reynolds heirs might appear to have been from the incapacitating fears of which Franklin Roosevelt would speak, wealth did not protect them from personal and family experiences—even genuinely tragic episodes, such as Smith's violent death at twenty[94]—that seem in retrospect to have reflected the troubled temper of the age.

Against this background, Reynolda survived in a sadly altered, spiritless state, perhaps best symbolized by the gradual filling in of Lake Katharine despite occasional efforts to restore it by dredging.

After Dick Reynolds married in 1933, he and his wife made their home on the estate while building a country house of their own in the mountains near Roaring Gap, where his family had so often vacationed when he was a boy. Since keeping up Reynolda had become more and more of a financial drain in difficult times, the trustees finally recommended that the property be sold. At that point, Mary and her husband, Charles Henry Babcock, a

Charlie and Mary Babcock with Charles Jr., Katharine, and Barbara, c. 1937.

Wall Street investment banker who had been introduced to the Reynolds family when he and Ed Johnston worked together at Guaranty Trust of New York, rescued the estate from sale and from further decline by buying out the shares of the other heirs. Babcock, a graduate of the Wharton School of the University of Pennsylvania who had established his own brokerage firm in New York just three years earlier, took on the annual operating deficit—more than $67,000 in 1934—as a bracing challenge, and set to work reorganizing the various enterprises capable of generating income for the estate.[95] At the same time, he and Mary began a comprehensive rehabilitation of the house, grounds, and greenhouse operations. Less than a year after their taking over, a report compiled by the estate manager summarizing work carried out within various departments was optimistic: "The entire property presents a much better appearance than it has for the last ten or twelve years, and the morale of the organization has been improved considerably due to the uncertainty of the future that previously existed."[96]

Just as needed major repairs were made to the infrastructure—roads and drives, electric and telephone systems, plumbing and heating—the list of landscape projects reflected a return to a program of long-range planning and conservation rather than merely routine maintenance of lawns, shrubs and trees, flower and vegetable gardens, greenhouse and nurseries. Robert Conrad had been responsible for such renewal efforts as digging, separating, and replanting the narcissus bulbs in the woods bordering the golf course, replacing cedars at the main entrance, purchasing fifty sugar maples "to eventually replace dead and dying maples along highway," and moving trees from the nursery to plant "around homes and along road in colored settlement . . . and in groups on knoll west of heating plant." Irvin Disher, who had continued to supervise commercial florist and landscape activities as part of his greenhouse management in the years since Katharine's death, reported an expansion of activities in that department as well: "In addition to the regular work . . . such as growing different flower crops in different seasons, design work, table and wedding decorations, corsages, planting window boxes, terrariums, cemetery decorations, and growing annuals and perennials for sale, we start in the greenhouse practically all of the annuals for the gardens in spring [and] are now also trying to raise enough perennials to take the place of the annuals in the garden."[97]

Mary Katharine Reynolds Babcock had received her mother's name at birth, and was sixteen when Katharine died. The influence of Katharine's personality, values, and way of life had earlier found expression in Mary's artistic pursuits; she had studied drawing and painting in Paris and in New York. Now that she was mistress of Reynolda, her love for this southern home and her respect for what her mother had achieved there guided a loving renewal of the estate that was also practical and stylish, as Katharine would have wished it to be. Mary, too, was a serious student of the landscape arts, horticulture, and flower arranging; the addition of both a painting studio and a flower workroom were among a number of architectural changes made to the house. But none of these remodeling projects, she had resolved from the first, must be allowed to compromise the original style of the bungalow: "In future," she had written at the top of a page of her notes listing the various improvements she intended to commission, "bungalow must keep present style."[98] Charles Barton Keen had died in 1931, but the New York architectural firm that the Babcocks hired followed the program that Mary had outlined in a way that preserved the integrity of Keen's design.[99]

Thomas Sears undoubtedly shared the general relief over Reynolda's return to active life. The Babcocks gave him the opportunity both to revisit work he had done years earlier, adding recommendations for needed improvements to his original plans, and to undertake such new projects as the design of a forecourt to replace the porte-cochère and a planting plan for an entranceway added to the front facade. Mary's responsibility for these projects is reflected in the way that Sears titled his plans—"Reynolda, Estate of Mrs. Charles Babcock."[100]

Since her husband's career was centered in New York, however, Reynolda initially served as the Babcocks' country house rather than their principal residence, which was in Greenwich, Connecticut, the same town in which Nancy and her family made their home. Mary and Charlie and their four children, for whom Reynolda became once again a paradise of outdoor play and parties, regularly visited during the holiday seasons of spring, fall, and winter, and again in summer. As much as possible, the couple tried to keep in touch with what was happening on the estate and with the social and civic life of Winston-Salem, but Reynolda was not yet their "home place" in the sense that Katharine had intended. Perhaps that difference bothered Mary, since by all accounts she favored her childhood home over the estate in Greenwich.

At some point early in 1940, the black community at Reynolda found a voice through which to convey the impact on their own lives of Katharine's death and the Great Depression. They produced and signed—under the heading "We the People"—a short history and "pictorial survey of the Negroes, their community activity, their achievement and daily work on the Reynolda Estate covering one quarter century," a typescript illustrated with captioned photographs that was presented to the Babcocks "in appreciation of their extensive good will." Written near the end of "the great shake up," when fewer workmen were needed on the estate or anywhere else, the narrative deliberately refers to the time when "Miss Katharine" lived as a kind of golden age: "'In those days it never rained.' For during those days every man wanting to work worked . . . and every man had an equal opportunity. . . . As the scale of living advanced their wages were raised." Besides frequent gifts and bonuses, "each family was given sufficient garden space and the necessary seed to plant." In making a plea for better wages and continued employment for older workers "who have given their years, their energy[,] in fact their all in helping to make Reynolda what it is today," the authors of the document provided eloquent testimony that Katharine's original vision of community was understood and appreciated by ordinary working people, who hoped to see it fostered once again in their children's generation: "Many . . . have come from neighboring counties and communities—working along as brothers with the people who live at Reynolda proper, striving as it were with one aim—doing their best in making Reynolda not only a progressive village, but a place where everyone shall have for his motto, 'Do unto others as you would that they should do to you.'"[101]

When the United States went to war after the Japanese attack on Pearl Harbor in December 1941, Charlie Babcock volunteered for the army, even though his age and family situation warranted exemption; he rose through the ranks to serve finally as major and chief financial officer of the American headquarters of the European Theater of Operations. In his absence, Mary decided to move to Reynolda. Rather than try to maintain a house as large as the bungalow in wartime, she and the children lived modestly in the electrician's cottage on the opposite side of Reynolda Road. She started a "victory garden" near the poultry run after educating herself through government publications as her mother would have done, did volunteer work at a local hospital and as a Red Cross worker, and taught arts and crafts in a public school. She also assumed responsibility for overseeing the estate, writing her husband almost every day for advice in matters outside the domestic and social ones with which she was most familiar.[102] This experience helped her to come to terms with the economic pressures that increasingly threatened not just her home, but the entire community of which Reynolda was a vital part.

Taxes on the estate were increasing, and the Babcocks' financial advisers were again concerned about the levels of expenditure required to maintain the entire place. In letters to her sister written early in 1945, Mary shared her anxieties about Reynolda's future: "We all know that the day of big estates is passing. I'm planning to sell off the church side of the road right after the war in pieces, selling as much as the town can absorb. Property around the Old Town Club will be sold after that, probably 10 or 20 years later. But the big house & gardens etc. are what cause upkeep expense." Although Charlie and she were convinced that the house might best be sold to a "university, orphanage or something before I was old enough to die," there had recently been an uproar in the town over a recommendation by a member of the Chamber of Commerce that five hundred acres of Reynolda land be purchased as the site for a proposed veterans' hospital. "So I guess," she concluded, "Reynolda will go on as is to live a long life and end as an ancient ruin, but with the charm of its homey atmosphere still there."[103]

A solution began to emerge, however, not longer after Charlie's return at the end of the war. Wake Forest College, a Baptist institution close to Raleigh, had moved its medical school to Winston-Salem in 1941. In the intervening years, Will Reynolds and a group of influential citizens had explored the possibility of getting the entire college relocated in their city; they offered substantial financial incentives for the move, including a gift of two million dollars for building costs anonymously proffered by Reynolds himself. Then, in July 1946, the Babcocks expressed their willingness to provide 350 acres of Reynolda land as a site for the campus. Agreement was reached, planning commenced, and in the fall of 1951 President Harry S. Truman was a luncheon guest at Reynolda on the day that he arrived in Winston-Salem to officiate at the ground-breaking ceremonies.[104] Sadly, however, Mary Babcock's hope that Reynolda's home place might also "go to a university, orphanage or something" before she was "old enough to die" was not to be realized. She and Charlie had made Reynolda their year-round home in 1948, but Mary died of cancer within five years. She was forty-four, the same age her mother had been, but hardly "old enough to die."

Charlie Babcock remarried, but continued until his own death in 1967 to work toward finding an adaptive reuse of the house and surrounding grounds that would as much as possible preserve their original form and character. Since Reynolda had been designed to accommodate active work and play, Wake Forest College (which became a university in 1967) seemed an ideal beneficiary, receiving additional donations of land and money from several family foundations, including the Mary Reynolds Babcock Foundation established by Mary's will. The village and gardens were deeded in this way, and subsequently redeveloped following criteria that Charlie, having educated himself in such matters through participation in a number of local historic preservation projects, had recommended.[105]

The physical fabric of the village has been largely unchanged by sensitive adaptive reuse, beginning with a 1978 master plan, of the various cottages, workshops, and farm buildings to accommodate offices, shops, cafes, and restaurants.[106] Even during the years of family ownership, Reynolda Gardens had served a public function, as Katharine intended, related to the village and town. Her daughter Mary, a dedicated member of the Garden Club of Amer-

Farm buildings, 2001.
Photo by Carol Betsch.

Barns and silo, 2001.
Photo by Carol Betsch.

Retaining wall and dairy, 2001. Photo by Carol Betsch.

ica, continued her mother's practice of welcoming visitors to a garden of which she was not ashamed to boast: "My . . . garden is open to the public without charge all year. It was said by a Japanese visitor that this planting of weeping Japanese cherry trees with boxwood and magnolia soulangiana and cryptomerias is even more beautiful than any in Japan. When the cherry trees are in bloom, thousands of visitors from all over the country come to see it. Many bus loads of children visited it last year."[107]

Over the course of three decades of management by Wake Forest University, the natural aging of trees and shrubs, weakening

and wear in structural elements, and the intervention of too many
hands inevitably compromised the visual and spatial qualities of
Thomas Sears's original design of the formal gardens. In 1995, a
1.2-million dollar rehabilitation project, based on a cultural landscape report and following guidelines and procedures endorsed by
the National Park Service Historic Landscape Initiative, selected
the years 1912–36 as the period to be interpreted, and replaced, re-
paired, or removed garden elements accordingly.[108] So many of the
Japanese cedars were diseased that the central allée was entirely removed, then replanted within five years using scions of the origi-

Path in the vegetable garden, along cut flower border, 2001.
Photo by Carol Betsch.

View toward teahouses in the vegetable garden, 2001. Photo by Carol Betsch.

nal trees. Other changes made to the gardens at this time represented programmatic responses to contemporary needs, such as improving accessibility for handicapped visitors. An additional million-dollar endowment for maintenance has made possible additions to staff commensurate with the restoration of more complex planting schemes in the greenhouse borders and parterres.[109] Although Katharine's gardens now welcome more than 100,000 visitors each year, the experience they offer remains grounded, as she and Sears intended it to be, in an atmosphere of gracious invitation, an invitation to discover how much the present moment—the beauty of the garden on this day, in this season—captures light and color from the prism of memory and tradition.

Planning a viable future for the house, which Mary had so feared might end in ruin of one sort or another, preoccupied

Charlie Babcock in the years prior to his own death. In 1963 he appointed a board of directors, made a gift on behalf of the Mary Reynolds Babcock Foundation of the house and its remaining nineteen acres, now incorporated as Reynolda House, Inc., and drew up a charter defining its dual mission as historic house museum—with collections of paintings, sculpture, furniture, and decorative arts—and "center for the encouragement of the arts and higher education." His daughter Barbara, an art historian, was appointed president. As an interim arrangement, Piedmont University Center, a consortium of North Carolina liberal arts colleges sponsoring conferences, cultural events, and other cooperative ventures, made their headquarters in the house for eleven years. During this time, renovations to the house in preparation for its new function continued, as did the assembling of a unique collection of American paintings; the American Association of Museums accredited Reynolda House in 1972.[110] John Wilmerding, a distinguished historian of American art, has described the museum's collection and its educational programs in language that suggests a remarkable continuity of commitment to education and to high standards over generations:

> One is struck by the sense of quality in the careful selection and presentation of the collection. These are American paintings at their best. Reynolda House pioneered study of art in context, whether through programs illuminating the connections to historical or cultural background, the parallels to literature and music, or the expressions of significant ideas in the American arts. The educational offerings are as fine-tuned and stimulating as the collection itself. Museums with much larger holdings may envy the polish and imagination Reynolda House brings to the study of American art.[111]

In 2004, Reynolda House Museum of American Art and its site became formally affiliated with Wake Forest University.

Katharine's home place and much of what had been the farm are now part of a university campus, although if one stands in the reception hall or Katharine's den or any of the other rooms of the house restored to their original appearance, the same conflation of past and present that strikes one on a walk in the gardens or through the woodland happens here as well. Katharine would not be surprised at all. "The good work is going on," she would probably say.

OPPOSITE:
Reynolda lamppost,
2001. Photo by Carol
Betsch.

Notes

INTRODUCTION

1. For a useful summary of American ideas about the biological and social roles of women, see Linda K. Kerber, "Separate Spheres, Female Worlds, Woman's Place: The Rhetoric of Women's History," in *Toward an Intellectual History of Women: Essays by Linda K. Kerber* (Chapel Hill: University of North Carolina Press, 1997), 159–99.

2. Norman T. Newton, *Design on the Land: The Development of Landscape Architecture* (Cambridge: Belknap Press of Harvard University Press, 1971).

3. See, for example, the essay by sculptor Robert Smithson, "Frederick Law Olmsted and the Dialectical Landscape," first published in the February 1973 issue of *Artforum*, and reprinted in *The Writings of Robert Smithson*, ed. Nancy Holt (New York: New York University Press, 1979), 117–28. Smithson discovered Olmsted's work and the theoretical foundations of his practice through a 1972 exhibition at the Whitney Museum of American Art, and particularly through the accompanying catalogue, *Frederick Law Olmsted's New York*, with text by Elizabeth Barlow Rogers and an illustrative portfolio by William Alex (New York: Praeger, in association with the Whitney Museum of American Art, 1972).

4. Deborah Nevins has pointed out that although "most histories state there were eleven original members . . . the introduction to the Society's *Illustrations of the Work of Members*, published in 1931, says there were ten charter members and that Frederick Law Olmsted, Jr., and Elizabeth Bullard . . . joined later in the year." Deborah Nevins, "The Triumph of Flora: Women and the American Landscape, 1890–1935," *Antiques* 127 (April 1985): 922n15.

5. Newton, *Design on the Land*, 385–86.

6. Beatrix Jones Farrand (1872–1959) belonged to a wealthy and distinguished New York City family. As a young woman she traveled widely in Europe, frequently visiting gardens in the company of her aunt, the highly acclaimed novelist Edith Wharton, whose 1904 study *Italian Villas and Their Gardens* influenced landscape design in the United States. Beatrix studied horticulture and the rudiments of landscape composition under the tutelage of Charles Sprague Sargent, founder and first director of the Arnold Arboretum in Boston and a family friend. Sargent encouraged her to prepare for a career as a garden designer through further travel and study abroad. Starting with commissions to develop landscape plans for estates in New York City, Westchester County, and Long Island, New York, and Newport, Rhode Island, Farrand soon expanded her practice to include major private projects such as the John D. Rockefeller Jr. estate at Seal Harbor, Mount Desert Island, Maine, and her most complex and brilliant work, lovingly developed over the course of a quarter-century, the gardens of Dumbarton Oaks, the Georgetown estate of Ambassador and Mrs. Robert Woods Bliss in Washington, D.C. Farrand was also recognized for campus design projects at Princeton, Yale, the University of Chicago, and other institutions. See Eleanor M. McPeck, "Farrand, Beatrix Jones," in *Pioneers of American Landscape Design*, ed. Charles A. Birnbaum and Robin Karson (New York: McGraw-Hill, 2000), 117–19.

7. Mrs. Schuyler Van Rennselaer, *Art Out-of-Doors* (New York: Charles Scribner's Sons, 1893), 8.

8. According to Beatrix Jones's biographer Jane Brown, Jones's mother was a friend of Mrs. Van Rennselaer. In spite of Van Rennselaer's reluctance to encourage young women to become landscape architects, her enthusiasm for the profession apparently did strengthen Jones's determination to prepare herself to practice. See Jane Brown, *Beatrix: The Gardening Life of Beatrix Jones Farrand, 1872–1959* (New York: Viking, 1995), 26, and 226 n. 29.

9. Van Rennselaer, *Art Out-of-Doors*, 358.

10. Quoted in Eleanor M. McPeck, "A Biographical Note and a Consideration of Four Major Private Gardens," in Diana Balmori, Diane Kostial McGuire, and Eleanor M. McPeck, *Beatrix Farrand's American Landscapes: Her Gardens and Campuses* (Sagaponack, N.Y.: Sagapress, 1985), 22.

11. Andrew Jackson Downing, *Treatise on the Theory and Practice of Landscape Gardening, Adapted to North America* . . . (New York: Wiley and Putnam, 1841); 2d ed., enlarged, revised, and newly illustrated (1844); 4th ed., enlarged, revised, and newly illustrated (1849; reissued 1850, 1852). No copies of a third edition are known to exist. Downing's *Cottage Residences; or, A series of designs for rural cottages and cottage villas, and their gardens and grounds, adapted to North America* . . . (New York: Wiley and Putnam, 1842); 2d ed. (1844); 3d ed. (1847); 4th ed., revised and enlarged (1852); and *The Architecture of Country Houses, including designs for cottages, farm houses, and villas* . . . (New York: D. Appleton, 1850; reissued 1850, 1852) were similarly influen-

tial, as were articles in *The Horticulturist, and Journal of Rural Art and Rural Taste*, which Downing founded and edited until his death in 1852.

12. For a fuller discussion of the self-effacing rhetoric used by many of these garden writers, see Diane Harris, "Cultivating Power: The Language of Feminism in Women's Garden Literature, 1870–1920," *Landscape Journal* 13 (Fall 1992): 113–23.

13. Quoted in Peter J. Schmitt, *Back to Nature: The Arcadian Myth in Urban America* (New York: Oxford University Press, 1969), 4.

14. See Virginia Lopez Begg, "Frances Duncan: The 'New Woman' in the Garden," *Journal of the New England Garden History Society* 2 (Fall 1992): 28–35. This essay is the source of the biographical information in the text on Duncan's career.

15. Clive Aslet, *The American Country House* (New Haven: Yale University Press, 1990), 144.

16. In spite of having had a remarkably successful professional career, which included not just a lifelong involvement with San Simeon but the design of hundreds of buildings in the Bay Area, Julia Morgan, too, was largely ignored by architectural historians until the 1970s. Her biographer found it astonishing, when she began research on Morgan, that there was no mention of her work in the leading architectural studies of the region. See Sara Holmes Boutelle, "An Elusive Pioneer: Tracing the Work of Julia Morgan," in *Architecture: A Place for Women*, ed. Ellen Perry Berkeley and Matilda McQuaid (Washington, D.C.: Smithsonian Institution Press, 1989), 107–16.

17. Ibid., 107.

18. Aileen S. Kraditor, ed., *Up from the Pedestal: Selected Writings in the History of American Feminism* (1968), quoted in Kerber, "Separate Spheres," 163.

19. Pamela Dean, "Learning to Be New Women: Campus Culture at the North Carolina Normal and Industrial College," *North Carolina Historical Review* 68 (July 1991): 286–306; Amy Thompson McCandless, "Progressivism and the Higher Education of Southern Women," *North Carolina Historical Review* 70 (July 1993): 302–25.

20. Leslie Rose Close, "A History of Women in Landscape Architecture," foreword to Judith B. Tankard, *The Gardens of Ellen Biddle Shipman* (Sagaponack, N.Y.: Sagapress in association with Library of American Landscape History, 1996), xvi.

21. Letter of February 25, 1894, from Frederick Law Olmsted to John Charles Olmsted, quoted in Laura Wood Roper, *FLO: A Biography of Frederick Law Olmsted* (Baltimore: Johns Hopkins University Press, 1973), 455n.

22. Wendy Kaplan, "Regionalism in American Architecture," in Elizabeth Cumming and Wendy Kaplan, *The Arts and Crafts Movement* (London: Thames and Hudson, 1991), 172.

23. Quoted in Berry B. Tracy et al., *Nineteenth-Century America: Furniture and Other Decorative Arts* (New York: Metropolitan Museum of Art, 1970), cat. no. 210.

24. Kaplan, "Regionalism," 172.

25. Mark Alan Hewitt, *The Architect and the Country House, 1890–1940* (New Haven: Yale University Press, 1990), 199.

26. Ibid.

27. The use of the term "Home Place" for this area of the estate appears in Katharine Smith Reynolds Johnston's will and on a site plan, "General Plan of Reynolda, Inc., Winston-Salem, N.C., Feb. 1925, J. E. Ellerbe, C. E. [Civil Engineer]." I assume that this designation was used informally within the family.

28. From Yeats's poem "A Prayer for My Daughter" of 1919. William Butler Yeats belonged to the circle of William Morris, and the two shared many of the same philosophical and political views.

1. KATE SMITH OF MOUNT AIRY

1. William Franklin Carter Jr. and Carrie Young Carter, "Footprints in the Hollows," photocopied manuscript (Mount Airy, N.C.: Surry County Historical Society, 1975), 106.

2. Zachary Taylor Smith was born February 19, 1847, in Patrick County, Virginia. According to his obituary in the *Winston-Salem Journal*, June 14, 1928, he enlisted in the Confederate army at seventeen and served as captain in the 72nd North Carolina regiment. He was taken prisoner after the battle of Fort Fisher, a Confederate stronghold at the mouth of the Cape Fear River, in January 1865.

3. Bertram Wyatt-Brown, *Southern Honor: Ethics and Behavior in the Old South* (New York: Oxford University Press, 1982), 34–38.

4. Quoted in ibid., 39.

5. Quoted in Numan V. Bartley, *The Creation of Modern Georgia* (Athens: University of Georgia Press, 1983), 84.

6. *The New South: Writing and Speeches of Henry Grady* (Savannah, Ga.: Beehive Press, 1971), 107.

7. Hester Bartlett Jackson, ed., *Heritage of Surry County, North Carolina*, vol. 1 (Winson-Salem: Hunter Publishing in cooperation with the Surry County Genealogical Association, 1983), viii–xi.

8. *Collections and Recollections: A Collection of Memories, Recipes, and Recollections That Reflect Our Early Beginnings* (Mount Airy, N.C.: Mount Airy Restoration Foundation, 1985), 90.

9. Ibid., 57.

10. Ibid., 28, 61.

11. Quoted in W. J. Cash, *The Mind of the South* (1941; reprint, Garden City, N.Y.: Doubleday, 1956), 190.

12. Quoted in *Winston-Salem Twin City Sentinel*, October 22, 1951.

13. Nannie Tilley, "Impact of the Tobacco Industry and the Reynoldses in the

Growth of Winston-Salem," speech to the Tobacco Institute, March 1974, typescript in Reynolda Archives (hereafter RA).

14. Quoted in Chester S. Davis, "How Richard J. Reynolds Made Folks Walk a Mile; The Story of the Man from No Business Mountain Who Parlayed a $7,400 Bankroll into Millions," *Winston-Salem Journal and Sentinel*, May 7, 1950. R. J. Reynolds was born and raised in Patrick County, Virginia.

15. See, for example, Barbara Mayer, *Reynolda: A History of an American Country House* (Winston-Salem, N.C.: John F. Blair for Reynolda House Museum of American Art, 1997), 5; Patrick Reynolds and Tom Shachtman, *The Gilded Leaf: Triumph, Tragedy, and Tobacco: Three Generations of the R. J. Reynolds Family and Fortune* (Boston: Little, Brown, 1989), 54.

16. R. S. Craven to Charles D. McIver, July 10, 1897, Collections of the Walter Clinton Jackson Library, University of North Carolina, Greensboro (hereafter JL).

17. Quoted in Hugh C. Bailey, *Liberalism in the New South: Southern Social Reformers and the Progressive Movement* (Coral Gables: University of Miami Press, 1969), 134–35.

18. Quoted ibid., 136.

19. Quoted in Rose Howell Holder, *McIver of North Carolina* (Chapel Hill: University of North Carolina Press, 1957), 69.

20. Ibid., 63, 71–73.

21. Ibid., 10–12, 35–36, 68.

22. Virginia L. Lathrop, "Mrs. Lula Martin McIver Accorded Special Honor," *Greensboro Daily News*, October 6, 1940, 1:1.

23. Holder, *McIver*, 63–66. Holder states that in spite of Lula's intentions, she and Charles McIver were married in his Presbyterian church because her church was undergoing repair. A Presbyterian minister substituting at the last minute read the traditional vows, to which the couple assented rather than create consternation among those attending the ceremony.

24. Quoted ibid., 75.

25. Quoted from the report of Edward Alderman, ibid., 108.

26. M. C. S. Noble, *A History of the Public Schools of North Carolina* (Chapel Hill: University of North Carolina Press, 1930), 436.

27. Quoted in Holder, *McIver*, 96.

28. Quoted ibid., 103.

29. Noble, *History of the Public Schools*, 438.

30. Alderman later served as president of Tulane University in New Orleans, and after that at the University of Virginia

31. Quoted in Holder, *McIver*, 94.

32. Ibid., 111.

33. Amy Thompson McCandless, "Progressivism and the Higher Education of Southern Women," *North Carolina Historical Review* 70 (July 1993): 312.

34. Lathrop, "Mrs. Lula Martin McIver."

35. Pamela Dean, "Learning to Be New Women: Campus Culture at the North Carolina Normal and Industrial College," *North Carolina Historical Review* 68 (July 1991): 289.

36. Holder, *McIver*, 115–16.

37. Quoted in McCandless, "Progressivism," 305.

38. Dean, "Learning," 290–91.

39. One of his contemporaries described McIver in this way. Quoted in Holder, *McIver*, 147.

40. Ibid., 143–61.

41. Ibid., 134–35.

42. From a poem by Owen Meredith, quoted ibid., 133. "Owen Meredith" was the pseudonym of the English statesman and poet Edward Robert Bulwer-Lytton, first earl of Lytton (1831–1891), son of the first Baron Lytton (1803–1873), English novelist and dramatist.

43. Dean, "Learning," 291.

44. Bertha M. Donnelly, quoted ibid., 294.

45. Alexander Garden, "Regeneration and the Testimony of the Spirit," quoted in *The Great Awakening: Documents Illustrating the Crisis and Its Consequences*, ed. Alan Heimert and Perry Miller (Indianapolis: Bobbs-Merrill, 1967), 59.

46. Letter of Kathrine [*sic*] Smith, July 12, 1897, JL.

47. Kate Smith to Charles D. McIver, July 12, 1897, JL.

48. See correspondence of July 6, 1897; July 11, 1898; December 11, 1899, JL.

49. Zachary T. Smith to Charles D. McIver, October 14, 1897, asking if his daughter should be sent home to recover, JL.

50. Holder, *McIver*, 190–91. Although Katharine's name is omitted from a fall 1899 chapel record listing the names of the students who died and those who survived typhoid fever, her name is included among those listed as having had "malaria fever." Letters of October 4 and December 11, 1899, from Katharine Smith to Charles McIver, suggest that she did not return to school until the following spring, JL.

51. Quoted in Holder, *McIver*, 193.

52. Lathrop, "Mrs. Lula Martin McIver."

53. Holder, *McIver*, 204; Dean, "Learning," 299.

54. Dean, "Learning," 287, 292.

55. *The Omega* (Roanoke, Va.: Stone Printing and Manufacturing, 1902).

56. Ibid., 82–83.

57. Zachary T. Smith, interview of April 30, 2000.

58. Undated letter from Cora Hollingsworth to Katharine Smith Reynolds (hereafter KSR) requesting a loan to help with purchase of a new kiln to be used by her students. She reminds KSR of the time when "we were painting [china] and you ask [*sic*] us all to help you by paying some in advance," RA, box 1, folder 65; Ruth Smith Lucas also remembered her sister's china-painting classes, Oral History Archives, Reynolda (hereafter OHA).

59. Katharine later inscribed the date December 20, 1902, at the place in her wedding book meant to mark the first meeting of the future bride and groom.

60. R. J. Reynolds was unhappy in his first experience of college life at the religiously conservative Emory and Henry College in rural Virginia. He had more success—and a welcome exposure to city life—at Bryant and Stratton Business College in Baltimore, where he could concentrate on those mathematical subjects for which he had a natural aptitude, while working in summer in his father's tobacco business. He was troubled throughout his life by a handicap that impaired his reading ability and made him a poor speller, the condition now described as dyslexia. Reynolds and Shachtman, *Gilded Leaf*, 31.

61. R. J. Reynolds (hereafter RJR) to Katharine Smith, April 14, 1903, RA, box 2, folder 154a.

62. LeGette Blythe, *Reynolda House* (Winston-Salem: s.d., n.d.), n.p., RA.

63. RJR to Katharine Smith, RA, box 1, folder 65. Letter on stationery from Hoffman House, Madison Square, New York City, undated except for year, 1905.

2. A MISSION FOR MRS. REYNOLDS

1. The list cited here is handwritten; another, typed list includes London, Paris, Geneva, Nice, Genoa, Milan, Venice, Florence, Rome, and Naples. Both are undated, RA.

2. Postcard of May 2, 1905, private collection of Barbara Babcock Millhouse (hereafter BBM).

3. Ruth Mullen, *The Paris Gowns in the Reynolda House Costume Collection* (Winston-Salem: Reynolda House, Museum of American Art, 1995), 7–14.

4. Thorstein Veblen, *The Theory of the Leisure Class* (New York: Macmillan, 1899).

5. Quoted in Wayne Andrews, *Architecture, Ambition, and Americans: A Social History of American Architecture* (New York: Free Press, 1964), 153.

6. John La Farge, "Mr. La Farge on Useless Art," *Architectural Record* 17 (April 1905): 347.

7. Norman T. Newton, *Design on the Land: The Development of Landscape Architecture* (Cambridge: Belknap Press of Harvard University Press, 1971), 413–17. See also the entry on Robinson by Amy Brown in *Pioneers of American Landscape Design*, ed. Charles A. Birnbaum and Robin Karson (New York: McGraw-Hill, 2000), 315–18.

8. The deed of sale transferring the property from William N. Reynolds to Richard J. Reynolds was filed in the county registrar's office on March 21, 1904.

9. W. J. Cash, *The Mind of the South* (1941; reprint, New York: Anchor Books, 1956), 201.

10. Ibid.

11. The *Mount Airy News* reported that after their wedding on February 27, 1905,

the Reynoldses traveled to New York City by train, departing for Liverpool on the ocean liner *Baltic* (White Star Line) two days later. The Paris edition of the *New York Herald* of March 11 noted that they were by then "among the passengers on the *Baltic* now stopping at the Carlton Hotel, London," and Katharine sent her sister Maxie a postcard from London also dated March 11; see Mullen, *Paris Gowns*, 5, 7. Since the crossing would have taken no more than a week, there would have been time between Liverpool and London to visit the Lake District. A c. 1906 advertising brochure distributed by the White Star Line emphasized the ease with which passengers disembarking at Liverpool might arrange such excursions on "luxuriously appointed express trains" connecting with "ancient towns" and "historical cities in the North of England." Gjenvick-Gjønvik Archives, http://www.steamships.org/index.php. Katharine's copy of Kurt Baedeker's *Great Britain: Handbook for Travellers*, 5th ed., rev. and enl. (New York: Charles Scribner's Sons, 1901), recommended Grasmere and three other villages as most appealing even to those having only one day to spend in the Lake District.

12. From the poem "London, 1802" (1808), addressed to Milton and lamenting the erosion of England's traditional values. See *William Wordsworth: Selected Poetry*, ed. Mark Van Doren (New York: Modern Library, 1950), 478.

13. "Home at Grasmere" is the title of what became book one of Wordsworth's unfinished *The Recluse* (1800), which he planned as "a philosophical poem, containing views of Man, Nature, and Society." See his preface to *The Excursion* (1814), in ibid., 604.

14. Jonathan Wordsworth, Michael C. Jays, and Robert Woof, *William Wordsworth and the Age of English Romanticism* (New Brunswick, N.J.: Rutgers University Press with the Wordsworth Trust, 1987), 146.

15. Wordsworth, *The Recluse, Selected Poetry*, 416.

16. From the poem *The Symphony* (1875), reprinted in Walter Blair, Theodore Hornberger, and Randall Stewart, *The Literature of the United States*, vol. 2 (Chicago: Scott Foresman and Co., 1953), 663.

17. Frederick Law Olmsted, *Walks and Talks of an American Farmer in England* (New York: G. P. Putnam, 1852). Reprint with intro. by Charles C. McGlaughlin, Amherst: Library of American Landscape History, distributed by University of Massachusetts Press, 2003.

18. *Winston-Salem Journal*, September 14, 1905.

19. Quoted in an editorial in the *Asheville Citizen*, reprinted in *Charles Duncan McIver*, memorial volume (Greensboro): North Carolina State Normal and Industrial College, [1907]), 53.

20. "Eulogy by Hon. William Jennings Bryan, Delivered in Greensboro on Monday Night, September 17," ibid., 22–23.

21. RJR was especially interested, well before his marriage to Katharine, in improving the local school system for blacks, demonstrating early support of the effort to establish graded schools for both races in Winston. He was elected to

the city commission in 1884, where he served as chairman of the sanitary and fire committees, and was subsequently appointed supervisor of roads in Winston Township, a post he held for several years. He was also instrumental in organizing a bank in Forsyth County designed to meet the needs of the community's factory workers, especially by encouraging savings accounts. Nannie M. Tilley, *The R. J. Reynolds Tobacco Company* (Chapel Hill: University of North Carolina Press, 1985), 52–54.

22. Kathleen Dalton, *Theodore Roosevelt: A Strenuous Life* (New York: Alfred A. Knopf, 2002).

23. Dewey W. Grantham, *Southern Progressivism: The Reconciliation of Progress and Tradition* (Knoxville: University of Tennessee Press, 1983), xv–xvi.

24. Ibid., xvii.

25. Tilley, *Reynolds Tobacco Company*, 177–80.

26. "She nursed us all . . . nursed some of [us] for a number of years." Nancy Reynolds, interview, OHA.

27. Tilley, *Reynolds Tobacco Company*, 525. *Winston-Salem Journal*, October 8, 1906; November 24, 1906; December 27, 1906.

28. *Winston-Salem Journal*, February 28, 1909.

29. Hugh C. Bailey, *Liberalism in the New South: Southern Social Reformers and the Progressive Movement* (Coral Gables: University of Miami Press, 1969), 89.

30. Ethel [Jackson] to KSR, February 27, 1907, RA, box 2, folder 114.

31. Postcard of August 10, 1907, BBM.

32. Mark Alan Hewitt, *The Architect and the Country House, 1890–1940* (New Haven: Yale University Press, 1990), 19.

33. Harry W. Desmond and Herbert Croly, *Stately Homes in America from Colonial Times to the Present Day* (New York: D. Appleton, 1903).

34. Charles A. Platt, *Italian Gardens* (New York: Harper & Brothers, 1893).

35. Hewitt, *The Architect and the Country House*, 61.

36. Postcards of March 11 and 19, 1908, BBM.

37. Postcards of October 18 and 29, 1908, BBM.

38. Letter of May 26, 1908, RA, box 1, folder 65.

39. *Winston-Salem Journal*, January 21, 1909.

40. *Winston-Salem Journal*, March 17, 1909.

41. Letter of August 11, 1909, RA, box 1, folder 65.

42. Letter of August 2, 1909, RA, box 1, folder 65.

43. Prosper Jules Alphonse Berckmans, Belgian émigré, and his equally distinguished horticulturist father, Louis E. Berckmans, established Fruitland Nursery in Augusta, Georgia, in 1859. Within just a few years their nursery was the largest of its kind in the South, famous for its importation and commercial introduction of the greatest variety of fruits, trees, and ornamental plants available in the region. Having survived the Civil War, the business continued to grow, sending out more than 25,000 catalogues a year by the turn of the century. By 1904 the nursery consisted of 500 acres, with 60,000 square feet of

greenhouse capacity. P. J. Berckmans served as president of the Georgia State Horticultural Society from its founding in 1876 until his death in 1910. His sons and grandsons continued to operate the internationally respected firm until the property was purchased by Robert Trent "Bobby" Jones in 1931 and converted into a golf course that is now the home of the Augusta National Golf Club, sponsors of the annual Masters Tournament. See Willard Range, *A Century of Georgia Agriculture, 1850–1950* (Athens: University of Georgia Press, 1954).

44. Probably RJR's brother-in-law James Stamper Dunn, who had married Katharine's sister Maxie in 1907.

45. Letter of August 5, 1909, RA, box 1, folder 65.

46. See Cynthia Rock, Susanna Torre, and Gwendolyn Wright, "The Appropriation of the House: Changes in House Design and Concepts of Domesticity," in *New Space for Women*, ed. Gerda R. Werkorle, Rebecca Peterson, and David Morley (Boulder, Colo.: Westview Press, 1980), 83–100.

47. This series of articles was subsequently published as a book, *The New Housekeeping: Efficiency Studies in Home Management* (New York: Doubleday, 1912).

48. Mrs. [Sarah T.] Rorer's *New Cook Book* (Philadelphia: Arnold and Co. [1902]), RA.

49. Lucy Maynard Salmon, *Domestic Service*, 2d. ed. (New York: Macmillan, 1911); Ellen H. Richards and S. Maria Elliott, *The Chemistry of Cooking and Cleaning: A Manual for Housekeepers*, 3d. ed. (Boston: Whitcomb and Barrows, 1912); H[erbert] W[illiam] Conn, *The Story of Germ Life* (New York: McClure, Phillips and Co., 1904), RA.

50. The Reynoldses were among the guests at a luncheon at which Poe was among those honored. *Winston-Salem Journal*, October 6, 1906.

51. Grantham, *Southern Progressivism*, 333.

52. Morland, "A Millionaire's Village: An Ideal Village in the Hills of North Carolina, Designed as a Whole and Built to Order," *House Beautiful* 14 (August 1903): 164–68.

53. Anne Firor Scott, describing members of the Women's Christian Temperance Union in "The 'New Woman' in the New South," *South Atlantic Quarterly* 61 (Autumn 1962): 477.

54. Tilley, *Reynolds Tobacco Company*, 139.

55. Quoted in Dolores Hayden, *Redesigning the American Dream: The Future of Housing, Work, and Family Life* (New York: W. W. Norton` 1984), 76.

56. Check dated March 4, 1910, from KSR to J. Van Lindley Nursery Company for grapes, raspberries, blueberries, rhubarb; check of April 12, 1910, to Cyphers Incubator Company for 100 chickens, RA, box 3, folder 248.

57. E. P. Powell, *The Country Home* (New York: McClure, Phillips & Co., 1904), 6–11 passim.

58. Letter of September 20, 1910, RA, box 1, folder 65.

59. Letter of September 22, 1910, RA, box 1, folder 65.

60. Letter of September 24, 1910, RA, unprocessed correspondence.

61. KSR to Eugene Smith, postcard, August 13, 1911, BBM.

62. Letter of August 9, 1911, RA, box 1, folder 65.

63. Letters of August 1 and 3, 1911, RA, box 1, folder 65.

3. CREATING REYNOLDA

1. See James S. Ackerman, "Thomas Jefferson," in *The Villa: Form and Ideology of Country Houses* (Princeton: Princeton University Press for the Trustees of the National Gallery of Art, Washington, D.C., 1990), 185–211.

2. *I'll Take My Stand: The South and the Agrarian Tradition*, by Twelve Southerners (1930; reprint, Baton Rouge: Louisiana State University Press, 1983), xiv, xvi–xvii.

3. Correspondence between KSR and a Washington, D.C., kitchen supply company relative to an invoice of July 1917 sent to R. J. Reynolds's secretary George W. Orr rather than to her. RA, box 1, folder 88.

4. Telegram to RJR at Knickerbocker Hotel, New York City, RA, box 2, folder 184.

5. Emma Bernard to KSR, referring to Katharine's protracted illness after the February wedding, April 15, 1912, RA, box 1, folder 74.

6. Letter of May 3, 1912, RA, box 2, folder 121.

7. Undated letter, RA, box 1, folder 63.1.

8. KSR to "Cousin Jeannie," June 10, 1912, RA, box 1, folder 114.

9. Letter of May 6, 1912, RA, box 2, folder 125.

10. Letter of May 27, 1912, RA, box 2, folder 125.

11. Letter of June 5, 1912, RA, box 2, folder 125. There is no evidence that the island was actually constructed.

12. KSR to Louise [Ludlow], June 17, 1912, box 2, folder 128.

13. Letter of June 14, 1912, RA, box 2, folder 166.

14. Letter of June 17, 1912 (dictated to an unidentified person), RA, box 2, folder 166.

15. KSR to Senah Reynolds, June 10, 1912, RA, box 2, folder 148.

16. Letter of June 20, 1912, RA, box 1, folder 121.

17. Letter of July 5, 1912, RA, box 1, folder 121.

18. KSR to Mrs. W. S. Fearrington, July 5, 1912, RA, box 1, folder 98.

19. Mrs. Haughton of Westminster, Md., to KSR, July 18, 1912, RA, box 1, folder 106.

20. Emma Louis Speight Morris quoted in Betty Ann Ragland Stainbacks, "Kate Smith Reynolds," *Alumnae News* [University of North Carolina, Greensboro] 52 (April 1964): 31, 41.

21. Nancy Reynolds, interview, OHA.

22. Quoted in Witold Rybczynski, *A Clearing in the Distance: Frederick Law Olmsted and America in the Nineteenth Century* (New York: Scribner, 1999), 380.

23. Quoted in ibid., 381.

24. Priscilla Brendler, quoted in Anne Raver, "A Great Estate Opens Its Gates," *New York Times*, May 15, 2003, D1, 8.

25. See my essay "After the 'Other' War: Landscapes of Home, North and South," in *The Architecture of Landscape, 1940–1960*, ed. Marc Treib (Philadelphia: University of Pennsylvania Press, 2002), 154–79.

26. Raver, "Great Estates," 8.

27. E. P. Powell, *The Country Home* (New York: McClure, Phillips & Co., 1904), 61.

28. "A Home in a Prairie Town," *Ladies' Home Journal* (February 1901), and "A Small House with 'Lots of Room in It,'" ibid. (July 1901).

29. For a discussion of the possible influence on Wright's style of the architecture of Robert C. Spencer Jr. see H. Allen Brooks, *Frank Lloyd Wright and His Midwest Contemporaries* (New York: W. W. Norton, l972), 57–6l.

30. Frank Lloyd Wright, *Modern Architecture* (1931), quoted in *Frank Lloyd Wright: Writings and Buildings*, selected by Edgar Kaufmann and Ban Raeburn (1960; reprint, New York: New American Library, 1974), 45.

31. Aymar Embury II, *The Livable House: Its Plan and Design*, Livable House series, vol.1 (New York: Moffat Yard and Company, 1917), 46.

32. Mark Alan Hewitt, *The Architect and the American Country House, 1890–1940* (New Haven: Yale University Press, 1990), 198–99.

33. Quoted ibid., 198.

34. Barbara Mayer affirms that the 1909 edition of Charles E. Hooper, *The Country House: A Practical Manual of the Planning and Construction of the American Country House and Its Surroundings* (New York: Doubleday, Page and Co. for the Country Life Press, [1904]), "is in the Reynolda House Library and almost certainly belonged to Katharine Reynolds" (Mayer, *Reynolda: A History of an American Country House* [Winston-Salem, N.C.: John F. Blair for Reynolda House Museum of American Art, 1997]), 54.

35. P[eter] H[arrison] Ditchfield, *The Charm of the English Village* (London, 1908); *The Cottages and Village Life of Rural England* (London, 1912); *Picturesque English Cottages and Their Doorway Gardens* (Philadelphia: J. C. Winston, 1905).

36. Ralph Adams Cram, preface to Ditchfield, *Picturesque English Cottages*.

37. Charles Barton Keen designed a house in Winston for Robert E. Lasater, a friend and business associate of the Reynoldses who was also married to a niece of R. J. Reynolds. Since the Lasater residence was completed in 1912, Barbara Mayer has speculated (*Reynolda*, 56) that Lasater may have introduced Katharine to Keen. It seems more likely, however, that since Katharine had begun planning her much larger project several years earlier, and was already familiar with Philadelphia's major design firms and the architecture and landscapes of its suburbs, the earlier date of completion simply reflects the difference in scale and complexity of the two commissions given to Keen.

38. Letter of August 1, 1912, RA, box 2, folder 121.

39. Letter of August 9, 1912, RA, box 1, folder 68.

40. Typescript dated July 29, 1912, RA, box 8, folder 516A. Although it is unsigned, the tone of these instructions is unmistakably Katharine's voice.

41. Quoted in KSR to Lord and Burnham, August 7, 1912, RA, box 2, folder 127.

42. Letter of August 20, 1912, RA, box 2, folder 125.

43. In a letter of January 2, 1913, KSR wrote Keen, referring to the site of the barn: "In excavating for this building, we were fortunate in striking a great quantity of the round stones, which we need so much in the foundation work, and I believe we will have plenty for use in the foundation of this building— as we have used them in the foundation of the greenhouse—if you think this would be a wise plan." Keen replied in a letter of January 14: "I am glad to know that you have found so many round boulder stone[s] in excavating for the foundation of the Farm building. I presume it is your intention to use these for the face work for the stone walls, which I think is the very best material we could use for this purpose." RA, box 2, folder 121.

44. Augusta Owens Patterson, *American Homes of Today: Their Architectural Style, Their Environment, Their Characteristics* (New York: Macmillan, 1924), 227.

45. Nannie M. Tilley, *The R. J. Reynolds Tobacco Company* (Chapel Hill: University of North Carolina Press, 1985), 193–94. Although the opportunity was theoretically open to all employees, Tilley notes that the enabling bylaw in the company's constitution stated that individuals might qualify for such purchases "in the discretion and at the option of the Board of Directors." Nevertheless, according to Tilley, "allocation of stock for purchase by officers and employees does appear to have been handled on a democratic basis."

46. Ibid., 266–72.

47. Among many acts of philanthropy throughout his adult life, R. J. Reynolds underwrote the establishment of a hospital and nurses' training department associated with Slater Normal and Industrial College, a Negro institution of which he was also a major benefactor; "led the drive" to build decent homes, with low-interest mortgages, for Negro employees of his company; and donated land for the site and a large contribution to establish a Methodist church for the local Negro community. According to Tilley, "the contributions of R. J. Reynolds generally went for projects intended to help the most neglected segment of the Winston-Salem population" (*Reynolds Tobacco Company*, 525–26).

48. Allen Tullos, *Habits of Industry: White Culture and the Transformation of the Carolina Piedmont* (Chapel Hill: University of North Carolina Press, 1989), 12.

49. Interviews with former residents of Five Row, OHA.

50. Neal Anderson to KSR, January 8, 1913, RA, box 1, folder 70.

51. "We all played together. . . . They'd play with us, we'd play with them. We didn't go to the same school, but we had the same books . . . paper and everything." Interviews with Harvey Miller, OHA.

52. Interviews, OHA.

53. Margaret Supplee Smith, "Reynolda: A Rural Vision in an Industrializing South," *North Carolina Historical Review* 65 (July 1988): 310–12.

54. Letter of December 10, 1912, RA, box 1, folder 102.

55. Letters of December 5, 1912, RA box 1, folder 82.

56. Letter of December 10, 1912, RA, box 1, folder 82.

57. KSR to "Christine," December 18, 1912, box 1, folder 79.

58. Letter of December 28, 1912, RA, box 1, folder 84.

59. Letter of January 14, 1913, RA, box 1, folder 102.

60. Letter of December 9, 1912, RA, box 2, folder 125.

61. Letter of January 2, 1913, RA, box 2, folder 125.

62. Letter of January 14, 1913, RA, box 1, folder 102.

63. Letter of February 18, 1913, RA, box 1, folder 74.

64. KSR to Miss A. M. Hall, February 18, 1913, RA, box 1, folder 106.

65. Postcard of February 28, 1913, BBM.

66. Letter of March 8, 1913, RA, box 1, folder 63.1.

67. Nancy Reynolds, interview, OHA.

68. Tilley, *Reynolds Tobacco Company*, 203–15 passim.

69. "Edith" to Henrietta van den Berg, April 28, 1914, RA, box 2, folder 166.

70. KSR wrote a check to the hotel dated May 26, 1914, RA, box 3, folder 253.

71. "Garden Planting Plan for Mrs. R. J. Reynolds," dated September 1913, by Louis L. Miller, Landscape Engineer, RA.

72. See correspondence between KSR and Louis L. Miller, RA, box 2, folder 125.

73. Legal notice filed with List of Liabilities and Assets, October 1, 1914, RA, box 8, folder 515.

4. THE LANDSCAPE OF HOME

1. Letter of May 27, 1912, RA, box 2, folder 127.

2. Letter of July 26, 1912, RA, box 2, folder 127.

3. Letter of October 14, 1977, from Philadelphia landscape architect George E. Patton to George Yarwood responding to Yarwood's request for information on the career of Thomas Sears for the archives of the American Society of Landscape Architects. Patton had interviewed a daughter of Sears, Eleanor Tibbetts, who mentioned the Philadelphia Museum of Art project as her father's earliest in that city. Archives of the American Society of Landscape Architects, Washington, D.C. See also Catherine Howett, "Sears, Thomas W. (1880–1966)" in *Pioneers of American Landscape Design*, ed. Charles A. Birnbaum and Robin Karson (New York: McGraw-Hill, 2000), 338–43.

4. Thomas Sears, photographer, *Parish Churches of England* (New York: Rogers and Manson, 1915).

5. Samuel Parsons Jr., *The Art of Landscape Architecture: Its Development and Its Application to Modern Landscape Gardening* (New York: Knickerbocker Press/ G. P. Putnam's Sons, 1915).

6. Sears and Wendell, "Planting Plan Near Chapel," March 29, 1915, and "Plan of Plantings around Chapel and Cottages," September 18, 1915.

7. Mark Alan Hewitt, *The Architect and the Country House, 1890–1940* (New Haven: Yale University Press, 1990), 197.

8. Patton to Yarwood.

9. See Robin Karson, "Manning, Warren Henry (1860–1939)," in Birnbaum and Karson, *Pioneers*, 236–42.

10. See Robin Karson, "Fletcher Steele, 1885–1971," ibid., 375–81; and Karson, *Fletcher Steele, Landscape Architect: An Account of the Gardenmaker's Life, 1885–1971*, rev. ed. (Amherst: Library of American Landscape History, distributed by University of Massachusetts Press, 2004).

11. Wilhelm Miller, *What England Can Teach Us about Gardening* (Garden City, N.Y.: Doubleday, Page & Co., 1911).

12. Ibid., 3, 18.

13. Glass-plate negatives of pictures Sears had taken at Gravetye were in his personal collection, later donated by his daughter Eleanor Tibbetts to the Archive of American Gardens Slide Library of Notable Parks and Gardens of the Smithsonian Institution, Washington, D.C.

14. Miller, *What England Can Teach Us*, 9–10, 17–21.

15. Ibid., 35, 40.

16. Such gifts and exchanges are documented in KSR's correspondence; for discussion of her interest in the art of flower arrangement and practice of it, see typescript of lecture by Sherold Hollingsworth, ASLA, presented October 30, 1995, to the Reynolda Flower Arranging Committee, RA.

17. John D. Sedding, *Garden Craft Old and New* (London: Kegan Paul, 1891); Reginald Blomfield, *The Formal Garden in England* (London: Macmillan, 1892).

18. "Property of Mrs. Kathrine [sic] S. Reynolds, Winston Salem, N.C.," A. F. Dean, Engineer, January 1915, RA.

19. Miller, *What England Can Teach Us*, 58

20. Wilhelm Miller, "The Prairie Style of Landscape Architecture," *Architectural Record* 40 (December 1916): 591; see also Miller, *The Prairie Spirit in Landscape Gardening*, circular no. 184 (Urbana: University of Illinois Agricultural Experiment Station, Department of Horticulture, 1915), reprinted with intro. by Christopher Vernon (Amherst: University of Massachusetts Press/Library of American Landscape History, 2003).

21. Charles Eliot, "The Waverley Oaks, A Plan for Their Preservation for the People," text originally published as a letter of February 22, 1890, to the editor of *Garden and Forest*, republished in [Charles W. Eliot], *Charles Eliot, Landscape Architect* (Boston: Houghton Mifflin, 1902); reprinted with intro. by Keith N. Morgan (Amherst: University of Massachusetts Press/Library of American Landscape History, 1999), 318.

22. "Uses of Native Plants" by Kenneth E. Gillett is listed as a "brochure" in

"Books and Magazines in K. S. Reynolds's Garden Library," Appendix II of Peyton F. Russ, "A Design History of Reynolda Gardens, 1910–1920: Garden for the Estate of Mr. and Mrs. R. J. Reynolds, Winston-Salem, North Carolina," undated unpublished ms., RA.

23. Nannie M. Tilley, *The R. J. Reynolds Tobacco Company* (Chapel Hill: University of North Carolina Press, 1985), 268. The first lunchroom for white employees of Reynolds Tobacco opened in April 1915; a lunchroom for Negro employees was provided in July of the same year.

24. Preston Stockton, manager of Reynolda Gardens of Wake Forest University, confirmed that several species that Thomas Sears apparently assumed would function as perennials (e.g., doronicum, delphinium, lupine) must be treated as biennials and replanted in the gardens each fall. Other species, such as aconitum and cerastium, proved so intolerant of the climate in summer that they are no longer grown. "The lilacs he chose probably struggled. We also have no luck with *Rhododendron vaseyi*. It is native to the higher elevations of the North Carolina mountains, so I guess that is not surprising. . . . I am interested to see how the [recently replanted] roses do when we finally get a cold winter. So far they have been perfectly hardy but I suspect that a few might not make it through single-digit [temperatures]." E-mail exchange with the author, May 3–4, 2006.

25. "Mrs. R. J. Reynolds State President of the Memorial," *Winston-Salem Journal*, September 15, 1915; Adelaide Fries, *Forsyth: The History of a County on the March* (Chapel Hill: University of North Carolina Press, 1949; reprint, 1976), 201–2, 210.

26. KSR's leadership role (including occasional teaching) in the Reynolda Presbyterian Church Sunday School is documented in an undated twelve-page typescript, "Reminiscences of Mrs. Richard Joshua Reynolds," by J. S[tuart] Kuykendall, the first elected elder of the church, RA, box 35.

27. Quoted in *Frank Lloyd Wright*, a film by Ken Burns and Lyn Novick, Public Broadcasting Service, American Stories series, 1998.

28. Elsie de Wolfe, *The House in Good Taste* (1913; reprint, Rizzoli, 2004), 3. De Wolfe, who had earlier aspired to a career as an actress, sought comfort for her lack of success by pouring her energies into a domestic project, the complete makeover—inspired by her reading of Edith Wharton and Ogden Codman Jr.'s *The Decoration of Houses* (New York: Charles Scribner's Sons, 1897)—of her New York City townhouse. Friends were so impressed with the freshness of its style that before long de Wolfe had reinvented herself as America's first professional interior decorator, with a client list drawn from the ranks of high society, including the duchess of Windsor. Her "modern" rooms replaced the dark wood paneling, richly colored and patterned wallpapers, and overstuffed furniture of an earlier time with white walls, mirrors, delicate French chairs, and fabrics and shades that helped to create a light-filled and lighthearted atmosphere.

29. Ibid., 4–9, passim.

30. Ibid., vii–viii.

31. William L. Bowers, *The Country Life Movement in America, 1900–1920* (Port Washington, N.Y.: Kennikat Press, 1974), 33.

32. Kenneth K. Bailey, *Southern White Protestantism in the Twentieth Century* (New York: Harper & Row, 1964), 41.

33. Page founded the highly respected and influential magazine *World's Work* in 1900, serving as its editor until 1913, when President Woodrow Wilson appointed him ambassador to Great Britain. When the First World War erupted in Europe the following year, Wilson was determined that the United States should maintain strict neutrality, a position that his successful and popular ambassador found untenable. The years leading up to America's finally joining the Allied cause in 1917 took a toll on Page's health, forcing his resignation in August 1918. He died a few months later, just weeks after the armistice ending the war.

34. Brendan Gill composed this description of Reynolda for a visitors' brochure distributed by Reynolda House Museum of American Art. Interview with Barbara Babcock Millhouse, September 5, 2004.

35. Tilley, *Reynolds Tobacco Company*, 314–18.

36. Evie Crim to KSR, May 28, 1918, RA, box 1, folder 86.

37. *Winston-Salem Journal*, July 5, 1916.

38. Among a number of references to the possibility of a California trip or to travel in Asia that occur in correspondence is a letter of January 1, 1913, to niece Ethel Reynolds, in which KSR remarks that she and her husband "are making our arrangements to take a trip somewhere. I have not decided yet whether it will be Augusta, Tampa, Vicksburg, or California," and a letter of May 29, 1913, from KSR to a Presbyterian missionary, Charles Pratt, who had written asking her for financial support; she closes with an expression of hope that she will have a chance to visit with him in Winston-Salem before his departure for Korea, "but anyway hope to see you sometime in Korea as we have not yet given out [*sic*] our oriental journey." RA, box 2, folders 146, 138.

39. The society column of the *Winston-Salem Journal*, March 7, 1915, noted the departure earlier that week of Mr. and Mrs. R. J. Reynolds on a trip to California that would include a visit to the Panama-California Exposition; the same column in the paper of April 7, 1915, announced their expected return that week from the West Coast trip.

40. See the itinerary for one of these trips, "Schedule of the Trogden North Carolina, Special Panama-California Exposition Standard Pullman Train," arranged by Mr. and Mrs. W. F. Trogden of North Wilkesboro, North Carolina, planned for June 8–July 16 [1915], RA, box 10, folder 681. See also photographs of a tour party visiting the Grand Canyon on horseback; Dick appears in at least two of these, and a woman believed to be Katharine stands close to him in another. RA, box 31. See also a set of four twentieth-century paintings

on silk of conventional Japanese landscape scenes, rolled and packaged in a slender carrying tube—the type of imported souvenir sold at the Japanese pavilions at both expositions. RA, box 26.

41. Josiah Condor, *Landscape Gardening in Japan* (Tokyo: Hakubunsha; Yokohama: Kelly and Walsh, 1893), and *Supplement to Landscape Gardening in Japan: Second and Revised Edition*, with collotypes by K. Ogawa (Tokyo: Hakubunsha; Yokohama: Kally and Walsh, 1912).

42. An earlier gift of cherry trees, presented to Mrs. William Howard Taft, wife of the president, in 1910, were found to be diseased, a source of considerable embarrassment to the Japanese government until the 1912 shipment was successfully installed.

43. Clive Aslet, *The Last Country Houses* (New Haven: Yale University Press, 1982), 56. See also Clay Lancaster, *The Japanese Influence in America* (1963; reprint, New York: Abbeville Press, 1983).

44. The best-defined landscape expression of this synthesis would emerge much later as a California "school," whose commitment to the principles of European modernism coexisted with an appreciation for the resonance of historic regional traditions, Japanese as well as Mediterranean. The willingness of Bay Area landscape architect Thomas Church (1902–1978) to experiment boldly with the integration and reinterpretation of new and old styles paved the way for the equally distinguished careers of such men as Garrett Eckbo (1910–2000), Lawrence Halprin (b. 1916), and Robert Royston (b. 1918). A seminal 1938 study, *Gardens in the Modern Landscape* by Christopher Tunnard (London: Architectural Press), also influenced the fusion of a Japanese sensibility with modernist forms in the distinctive regional style associated with these designers. Tunnard was open to a selective borrowing of aesthetic principles associated with certain historic styles and specifically urged Western designers to learn from Eastern landscape traditions the lessons of a more reverent, philosophic, and revelatory approach to the manipulation of the natural world.

45. Ruth Smith Lucas, interview, February 7, 1977, OHA.

46. Thomas W. Sears, "Planting Plan for Greenhouse Garden, Estate of Mrs. R. J. Reynolds, Winston-Salem," a set of five plans labeled A through E, dated September 25, 1917, RA. Irvin M. Disher, manager of Reynolda's greenhouse operations from shortly after his employment in 1910 until his retirement in 1959, remembered a delivery of fifty weeping cherry trees shipped by Andorra Nurseries of Pennsylvania in February 1917. Interview with I. M. Disher, *Winston-Salem Journal*, March 11, 1951, quoted in "Garden History and the Renovation of the Formal Gardens," *Gardener's Journal* (newsletter of Reynolda Gardens of Wake Forest University) (Summer 1996): 3.

47. Bill of lading dated November 11, 1912, from Bloodgood Nurseries, Flushing, N.Y., RA.

48. There seems to be no extant planting plan that includes the wisteria vine cov-

ering the east entrance pergola, although the Sears Plan D of September 25, 1917, specified eight *Wisteria chinensis* vines, two each planted to cover four of the five shelters joined by pergolas; the central, recessed pergola was to be planted with "Japanese Virgin's Bower" (*Clematis paniculata*) and grapevines.

49. Charles Henderson, *Henderson's Picturesque Gardens and Ornamental Gardening Illustrated* (New York: Peter Henderson, 1908), 70–72. Henderson devoted one section to a general description of the gardens of Japan and another to Japanese iris gardens.

50. Katharine apparently wanted to grow even more peonies than Sears had specified in the 1917 set of planting plans for the formal gardens. In 1920 he submitted a second plan for beds immediately in front of the greenhouse that had originally been planted with the mixture of annuals and perennials shown in his Plan D. In his later design, ten species of herbaceous peonies in shades of pink and white dominate the border, with only two varieties each of Japanese anemones and chrysanthemums in the same color range to provide a fall display. Camilla Wilcox, "The Year of the Peony at Reynolda Gardens," *Gardener's Journal* (Summer 2000): 2.

51. Thomas Sears, "Planting Plan for Material around Teahouses A & B in Vegetable Garden," December 6, 1921, RA.

52. Thomas W. Sears, "Details of Shelters & Pergolas," revised plan, October 25, 1916, RA.

53. In a letter of January 24, 1918, related to his final bill for design work on the bungalow and additional oversight of subcontracts unrelated to his original agreement, Charles Barton Keen returned to the subject of a discussion in which he had explained to KSR that the additional work involving subcontractors handled through his office warranted an increase in his payment for services, originally based on 6 percent of the cost of construction: "[It] is usual and proper to charge the sum of 10% where work is handled under individual contracts, to compensate for the additional work involved. . . . In fact my position and the work performed by me was practically that of General Contractor, for which the usual percentage or profit charge is 10%." After suggesting a compromise figure of 8 percent, Keen reminded her of another service for which he deserved compensation, "the time spent and advice given in considering the question of decoration and furniture. You will recollect the consideration given to the schemes of W. and J. Sloane and Wanamakers and I feel quite sure that you will agree that I am entitled to compensation for these services and would appreciate an expression of opinion on the subject. He closed the letter tersely, "Trusting I have made myself clear." RA, box 2, folder 121.

54. Camilla Wilcox, "A Modern Rose Garden," *Gardener's Journal* (Winter 1997): 8.

55. Sears used an earlier botanical name for this plant, *Pyrethrum roseum*.

56. Sears listed this plant on his plan as *Phlox amoena* "Miss Lingard" and de-

scribed its color as pink. Although "Miss Lingard" is classified at the present time as a cultivar of *P. maculata*, its parentage is uncertain and it may actually be the product of a cross between this species and *P. carolina*. See Alan M. Armitage, *Herbaceous Perennial Plants: A Treatise on Their Identification, Culture, and Garden Attributes* (Athens, Ga.: Varsity Press, 1989), 457–58.

57. KSR to Ludowici-Celadon Co., October 3, 1916, RA, box 9, folder 620.

58. Thomas W. Sears, "Planting Plan around Bungalow, Property of Mrs. R. J. Reynolds," February 23, 1916, RA. Sears specified on this plan that each column be planted with one of three recommended species of flowering vine, but later photographs of the house show that climbing roses were substituted in these locations.

59. This species is listed by Sears as *Andromeda japonica*.

60. RJR paid 1916 income taxes of $66,000, more than twice the amount paid by any other resident of North Carolina. *Winston-Salem Journal and Sentinel*, May 14, 1950.

61. Ibid., January 2, 1917.

62. Telegram dated February 2, 1917, from RJR to Belview Hotel, Bellair, Florida, requests "four good outside rooms" for a party of eight arriving March 17; a letter dated May 8, 1917, from H. Martin to KSR refers to the Reynoldses having recently vacationed in "Palm Beach." RA, box 1, folder 61, and box 2, folder 131.

63. *Twin City Sentinel*, September 27, 1917; Minnie L. Blanton to KSR, September 13, 1917, RA, box 1, folder 75.

64. *Winston-Salem Journal and Sentinel*, June 9, 1917.

65. *Winston-Salem Journal and Sentinel*, July 7, 1917.

66. Letter of July 8, 1917, RA, box 1, folder 70.

67. Letter of July 9, 1917, RA, box 1, folder 70.

68. William Martin to KSR, July 18, 1917, RA, box 2, folder 131.

69. *Winston-Salem Journal and Sentinel*, July 7, 1917. All quotations are from this source.

70. KSR to Henrietta van den Berg, September 28, 1917, box 2, folder 166.

71. Telegrams dated July 13 and July 31, 1917, RA, box 1, folder 63.

72. See for example, July 30, 1917, receipt to KSR from Riverside and Dan River Cotton Mills of Danville, Virginia, for purchase of three notes of deferred payment on subscription to 120 shares of common stock. RA, box 1, folder 88, and 1917–18 correspondence with stockbrokers, F. C. Abbot and Co., RA, box 1, folder 99; correspondence with James T. Catlin, RA, box 1, folder 79.

73. Letter of November 9, 1917, RA, box 2, folder 166.

74. Invitation to dedication scheduled on October 17, 1917, RA, box 2, folder 136. September 27, 1917; letter of Mary Gertrude Fendall, Treasurer, National Woman's Party, to KSR, RA, box 21, folder 98.

75. Letter of November 21, 1917, RA, box 1, folder 75.

76. Letter of November 24, 1917, RA, box 1, folder 75.

77. Letter of November 26, 1917, RA, box 1, folder 75.

78. Telegram dated November 30, 1917, RA, box 1, folder 75.

79. Telegram dated December 1, 1917, RA, box 1, folder 75.

80. Dr. Thomas R. Brown to "Doctor H. Vandenberg," telegram dated December 1, 1917, RA, box 1, folder 75.

81. Telegram dated December 4, 1917, RA, box 2, folder 166.

82. Postcard of December 7, 1917, RA, box 2, folder 178.

83. Telegram dated December 7, 1917, RA, box 2, folder 166.

84. *Sorosis Year Book, 1917–1918* (Winston-Salem, N.C.: privately printed), 11, RA, box 2, folder 157.1–01. Sorosis clubs originated in an 1868 protest against the exclusion of women journalists from the New York Press Club. See Linda K. Kerber, "Separate Spheres, Female Worlds, Woman's Place: The Rhetoric of Women's History," in *Toward an Intellectual History of Women: Essays by Linda K. Kerber* (Chapel Hill: University of North Carolina Press, 1997), 189.

85. KSR to Mrs. Eugene Reilley, January 23, 1918, RA, box 9, folder 592; *Winston-Salem Journal*, October 24, 1917.

86. See KSR's correspondence with lighting manufacturer E. F. Caldwell, RA, box 1, folder 96; KSR to Frank Taft, Aeolian Organ Company, February 25, 1918, RA, box 1, folder 69.

87. Letter of February 19, 1918, RA, box 2, folder 152.

88. Letter of February 22, 1918, RA, box 2, folder 152.

89. J. W. [?] Conrad to KSR, June 27, 1918, RA, box 1, folder 85.5.

90. William Hollis Hatfield to KSR, September 9 and 30, 1917, and June 3, 1918, RA, box 1, folder 106.

91. Nadeina Gibson Buchanan, interview, OHA.

92. KSR to Hardin William Reynolds, M.D., February 25, 1918, RA, box 2, folder 142.

93. *Winston-Salem Journal and Sentinel*, August 18, 1918, citing affidavits for will of Richard Joshua Reynolds that stated that "R. J. Reynolds had been ill for more than a year prior to his death on the 29th of July 1918; that on account of the seriousness of his condition he entered a hospital in Philadelphia about the fifth day of April, remaining there until his return home on the nineteenth day of July, 1918."

94. Jessie B. Hill to KSR, May 1, 1918, RA, box 1, folder 106.

95. Letters exchanged between KSR and Minnie Morrison of Statesville, N.C., during summer and fall 1918, RA, box 2, folder 135.

96. Senah Critz to KSR, undated, RA, box 1, folder 87.

97. Henrietta van den Berg to Senah Critz, May 27, 1918, RA, box 2, folder 166.

98. Adelaide Douglas to KSR, undated, RA, box 1, folder 88.

99. Letter of May 28, 1918, RA, box 1, folder 86.

100. James Dunn to KSR, June 2, 1918, RA, box 1, folder 93.

101. Undated, RA, box 1, folder 87.

102. Evie Crim to KSR, June 17, 1918: "Everyone here is well and the servants in-

quire of me each day if I have heard further from Mr. Reynolds. They are glad the operation is over," RA, box 1, folder 86.

103. Letter to Neal L. Anderson, July 19, 1918.

104. Letter of July 18, 1918, RA, box 1, folder 86.

105. Private Robert C. Conrad to KSR, July 7, 1918; KSR to Conrad, July 18, 1918, RA, box 1, folders 79, 85.5.

106. Letter of July 18, 1918, RA, box 1, folder 70.

107. Neal L. Anderson, D.D., "Richard Joshua Reynolds," typescript, RA, box 1, folder 70.

5. CHANGING SEASONS, A VISION RENEWED

1. Letter of August 6, 1918, RA, box 1, folder 68.

2. Ruth Smith Lucas, sister of KSR, recalled that after RJR's death, "huge federal and state taxes" were owed on the estate, but Katharine "worked with it herself and managed to avoid disposing of a lot of capital to pay the taxes." Lucy Hadley Cash, one of the original group of Reynolda School teachers who lived on the estate, reported that when Katharine was in New York City, she would "go down in the business district and manipulate things herself" and frequently boasted "about putting something over on Wall Street, that she'd made a good deal, or she'd out-talked them." OHA.

3. KSR to Miss A. C. Meeley, August 6, 1918, RA, box 2, folder 132.

4. Virginia Woolf, *A Room of One's Own* (London: Hogarth Press, 1929), 110–11.

5. Ibid., 135.

6. Charles Barton Keen, "Cottage 2 and Temporary School House at Reynolda," August 8, 1918.

7. Educated at Cornell University, Humphreys subsequently worked in the offices of both George W. Post and Bradford Gilbert before setting up his own practice. Clarence E. Weaver, *Winston-Salem, "City of Industry"* ([Winston-Salem]: Winston Printing Company [1918?]). The spelling of his name in Weaver and on a relevant website, www.emporis.com, is "Humphries."

8. Letters of September 10, 1918, RA, box 2, folders 112 and 135.

9. Henrietta van den Berg had reported to army headquarters in Washington, D.C., for a physical examination. In a telegram sent from Baltimore on August 9, 1918, she informed KSR that she had been unable to "get a further extension of time, but they promise not to call me if not absolutely necessary," RA, box 2, folder 166.

10. Undated letter from Sophie Norfleet to KSR refers to the latter's sadness over the death of Miss Hill: "I know you will miss her love and friendship," RA, box 2, folder 136.

11. An article in the *Winston-Salem Journal and Sentinel* of October 20, 1918, reports the death from flu of Miss Jessie Hill from Jefferson Hospital, Philadelphia, who had nursed R. J. Reynolds before his death.

12. A letter of November 1, 1918, from S. Mamie Carter to KSR refers to "the awful flu. So many cases in Winston-Salem makes me feel anxious to hear from you," RA, box 1, folder 79.

13. Rev. Neal Anderson to KSR, January 2, 1919, RA, box 1, folder 70.

14. On January 13, 1919, Evie Crim wrote to KSR, "I regret to hear from Mr. Orr that you are not well and that you were really ill in Jacksonville," RA, box 1, folder 86.

15. Rev. Neal Anderson to KSR, February 12, 1919, RA, box 1, folder 68.

16. See John M. Barry, *The Great Influenza: The Epic Story of the Deadliest Plague in History* (New York: Viking, 2004).

17. There are only three extant Sears plans for 1918, two done in January and another in December, the latter a design for a stairway leading from the schoolhouse to playgrounds in back of the building, although a letter of November 18 to KSR accompanied "two blueprints showing the grading and treatment of walks, etc.," RA, box 2, folder 152.

18. Thomas W. Sears, "Planting Plan for Cottage Near Blacksmith Shop," undated, RA.

19. Thomas W. Sears, "Grading Plan; Teacher's [*sic*] Cottage Garden" undated; Thomas W. Sears, "Study for Cut Flower and Nicer Vegetable Garden," February 5, 1919, RA.

20. Letter from a woman [signature undecipherable] in Dearborn, N.C., to KSR, RA, box 1, folder 79; *Twin-City Sentinel*, May 10, 1919.

21. Hilda Loines, Acting President, Woman's National Farm and Garden Association, to KSR, February 19, 1919, RA, box 2, folder 122.

22. Letter of March 13, 1919, RA, box 2, folder 136.

23. "Vocational School to Be Built at Reynolda Equipped for Day Pupils," *Winston-Salem Journal and Sentinel*, March 9, 1919.

24. Letter of December 26, 1918, from Laura Coit, Secretary of the Association, to KSR. RA, unprocessed correspondence.

25. R. H. Latham, Superintendent, to KSR, March 19, 1919, RA, box 1, folder 122.

26. KSR to Mayor and Board of Aldermen, City of Winston-Salem, July 3, 1919, referring to an earlier offer: "Regardless of which site is selected, my offer holds good not only as to the land but also as to the erection of a large memorial auditorium." Letter published in *Winston-Salem Journal*, July 4, 1919.

27. This commission represented a turning point in Keen's career. In addition to the many residences designed for North Carolina clients, he received commissions for the R. J. Reynolds High School (1921), the Winston-Salem Hospital (1921), and the Greensboro Country Club (1922). His practice in the region became so extensive that in 1923 he moved his home office to Winston-Salem and resided in the city for a period of time. Sandra L. Tatman, "Keen, Charles Barton (1868–1931)," Philadelphia Architects and Buildings Project website, www.philadelphiabuildings.org, 2003.

28. Newspaper clipping dated June 1919 [source unidentified], "Pageant, 'Bird's Ball' Proved Great Success," RA, box 8, folder 541.

29. F. B. Dresslar, Special Agent of the Bureau of Education, Department of the Interior, Washington, D.C., to KSR, February 24, 1919, RA, box 1, folder 88.

30. "Vocational School to Be Built."

31. R. H. Latham, Superintendent, to KSR, March 19, 1919, RA, box 1, folder 122. Another letter of March 20 from H. H. Boyden of Salisbury, N.C., asked KSR for more information "about the vocational School you are going to give your people," RA, box 1, folder 75.

32. See the letter of March 14, 1919, from KSR to U.S. Bureau of Education requesting the "bulletin of rural schools and buildings and also volumes of American school architecture . . . by F. B. Dresslar," RA, box 1, folder 88. Fletcher B. Dresslar, *Rural School Houses and Grounds* (Washington, D.C.: U.S. Bureau of Education, 1914); Fletcher B. Dresslar, *American School Houses* (Washington, D.C.: U.S. Government Printing Office, 1911).

33. The March 19, 1919, letter from Latham to KSR closes, "I would certainly be glad to have the opportunity to talk with Dr. Dresslar, if he comes to Winston-Salem."

34. *Winston-Salem Journal*, July 31, 1919.

35. See interview with Lucy Hadley Cash, one of the original group of teachers at the new school, describing his arrival in uniform, OHA.

36. *Winston-Salem Journal*, July 31, 1919.

37. *Winston-Salem Journal*, August 31, 1919.

38. *Winston-Salem Journal*, September 14, 1919.

39. Lucy Hadley Cash, interview, OHA.

40. Once the family had moved to Reynolda, Katharine provided regular bus service for the convenience of those employees whose homes were in the city as well as for children commuting to the school.

41. Interview with Ethel Brock Sloan, OHA.

42. Interview with Mary Martha Lybrook Spitzmuller, OHA.

43. "Woman Handles and Counts Vast Sums at the Mint," *Philadelphia Public Ledger*, February 11, 1921. The color was named for Joseph Jacques Joffre, French marshal who served as commander of Allied forces during the First World War.

44. File on the R. J. Reynolds Professorship (which effectively created the first Department of Biology at Davidson), E. H. Little Library, Davidson College, Davidson, N.C.

45. *Winston-Salem Sentinel*, March 8, 1920.

46. Letter of January 20, 1921, Katharine Smith Reynolds Johnston and J. Edward Johnston Personal Correspondence Collection, 1920–1923, Zachary Smith Reynolds Library, Wake Forest University (hereafter ZSRL).

47. JEJ to KSR, letters of November 4, 7, 8, and 9, 1920, ZSRL. In the letter of November 9, Ed commented on Katharine's report of a conversation with Will

Reynolds: "I can imagine how interested he is and how anxious he is to learn the truth, however much he may suspect. I also know that he, like everyone else there, is wondering about your coming to Wilson. . . . My path will not be a smooth one working for the company."

48. Letter of December 6, 1920, ZSRL.

49. KSR to JEJ, letter of January 15, 1921, ZSRL.

50. Letter of January 25, 1921, ZSRL.

51. Letter of January 29, 1921, ZSRL. In a letter of January 4, 1921, Katharine had written Ed: "It is very hard to see Papa and Mamma alone, but it will not be as hard to talk with them as it was to tell Dick. But Dick has been lovely," ZSRL.

52. Diary of Mary Katharine Reynolds, entry for January 24, 1921, Babcock Family Papers, RA, box 2, folder 79.

53. Gertrude Jekyll, *Children and Gardens* (London: Country Life, 1908).

54. Thomas W. Sears, "Planting Plan for Fruit, Cut Flower and Nicer Vegetable Garden, Estate of Mrs. R. J. Reynolds," dated February 17, 1921, RA.

55. Although he had been made an officer of the Reynolds Tobacco Company, Richard ["R. S."] Reynolds left in 1912 to seek his fortune elsewhere; he was a founder of Reynolds Metal, later the Reynolds Aluminum Company.

56. *Winston-Salem Journal*, June 9, 1921.

57. Entry for June 11, 1921.

58. KSRJ to Mary, postcard dated July 16, 1921, RA, box 2, folder 178.

59. JEJ to Mary, postcard dated July 9, 1921, RA, box 2, folder 178.

60. KSRJ to Mary, postcard dated June 29, 1921, RA, box 2, folder 178.

61. Interview with Elizabeth Wade, switchboard operator at Reynolda, OHA.

62. Letter of September 7, 1921, ZSRL.

63. *Winston-Salem Journal*, March 9, 1919.

64. Interviews with former Reynolda School teacher Ethel Brock Sloan and former students Nadeina Gibson Buchanan, Nancy Reynolds, Tippy Ruffin, Aurelia Spaugh, Elizabeth Lybrook Wyeth, OHA.

65. Katharine had planned from the beginning that Reynolda Presbyterian Church should one day have a handsome manse, the largest private residence on the estate except for her own family's home. In a letter of July 1, 1916, in the archives of Reynolda Presbyterian Church, she explained that although she planned eventually to transfer ownership of an appropriate portion of adjacent property to the church, she intended first to put the site "in excellent condition, with a manse that will accommodate any ordinary-sized family. It perhaps will be a couple years before I will be in a position to do this." In the meantime, Katharine had allowed the first minister of Reynolda Church, Rev. T. W. Simpson, to live rent-free with his family in a cottage on the estate. Nadeina Gibson Buchanan, daughter of Reynolda's resident electrician, remembered the morning in her childhood on which the almost finished manse caught fire, after which the building "had to be reworked. . . . It was a beauti-

ful home, just gorgeous. And it was completely furnished all over with the finest furniture you can imagine," OHA. Thomas Sears produced a "General Planting Plan for the Manse" and "Planting Plan for Manse Garden," both dated March 31, 1920, RA. In December of the same year, Katharine met with her Philadelphia decorator to review "materials and designs" for the manse, and by January was supervising the arrangement of new furnishings. Letters to JEJ dated December 13, 1920, and January 10, 1921, ZSRL. Mary Reynolds noted in her diary entry on January 16, 1921, that "the teachers are going to spend their first night in the manse."

66. Letter from JEJ to KSRJ, September 7, 1921, ZSRL.

67. Nancy Reynolds, interview, OHA.

68. Letter of October 17, 1921, ZSRL.

69. Emma Kaminer to KSR, July 10, 1921, RA, box 1, folder 119.

70. *Winston-Salem Journal*, March 31, 1922.

71. Letter of May 31, 1922, addressed to KSR at Marlborough Blenheim, RA, box 2, folder 183.

72. *Winston-Salem Journal*, June 24, 1922.

73. Thomas W. Sears, "Study Beyond Vegetable Gardens," June 8, 1921, RA.

74. Thomas W. Sears, "Bulb Planting for Cedar Walk," August 8, 1922, RA.

75. *Winston-Salem Journal*, July 11, 1922.

76. OHA.

77. Telegram dated July 28, 1922, from John Walker [camp director?] to James S. Dunn, Sr., describes "baffling" infection in the boy's heel; "James S. Dunn, Jr., Died at Charlottesville, Va.," undated and unidentified newspaper clipping reporting the boy's death at the University of Virginia Hospital, return of his body to Winston-Salem, and funeral arrangements planned for the following afternoon. Richard Reynolds, Jr., is listed among the pallbearers, RA, unprocessed materials.

78. *Winston-Salem Journal*, September 26, 1922.

79. Keen produced three drawings dated March 12, 1923, for a project described as the "Temporary Grade School House" at Reynolda. In May of the same year, he moved his firm's main office to the Wachovia Bank and Trust Company building in Winston-Salem.

80. *Winston-Salem Journal*, March 31, 1923.

81. *Winston-Salem Journal*, July 4, 1919.

82. Interview with Nadeina Gibson Buchanan, OHA.

83. "Musical Program for Garden Party, Reynolda," July 6, 1923, RA, box 8, folder 536.

84. *Winston-Salem Journal*, July 7, 1923.

85. *Winston-Salem Journal*, November 15, 1923.

86. Tiffany & Company 1924 pocket calendar, RA, unprocessed material, box U126.

87. Ibid.

88. Will of Katharine Smith Reynolds Johnston, dated March 29, 1924, filed for probate in the office of the Clerk of the Superior Court, Forsyth County, North Carolina, May 29, 1924.

89. Ibid.

90. Telephone interview with Zachary Taylor Smith, October 24, 1995.

91. Colonel J. Edward Johnston died in 1951 at age 57, having served during World War II as a military intelligence officer at the Pentagon and overseas. In 1948 he was awarded the Order of the British Empire; the citation accompanying the medal credited him with being "mainly responsible for the intelligence agreement covering British and American prisoners of war. Delicate situations vital to the lives of British subjects and American citizens arose from time to time, situations made all the more delicate by the secret nature of the work involved and the local interests of the various commanders outside America." At the time of his death, Johnston was serving as a trustee of Johns Hopkins Hospital, a member of the board of directors at Safe Deposit and Trust Company of Baltimore, and director and fellow of the American Institute of Management, among other activities. He was survived by his and Katharine's son, whom he had raised, as well as two daughters from a second marriage that ended in divorce. Obituary, undated, RA, unprocessed material, box U13.

92. Letter to Nancy, May 30, 1927; letter to Mary, April 25, 1927; letter from Mary to Maxie Dunn, January 18, 1929, RA, Nancy Susan Reynolds Papers, unprocessed, box 1.

93. Barry Alan Lawing, "A History of Aviation in Winston-Salem," Master's thesis, Wake Forest University, 1984.

94. *Winston-Salem Journal*, July 7, 1932.

95. Barbara Mayer, *Reynolda: A History of an American Country House* (Winston-Salem: John F. Blair, 1997), 105.

96. Stewart Warnken, "Balance Sheet for Reynolda, Inc.," and "Comments on Operations at Reynolda During the Year 1935," RA, unprocessed material, box U104.

97. Ibid.

98. Notes in Mary's handwriting, RA, unprocessed material, box U15.

99. Johnson & Porter, Architects, New York City. Series of plans for Reynolda, 1936–37, RA.

100. Thomas W. Sears, "Study for New Forecourt, Reynolda," April 29, 1936, and "Grading Plan of New Driveway and Forecourt, Reynolda Estate of Mrs. Chas. Babcock, Jr.," [undated].

101. Typescript with pen and ink title page; photographs wanting. RA, box 4, folder 345 (oversize).

102. Mayer, *Reynolda*, 112–18.

103. Letters of February 6 and 16, 1945, RA, Nancy Susan Reynolds Papers, unprocessed, box 1.

104. *Winston-Salem Journal*, October 16, 1951.

105. Mayer, *Reynolda*, 123–24.

106. "Reynolda Village Master Plan," Wake Forest University, Winston Salem, E. E. Bouldin, Architect, [1978–1984].

107. Manuscript draft and notes for letter supporting admission of the Winston-Salem Garden Club to the Garden Club of America, undated [c. March 1951], RA, unprocessed material, box U020.

108. The Jaeger Company, Gainsville, Georgia, "Reynolda Gardens Cultural Landscape Report, R. J. Reynolds Estate, Wake Forest University . . . ," 1996.

109. NPS report and website, "The Reynolda Gardens," *Currents*, [undated], http://www.cr.nps.gov/hps/hli/currents/reynolda/intro.htm.

110. Mayer, *Reynolda*, 122–32.

111. Quoted in "At Home with Art; The Campaign for Reynolda House, An American Museum of American Art," produced by Jan Krukowski Associates (Winston-Salem: Reynolda House, Museum of American Art, 1990). RA, unprocessed, oversize.

Illustration Source Credits

Illustrations not otherwise credited are courtesy of Reynolda House, Museum of American Art, Winston-Salem, N.C.

21: Artisans cottages. Courtesy Rose Valley Museum & Historical Society, Moylan, Pa.

29: United Daughters of the Confederacy parade, Mt. Airy. Courtesy North Carolina Collection, The University of North Carolina Library at Chapel Hill.

40: Charles Duncan McIver. Courtesy Charles Duncan McIver Records, University Archives & Manuscripts, Jackson Library, The University of North Carolina at Greensboro.

43: Charles and Lula Martin McIver with their children. Courtesy Susan McIver Abernathy.

46: "Normal College Avenue and College Buildings." Courtesy Postcard Collection, University Archives & Manuscripts, Jackson Library, The University of North Carolina at Greensboro.

50, 52, 53, 55, 57, 58, 63, 86: "Faculty," "Girls' Rooms," Sue May Kirkland ("Charter Members of the Faculty"), "Y.W.C.A. Cabinet," "The Cats," "On the Field—Hockey," "To Sunny Fields Beyond. Peabody Park," frontispiece, "Where Nature Teaches. Peabody Park," from *The Carolinian*, Edited by the Senior Class, 1909. Courtesy Documenting the American South (http://docsouth.unc.edu), The University of North Carolina at Chapel Hill Libraries, North Carolina Collection.

73: "View from Standpipe Southward," "Street Scene," from *Winston-Salem, North Carolina . . . the natural geographical gateway . . . illustrations selected and facts* comp. and written by Col. G. Webb and L. E. Norryce [Roanoke, Va., The Stone Printing and Manufacturing Company, 1905?].

79: "On the Roof of Manufactures Building," from *The Magic City: A Massive Port-folio of Original Photographic Views of the Great World's Fair, with descriptions by J. W. Buel* (St. Louis: Historical Publishing Company, 1894).

79: "The Civic Center That Denver Is About to Realize," from *Los Angeles, California: The City Beautiful: Suggestions by Charles Mulford Robinson: Report of the Municipal Art Commission for the City of Los Angeles, California* (Los Angeles: William J. Porter, 1909).

81, 113, 138: Biltmore Estate. Courtesy Images of America: Lantern Slide Collection, Harvard University Graduate School of Design, Frances Loeb Library.

83, 84: "Dove Cottage," "Grasmere," "A Leafy Bower: Rydal," from William Angus Knight, *Through Wordsworth Country: A Companion to the Lake District,* 2nd ed. (London: S. Sonnenschein, 1890).

88, 89: frontispiece, "Old Timber Farm-House" (p. 119) by J. W. Orr, N.Y., from Frederick Law Olmsted, *Walks and Talks of an American Farmer in England* (1852; rpt. Amherst, Mass.: Library of American Landscape History, 2002).

102: "Mt. Washington from Pinkham Notch, White Mts., N.H.," "No. Wood-stock & Franconia Mts. from Parker Ledge, N.H., 1905," "Hood Farm, Derry, N.H.," postcards. Courtesy private collection.

125: Aerial photo of Monticello, 1985. Courtesy William Rieley.

139: "A Proposed Country Residence at Somerville, New Jersey, Horace Trum-bauer, Architect." Courtesy James B. Duke Collection, Rare Book, Manu-script, & Special Collections Library, Duke University, Durham, N.C.

146: House of the Democrat, Rose Valley. Photo courtesy Robert Linzer Edwards.

186: Conservatory and Lily Pond, c. 1925. Courtesy The LuEsther T. Mertz Library of The New York Botanical Garden, Bronx, New York.

201: Millmead, from Gertrude Jekyll and Lawrence Weaver, *Gardens for Small Country Houses,* 4th ed. (New York: C. Scribner's Sons, 1920).

203: "Estate of William Robinson, Sussex," by Thomas Sears. From the T-Square Club and Philadelphia Chapter of the American Institute of Architects, *Yearbook and Catalogue of the Fifteenth Annual Architectural Exhibition* (1909). Courtesy of the Athenæum of Philadelphia.

237: The Japanese Pavilion, from *Official Miniature View Book of the Panama-Pacific International Exposition* (San Francisco: Robert A. Reid, 1915). Courtesy Advertising Ephemera Collection, Rare Book, Manuscript, & Special Collections Library, Duke University.

Index

Page numbers in *italics* indicate illustrations or material contained in their captions.

and, 11, 14; on Japanese landscape design, 237, 241, 320; KSR as reader of, 103, 146, 200; Miller (Wilhelm) in, 201, 205, 212, 217; on "prairie style," 212; on "wild gardening," 217
Country Life movement, 125, 225
Cram, Ralph Adams, 150
Crim, Evie, 128, 233, 288, 289, 371n14
Critz, Robert, 72
Critz, Ruth, 121
Critz, Senah, 121, 287–88
Croly, Herbert, 103, 104, 145
cryptomerias, *239*, 241, 242, 320, 335, 341–44
Cyclopedia of American Horticulture (Bailey), 201

dairy farming, 112. *See also under* Reynolda Estate farming operations
Daughters of the Confederacy, *29*
Davidson College, 270, 304; R. J. Reynolds Professorship at, 308, 372n44
Decoration of Houses, The (Wharton and Codman), 364n28
Democratic Party, 93–94, 171, 177
Depression, Great, 332, 337
Design on the Land (Newton), 4
De Wolfe, Elsie, 221–25, 227–28, 364n28
Diamond Ring Club (Sullins College), 69
Disher, Irvin, 335, 366n46
Ditchfield, Peter, 150
domestic engineering, 110–11, 114, 144, 167–68
Domestic Service (Salmon), 111
Dove Cottage (Grasmere, England), 82–85, *83*
Downing, Andrew Jackson, 10, 188, 201–2, 218, 350–51n11

Dresslar, Fletcher B., 302–3, 306, 372nn32–33
Duke, James B. ("Buck"), 93, 116, 117, 138–40
Duke Farms (N.J.), 138–40, *139*, 145, 172, 173
Dumbarton Oaks (Washington, D.C.), 350n6
Duncan, Frances, 13–15
Dunn, James S. (brother-in-law), 97, *97*, 311, 374n77
Dunn, James S., Jr. (nephew), 322, 374n77
Dunn, Maxie Smith (sister), 90, 311; in Mount Airy, 70; at Sullins, 61, 65; visits to Fifth Street house, 97, *97*

Eckbo, Garrett, 366n44
eclecticism, 208
educational reform, 38–39; agricultural reform and, 39; City Beautiful movement and, 79–80; KSR and, 301–2; Normal School and, 39–46, 52–53; RJR and, 356–57n21
electrification, 143–44
Eliot, Charles, 6, 212
Ellerbe, J. E., *158*, *162*
Embury, Aymar, II, 148, 150
Emerson, Ralph Waldo, 87
Emory and Henry College (Va.), 355n60
Engelhart, W. L., 308
English Flower Garden, The (Robinson), 202
epidemics, 59–60, 110, 142–43, 298–99, 354n50, 370–71nn10–12
Eseola Inn (Linville, N.C.), 121–22

Fairesonian Literary Society (Sullins College), 65
family planning, 309
Farmers' Alliance, 94, 111

and, 274; pageants/performances on, *312*, 312–13; pathways near, *280*; plans for, 132; recreation facilities on, 324; Reynolda water supply and, *143*, 143; site preparation, *124*, 152; woodland drive near, *278*

Katrine, Loch (Scotland), 132

Keen, Charles Barton, *23*, 308; architectural style of, 149–50, *151*, 157, 180; career background of, 23; as church architect, 195–97; compensation received by, 367n53; death of, 336; English influence on, 199, 208, 217; KSR and, 231, 360n37; KSR's correspondence with, 130, 134–35, 151–52, 209, 361n43, 367n53; master plan revisions and, 183; Miller replacement and, 192; Reynolda school building designed by, 296–97, 302, 318, 323, 374n79; southern landscape traditions and, 216–17; as village architect, 296; Winston-Salem projects of, 308, 371n27

Keen, Charles Barton, bungalow plans of: architectural style of, 147–48, 153–57; KSR hires, 23, 129; KSR's oversight of, 179, 270; bungalow siting in, 131–32, first floor plan, *158*; front/rear elevations, *131*; interior design, 262, 270; preliminary plans, 129–30; revisions to, 134

Keith's Magazine on Home Building, 10

Kentucky, 314

Kentucky Belle (horse), 141

Kew Gardens (London, Eng.), 187

Kings College (Bristol, Tenn.), 67

Kirkland, Sue May, 51, *53*

Kykuit (Pocantico Hills, N.Y.), 237

Ladies' Home Journal, 10, 13, 14, 110–11, 145–46

"Lady of the Lake, The" (Scott), 132

La Farge, John, 78

landscape architecture, American: colonial heritage and, 207–9; feminism and, 12–15; influence on Reynolda, 137–40; Japanese influence on, 366n44; magazine publishers and, 10–11; prairie style, 211–12; professionalization of, 6, 349n3; renaming of, 7, 8, 10; as replication of rural scenery, 87–89, 88, 89; southern traditions, Reynolda and, 216–19; values of, 204–5; women in, 4–5, 6–10, 11–12, 349n4, 350nn6, 8, 351n16

landscape architecture, British, influence of, 200–209; American adaptations, 137–40, 145, 148–49, 199; on gardens, 202–4; on Reynolda, 136, 180

landscape architecture, Japanese, influence of, 237–44, 320, 366n44

Landscape Gardening in Japan (Condor), 236

Lanier, Sydney, 87

Lasater, Robert E., 330, 360n37

Lash, Ed, 165

Latham, R. H., 308, 372n33

League of Nations, Southern Congress for a, 301

Lee, Robert E., 28

liberalism, 100

Library War Council, 268

Linville (N.C.), *121*, 121–22

Livable House, The (Embury), 148

London (England), 187

Lord and Burnham, 133–34, 152, 184–87

Loudon, John Claudius, 188

Lucas, Ruth Smith, 70, 316, 354n58, 370n2

Luytens, Edwin, 150, 200, *201*, 207, 218–19, 253

Lyndhurst (Tarrytown, N.Y.), 187

torical evolution of, 221–23, 364n28; Reynolda bungalow and, 221, 224, 227–30

Reynolda Archives, 82–83

Reynolda Estate, 3, 5–6; amphitheaters at, *234*, 235, *235*; borders at, 214–15, *215*; children's playhouse at, *313*, 313; employee treatment at, 159–60, 161–67, 337, 372n40; expenditures for, 183–84; financial difficulties of, 322–23, 338; Five Row neighborhood, 161–66, *162, 163*; "General Plan of Reynolda," *162*, 352n27; goals of, 159, 224; golf course at, 141, 152, *277*; as "home place," 136, 149, 224–25, 226–30, 352n27; impact of RJR's death on, 294; impact of WWI on, 232, 262, 285–86; after KSR's death, 330–31, 332–33; KSR's expectations of, 25, 123, 337; KSR's remarriage at, 314–15; KSR's travels and, 103–5; in KSR's will, 328; lampposts at, *347*; land purchases for, 91, 106, 107–8, 109–10; landscape architect for, 23–24; landscape design at, 179–81, 213–15; management philosophy of, 140; as model, 15, 26, 140–41, 220, 224–25; naming of, 181; native species planted at, 214–15; pageants/performances at, *312*, 312–13; 131–32, 133–34, 151–52, 157, *158*, 179; polo fields at, *324, 325*; property sold to Wake Forest College, 338–39; renewal of, 333–36; road layout at, 209–10, *210*, 214–15; site engineering, 142–45, 184; social events at, 232–35, *233*, 311, 320–21, 324–26, 331; stonework at, 144, 153–57, *154*, 185, 188, *341*, 361n43; superintendents at, 131–32, 152–53, 285–86, 318;

swimming pool, *325*; taxes on, 338, 370n2; water supply at, 142–43, 273. *See also* Buckenham and Miller master plan; Katharine, Lake; *specific part of estate*

Reynolda Estate bungalow, *147, 227, 228, 334*; architectural influences on, 145–48; construction of, 209, 232–35, *233*, 277, 281–82, 284; expenditures for, 183, 367n53; family moves into, 148, 283, 290–91; furnishing of, 282, 284; greenhouses and, 185; as historic house museum, 344–46; "hospital" room in, 270; interior design in, *229, 230*, 262; KSR's expectations of, 124; plans for, *131*; planting schemes near, 368n58; porte-cochère of, *264*, 336; renovation of, 336; residential design and, 221, 227–30; Reynolda landscape and, 145; RJR's death in, 291; site preparation, 183; stonework of, 153–55; terrace garden of, 263–67, *265, 266, 267*; topographical plan of, *197*; Tuscan columns of, 155, *155*; woodland drives, 262–63, *263, 264, 265, 278*; during WWII, 337–38. *See also* Keen, Charles Barton, bungalow plans of

Reynolda Estate farming operations: construction of supporting facilities, 123–24, 152, 361n43; dairy farming, 152, 153, *154, 156*, 269, *269, 272*, 272–73, *276, 341*; KSR's expectations of, 25, 117, 126–28; as model, 114, 268–69, 271–81; poultry, 273; scientific management and, 125–26; sheep, *277*; southern influences on, 126–28, 226

Reynolda Estate gardens: Blue and Yellow Garden, 254, *255*; construction materials in, 245–48, *247*, 285;

301–2, 308; courtship of, 70–74; death of, 26, 327, 337; educational initiatives of, 167–68; education of, 17–18, 38; employees as treated by, 159–60, 161–67, 337, 372n40; family life of, 97, 97–98, 99, 106, *127*; family of, 18; female landscape architects and, 15; flowers and, 205–6, 241–42, 252; flu pandemic (1918) and, 298–99; as homemaker, 80; honeymoons of, 75–77, *76*, 82–85, *83*, 88–89, 315, 355n1, 355–56n11; impact of WWI on, 269–70; landscape tastes of, 86–88, 141, 320; leisure activities of, 133, 141, 233, 306–7; managerial ability of, 90, 110–12, 128–29, 168–69, 269–70, 281, 370n2; marriage of, 18, 37–38, 74, 268, 293; McIver's influence on, 19, 82, 91, 95–96, 224; name change of, 59; as New Woman, 141, 219–20, 294; nurse hired by, 118–19, *119*; personal secretary hired by, 128, 151; pregnancies/childbirths of, 90, 97, 98, 105, 110, 118–19, 120–22, 178–79, 319, 320, 326–27; public recognition of, 4–5; religious faith of, 106, 127, 159, 160, 177, 210, 232; remarriage of, 314–15, 373n51; Reynolda construction coordinated by, 23–26; social conscience of, 92–93, 95, 100, 114–15, 160, 224–26, 301–2; as society matron, 89–90, 105, 106, 120, 167, 170–71, 232–35, 322; southern background of, 16–20, 82; travels of, *101*, 101–5, *102*, 119–20, 235–36, 315–16, 322, 326, 365–66nn38–40; as widow, 293–96, 299–300, 307–9; will of, 327–29, 330, 352n27, 374n88

Reynolds, Katharine Smith, health problems of: childbearing and, 98,

319; chronic heart problems, 61–62, 96; contemporary remedies for, 96–97; fatal embolism, 327; KSR's coping strategies, 232; KSR's fears concerning, 321–22, 371n14; at Normal School, 17, 59–60, 354n50; overwork and, 106–7, 170, 176–77; physical culture and, 171–72; physical exercise and, 133, 233; RJR and, 121–22; rheumatic fever, 61–62, 96; "rheumatism," 100–101; RJR's hospitalization and, 283, 286–87; surgeries, 129–30, 130–31, 231

Reynolds, Lucy (cousin), 61, 72

Reynolds, Mary Katharine. *See* Babcock, Mary Katharine Reynolds

Reynolds, Nancy Susan (daughter), 288, *316*; birth of, 98, 110; education of, 311, 322; family life of, *233*; illnesses of, 298, 326; on KSR's health fears, 322; in KSR's will, 327–29, 330; marriage of, 332; in New York, 318–20; religious confirmation of, 270; summer camp attended by, 315, 320; travels of, 331–32

Reynolds, Richard Joshua (R. J.), *19*; automobile of, *101*, 101; business success of, and southern mores, 82; Camel cigarettes launched by, 177–78; character of, 35–37, 70–71, 93, 219; as civic leader, 356–57n21; death of, 291; education of, 355n60; family life of, 97, *97*, 99; health/illnesses of, 270, 281-84, 286, 288–91, 369n93; home of, *36*; honeymoon of, 75–77, *77*, 355n1, 355–56n11; KSR courted by, 37–38, 70–74, 355n59; KSR's correspondence with, 108–9, 129, 130, 282–83; marriage of, 18, 268, 293; memorial to, 302–4; religion and,

Salem Academy (Salem, N.C.), 42

Salmon, Lucy Maynard, 111

San Diego (Calif.), Panama-California Exposition (1915), 236, 365–66nn39–40

San Francisco (Calif.), 186; Panama-Pacific International Exposition (1915), 236, *237*, 365–66n40

Sanger, Margaret, 309

San Simeon (Calif.), 15–16, 351n16

Sargent, Charles Sprague, 7–8, 212, *213*, 350n6

Savannah (Ga.), 298

Scientific American Building Monthly, 10

scientific management, 110–12, 114, 125–26, 140–41

Scott, Walter, 67–68, 132

Sears, Thomas Warren, *23*; career background of, 192–95, *194*, 200, 362n3; English influence on, 199, 202; greenhouse complex plans of, 314; improvement projects of, 323–24, 336; influences on, 212–14; KSR and, 231; KSR's correspondence with, 285; KSR's *japonisme* and, 241–43; landscape design style of, 199–200, 208, 208–9; Miller replaced by, 180–81, 198–99, 209; photographs of, *275*, 363n13; as Reynolda landscape designer, 23–24, 197–98, 209–10, 213–15, 262–67; southern landscape traditions and, 216–18; terrace garden plans of, 262–67; village planting schemes of, 300–301, 371n17, 374n65; wooded entry drive plans of, 262–63

Sears, Thomas Warren, formal garden plans by: cedar alley, 320; construction materials, 245–48, *247*; "Fruit, Cut Flower and Nicer Vegetable Garden," 245, *246*, 314; geometry of, 244–45; implementation of, 297, 314; influences on, 252–54; Plan A, *246*; Plan D, *245*, 367n48; planting schemes, 254–62, *255*, *256*, *258*, *259*, *260*, 366n46, 367n50, 368n58; problems facing, 257–62, 364n24; restraint as governing principle of, 245–52; water features, 248–49, *250*

Sedding, J. D., 206–7

segregation, racial, 161, 165–66

Shipman, Ellen Biddle, 5, 103

Shipman, Louis, 103

Silas Creek, 117

Silva of North America, The (Sargent), 212

Simonds, Ossian Cole, 211

Simpson, T. W., 373n65

single-season displays, 257

Slater Normal and Industrial College (N.C.), 361n47

slavery, 28, 32

Smith, Eugene ("Gene"; brother), 70, 121, 312

Smith, Irene (sister), 70, 97, 175, 311

Smith, Mary Jackson (mother), 107; children borne by, 97, 319; garden of, 219; KSR's college education and, 38; KSR's correspondence with, 101–3; KSR's remarriage and, 311–12, 373n51; in KSR's will, 327; marriage of, 28–29

Smith, Mary Katharine ("Kate"). *See* Reynolds, Katharine Smith

Smith, Maxie (sister). *See* Dunn, Maxie Smith

Smith, Ruth (sister). *See* Lucas, Ruth Smith

Smith, Zachary Madison ("Matt"; brother), 70, 107, 316

Smith, Zachary Taylor (father), 28; biographical overview of, 352n2; class status of, 33–34; KSR's education and, 38, 61–63; KSR's remarriage